WEAK NATIONALISMS

Weak Nationalisms

Affect and Nonfiction

in Postwar America

DOUGLAS DOWLAND

UNIVERSITY OF NEBRASKA PRESS   *Lincoln*

© 2019 by the Board of Regents of
the University of Nebraska

Acknowledgments for the use of copyrighted
material appear on page 225, which constitutes
an extension of the copyright page.

All rights reserved

Library of Congress Cataloging-in-Publication Data
Names: Dowland, Douglas, author.
Title: Weak nationalisms: affect and nonfiction
in postwar America / Douglas Dowland.
Description: Lincoln: University of Nebraska Press,
[2019] | Includes bibliographical references and index.
Identifiers: LCCN 2018046954
ISBN 9781496200501 (cloth: alk. paper)
ISBN 9781496215482 (pbk.: alk. paper)
ISBN 9781496215994 (epub)
ISBN 9781496216007 (mobi)
ISBN 9781496216014 (pdf)
Subjects: LCSH: American literature—History and
criticism. | Nationalism in literature. | National
characteristics, American, in literature. | Synecdoche.
Classification: LCC PS169.N36 D69 2019 |
DDC 810.9/3581—dc23 LC record available
at https://lccn.loc.gov/2018046954

Set in New Baskerville ITC by Mikala R. Kolander.
Designed by N. Putens.

CONTENTS

Acknowledgments vii

Introduction: Affected Readers in an Imagined Community 1

1. Moodiness: The Everyday America of Beauvoir's *America Day by Day* 37

2. Curiosity and Its Discontents: Steinbeck's *Travels with Charley* and *America and Americans* 71

3. Hopefulness: *On the Road with Charles Kuralt*. 117

4. Incredulity: Reading Sarah Vowell 165

Conclusion: Affected Critics, the Nation, and the Limits of Critique 209

Source Acknowledgments. 225

Notes 227

Bibliography. 253

Index 265

ACKNOWLEDGMENTS

A book is, if anything, an index of narratives. This book is also an index of my intellectual career: it began as an undergraduate honors thesis on John Steinbeck, which I undertook at Michigan State University under the codirection of Ellen McCallum and the late David T. Bailey. The issues of national identity in my thesis continued to blossom throughout my graduate studies at the University of Iowa and eventually became my dissertation, directed by Brooks Landon. My thanks as well to David Wittenberg, Claire Fox, Loren Glass, Naomi Greyser, Daniel M. Gross, and the late Kenneth Cmiel for their guidance.

The Getty College of Arts and Sciences at Ohio Northern University has approved reductions in teaching load as well as faculty research grants that accelerated the development of this book. My appreciation to Holly Baumgartner, dean, and Catherine Albrecht, former dean, and Lisa G. Robeson, chair of the Department of English, for helping me in this way.

The University of Nebraska Press has maintained a steady faith in this book from its inception to its publication. My thanks to Alicia Christensen and to the two superb readers commissioned by the press, and to Wayne Larsen for his judicious copyediting.

My thanks as well to Joshua Gooch, who read far too much of this book in each of its stages and provided generous feedback each step of the way.

Most of this book has been written in the presence of Joanie, a rescued Chihuahua, who dozed as I typed and attentively listened as I read the draft manuscript aloud—though I admit she may have dozed while I read it aloud as well.

INTRODUCTION

Affected Readers in an Imagined Community

Since the Second World War, defining "America" has become one of nonfiction's urgent tasks. One way of understanding how postwar nonfiction, broadly conceived, negotiated this urgency is by examining the way in which affect—and the pervasive use of synecdoche as a means to evoke affect—shaped the textual construction of the nation. How do theories of affect illuminate, for example, the intensities of an essay like Jane Smiley's "The Unteachable Ignorance of the Red States"? Published in *Slate* less than forty-eight hours after the polls closed upon the 2004 presidential election, Smiley's essay declared, "The election results reflect the decision of the right wing to cultivate and exploit ignorance in the citizenry."[1] Relying on her experience of growing up in Missouri to anchor her argument, and certain that most of her family in that state voted for George W. Bush, Smiley insisted that while citizens of the "blue states" are good but naive, those who live in the "red states" are "full of original sin and . . . have a taste for violence."[2] Even worse, Smiley went on to lament, is that red state Americans "prefer to be ignorant. As a result, they are virtually unteachable."[3]

In moments of strong affect, synecdoches of nationalism often presume an us/them dichotomy. Typically, this presumes an interpretation in which "us" (or "we") are "true" nationalists, whereas "them" (or "they") are "false" representatives. Smiley's evocation of "blue state" and "red state" citizens is further synecdochical, reducing complex politics to simple, primary colors. In her schema, individuals—who undoubtedly have contradictory and inconsistent political positions—are little more than citizens of the states in which a majority of those citizens vote for a particular party (which undoubtedly have contradictory and inconsistent positions of their own.) The driving force behind Smiley's essay—that blue and red state citizens have diametrically opposing human natures—rests fundamentally on a perspective that political parties are truly representative of individual Americans, that part and whole are the same. Such synecdoches—and the dichotomies they encourage—perpetuate an extreme reading of the nation: it is not just that red state citizens believe in original sin but that they are "full" of it, not just that they are violent but that they savor, have a "taste" for violence.

Synecdoches that evoke an us/them dichotomy almost always place readers in the "us" position. "Unteachable" is an educator's lament, the washing of one's hands of an incorrigible student. The phrase suggests a relationship in which Smiley becomes the teacher, in which the "red state types" become students. (And I presume, as readers of *Slate*, we are colleagues in the know. After all, who else would use the phrase "unteachable" but one teacher to another?) Her experience growing up in Missouri and her awareness of her family's voting record evokes a long tenure among such red state types. And her diagnosis makes her superior to them: positioned as a teacher, Smiley gives herself the authority to dismiss the red state types from her purview through the evaluation of their incorrigibility.

But such diagnoses can take place only through the theories of affect that support them. Smiley's conception of who red state Americans are, and the ignorance they perpetuate, is also a theory of affect. Such ignorance, according to Smiley, begins by instilling fear that "if you don't believe in the literal word of the *Bible*, you will burn in hell," a belief that can be instilled only by abdicating critical thinking and realizing that "Satan resides in the toils and snares of complex thought."[4] Smiley's conception of right-wing ignorance is premised on a teacher's—an English professor's, no doubt—conception of ignorance: a bad, literal reading of a text that critical thinking would otherwise interrogate. At the same time, such simple reading is emotionally motivated through fear: the fear of God is also a fear to question; complex thought becomes an act of sin. Smiley's theory of affect places complex thinking and intense feeling on opposite ends of each other: for her, it is the difference between Democrats and Republicans. Smiley's suggestion for a left-wing response also contains a theory of affect, a theory of reaction to right-wing ignorance. She implores progressives to "assume the worst" about every red state policy and to react to these outrages, which prove that red states "love to cheat and intimidate."[5] But by using reason, common sense, and the law, blue state citizens can give "them more to think about than they can handle."[6] If the left is persistently thoughtful and vigilantly reactive, Smiley suggests, they can overwhelm the unteachable, one presumes, even if doing so does not teach them a thing.

Soon after the article appeared in *Slate*, Smiley made two corrections. The day after it was published, a family member informed Smiley that her family did not vote as she assumed. Smiley had originally presumed that 75 percent of her family had voted Republican and that 25 percent had voted Democratic. Indeed, according to her revised tally, Smiley's family had shifted substantially leftward: 55 percent of her family had voted Republican, and 45 percent of her family had voted Democratic. A month after the article was posted, Smiley realized that a historical event described in the essay, "Quantrill's Raid" in Lawrence, Kansas, had occurred in 1863 and not 1862 as she had originally written, and that the death count from the raid was at least one hundred fewer than she had originally written. The latter correction was made without comment.

Neither of these corrections led Smiley to revise the argument—or reconsider the affects—of her essay. Perhaps this is unsurprising: what we sense most from her essay are her intense affects seeking a language, a frustration about America in need of release regardless of its factuality, a feeling that is both individual and tethered, through synecdoche, to the nation. And I suspect that most readers of Smiley's essay, of politics both left and right, find something ridiculous in it—yet they might have felt something akin to the emotion Smiley expressed. It could be said that Smiley's essay demonstrates what Sianne Ngai would describe as an "ugly feeling": it performs Smiley's feelings of "obstructed agency."[7] What makes Smiley's feeling so ugly is that its resolution is a modus operandi of the very problem that inspired it, a call for a liberal intolerance in a language similar to the conservative intolerance she derides. It barely conceals the us-versus-them antagonism that we dismiss (and which I presume that Smiley herself would find repulsive) as the trademark of the uneducated. In fact, this very sort of antagonism was explicitly critiqued, with much success, by then-senator Barack Obama in his 2004 keynote address to the Democratic National Convention just five months before, when he said, "The pundits like to slice and dice our country into Red States and Blue States; Red States for Republicans, Blue States for Democrats. But I've got news for them, too: We worship an awesome God in the Blue States, and we don't like federal agents poking around in our libraries in the Red States. We coach Little League in the Blue States and have gay friends in the Red States."[8] In effect, Smiley's essay is the opposite of Obama's speech, for hers is a left-wing call for right-wing tactics.[9] Smiley asks the left to act more like the right. More precisely: she asks the left to act like the right that she, an adherent of the left, perceives the right to be.

One can agree or disagree with Smiley's characterization of red state citizens, or with her characterization of the nation as a whole. Rather than examining it for its correctness, however, I have attempted to read it for what it is: a way of answering the question "What is America?" by promulgating a theory of America. One could say then, as the affect theorist Silvan Tomkins might, that Smiley has a "strong theory" of America, one that led Smiley astray to incorrect presumptions about her family, the facts, and the nation. The intensity of her affect led to the confusion of parts for wholes. But it is not fair to say—and it would play into a persistent Cartesian dichotomy between reason and emotion, one that Smiley herself perpetuates in the essay—that she got her facts wrong because she was overly emotional. Rather, Smiley's synecdochical reasoning led the transformation of an otherwise weak theory of the nation into a strong, monopolizing theory, complete with an us/them dichotomy. It is not that she is merely angry: after all, anger can make us acutely aware of an injustice, can spur the otherwise sluggish into action. Rather, Smiley's anger has the opposite effect of revealing her own inflexibility. If anything, by entrenching herself in the dichotomy of left and right, Smiley herself became the unteachable other she so dreads in the essay.

My reading of Smiley's essay serves as a primer to the readings of texts that I perform in greater detail throughout this book. Though I explore each component later in this introduction, it might be helpful to outline the driving argument behind my reading of these texts first. What I examine in this book are textual moments of weak nationalism. This is not the hot or strong variety of nationalism we are used to associating with that word, but a type that is nascent and nimble, one that perpetually struggles between evoking the nation as a horizon of possibility and reading the nation as an absolute, concrete certainty. Strong nationalisms are by nature reductive, whereas weak nationalisms are inductive. They are not polar opposites then; their synecdochical techniques generate different rhetorical trajectories and affective valences. Smiley's essay, for example, captures the affective intensities that elections often evoke. But the nation is more than these intense moments: it consists, for the most part, of a smoothly flowing, weak nationalism that threads intense moments together and functions like an integument to keep the nation together in barely noticed, seemingly banal ways by substituting a part for the whole of the American experience. The common thread of the texts studied in this book is that each contains such moments: moments of affect that articulate an imagined community—an America—of which they are a part. Thus the affects of weak nationalism provide a counterpoint to the pernicious characterization of nationalism we take for granted today. Nationalism is not the sole property of the ideological extremist but is tacitly infused in a range of discourses and evokes a spectrum of affects.

The argument of this book, it could be said, strikes a nerve within

INTRODUCTION 5

literary and cultural criticism because it takes seriously texts that critics thought they had easily dismissed. Of these texts' synecdochical mode, for example, Clifford Geertz once wrote, "The Jonesville-is-America writ small (or America-is-Jonesville writ large) fallacy is so obviously one that the only thing that needs explanation is how people have managed to believe it and expected others to believe it. . . . The notion that this gives you the thing entire . . . is an idea which only someone too long in the bush could possibly entertain."[10] But if it is a fallacy, why does it endure? Perhaps because, for a certain archive of texts, it is not a fallacy but a feeling toward the nation that critics—even critics who pioneered "thick description" and, as we will see below, "close reading"—typically avoid examining. It is not "obvious"—and critics should be careful of their own common sense that dismisses these texts as obvious—how synecdoches offer a way of imagining a nation from a single, subjective perspective. The connection between a person and the nation is emotional. Its writers "manage to believe it" because they feel it, read it in objects that evoke a synecdochical relationship between the object and the nation. After all, the affects organize and, in doing so, shape our social lives, of which the nation is a part. It may not always be the most prominent component of the social: in fact, what interests me in this book is how affects are fused to the national and, in their synecdochical fusing, become more prominent than they were before. Thus these texts are not a sign that someone has been "too long in the bush"; it is a sign of their being in the bush, of seeing and interpreting connections that are anchored in an object but also something more than the object itself. The nation is, after all, an affective attachment.

So to answer the question I raised at the beginning of this chapter: theories of affect allow for a reading of texts like these that rearticulate them not as fallacious reasoning but as the articulation of affect itself. In other words, affect theory allows us to witness the emotions that engender a synecdochical reading of the nation, and it does so in a way that makes sense of any "citizen's sense of the national world" that gives them their "bearings, situating them in their own imagined public" while accounting for "the passion with which they protested findings that threatened to undermine their personal certainties."[11] "Bearings" and "certainties" rely on the sort of synecdoche that Geertz too readily criticized: they are feelings that spur the connection between self and other, that form the affective bonds of community through which individuals understand their national world. The claim that "Jonesville-is-America" is fallacious rests in part on a rather jaded assumption that, as E. L. Doctorow once wrote, "we are taught that facts are to be distinguished from feeling and that feeling is what we are permitted for our rest and relaxation when the facts get us down."[12] The tactics of critical analysis make it easy to be jaded toward synecdochical assumptions, to underestimate the complex affective reading practices that occur for weak nationalism to construct an imagined community and keep the embers of the nation glowing. Yet for the authors that I examine in this book, even when they feel incredulous toward it, there is a complexity of feeling that evokes affects both negative and positive.[13] For such enjoyment to persist as part of a citizen's "competence," Lauren Berlant notes, requires a great deal of interpretation, to "read conveniently and flexibly between the lines [of nationalist rhetoric], thus preserving both utopian national identification and cynical practical citizenship."[14] As much as the nation is a site of feeling, it is also a site of reading, where objects and events are interpreted into something valuable for its denizens. To acknowledge the role of affect in how these readings are produced, and the rhetoric that allows such readings to become narratives, is to acknowledge the central role of affect in archives that otherwise seem unworthy of critical attention.

The way in which I illuminate this archive is to consider the complexity of weak affect. According to Tomkins, each person develops a theory of affects. Ideally, these theories, over time, coalesce into a sense of self. This can take place, however, only when one's theory of affects is relatively weak, when there is no predominant affect that monopolizes the others. Such monopolizing is a sign of a "strong theory" of affect. For example, "The individual who has a strong fear theory is an anxiety neurotic or a schizophrenic, for whom fear is an ever-present threat which must be anticipated and dealt with."[15] But for the most part, what makes affects effective are their very weaknesses, "developed to account for and organize very specific experiences which are neither intense enough nor recurrent enough to prompt the generation of more than a crude general description of the phenomena themselves."[16] Weak affects, then, provide strength to the system, making it effective. "A weak theory then must be a relatively effective one to remain weak. If it breaks down only occasionally, it can be revised and yet remain relatively weak."[17]

I presume that the texts that I study in this book have their own individual theories of affect. Following affect theory I also presume that affects—including the affects of nationalism—are most effective when they are weak. Accordingly I argue that the texts I examine in this book, in their attempts to synecdochically connect the imagined community with concrete signs, reveal the problematic of affective intensity toward the nation. Synecdoche and its weak affects allow for the construction of weak nationalisms, yet synecdoche also risks turning weak affects of the nation into strong ones. And as Tomkins elaborates throughout *Affect-Imagery-Consciousness*, what makes even the weakest of affects fascinating is their ability to be read, the joy and shame in reading others' emotions and having one's emotions read, in the inventive and unexpectedly intense relations of feeling that emerge through the act of reading.[18] To investigate how affects are generated through a trope like synecdoche is to renew the questions literary criticism asks of texts. By doing so, reading affects for what "may have been previously invisible, opaque, difficult, abstract" transforms texts that may be otherwise banal or invisible into ones that are "interesting, that solicits and rewards one's attention."[19]

It is, after all, what the authors who I study in this book do with the affects they feel that makes those affects American. And what they do with these affects—their attempt to answer the question "What is America?"—reminds us that affects are an "angle of participation in processes larger than ourselves."[20] What the authors I examine in this book have in common is their object: the nation. Where they diverge is in their individual theory of the nation and in the unique affects their work displays. Affected by her moodiness, itself a combination of sensory experience and academic training, Simone de Beauvoir extrapolates the nation from the parts she reads. Affected by a feeling of no longer knowing his country, John Steinbeck becomes curious about it, and seeks to read it and know it again. And affected by what he sees on his travels, he later reveals his discontent toward what he found. Affected by a nation that is losing its place in the world, a loss being represented in the evening news, Charles Kuralt scripts a hopeful portrait of the nation, an evocative, emotional portrait that feels hopeful but never reaches the true political radicalism of hope. The incredulity Sarah Vowell expresses toward the Reagan-era Cold War triumphalism in which she came of age also comes to define her as a writer. Yet that incredulity ricochets back to the very credulity of that exceptionalism, thus trapping Vowell in the terms she seeks to define herself against.

This archive of texts has been, for the most part, invisible to the critical eye. In what follows, I explore why this invisibility has occurred and how studying these texts for their weak nationalism brings them to light. Much of this invisibility stems from the very dichotomy that Smiley outlined in her essay: that reason and emotion are irreconcilable, that anyone who writes of the nation in even the slightest appreciative way is both unreasonable and unteachable, that the only way to negotiate such texts is through intense, if not aggressive, critical suspicion. In this book I try to avoid an analysis that might lead to similar, obviously reductive conclusions in the hope that the conception of nationalism widens in ways that are productive for the study of texts and their affects. And accordingly, the affects of these texts come to the fore in a way that widens our sense of nationalism. Through the study of weak nationalism, perhaps critics can reclaim their space in a discussion in which they have mostly been absent, a space that allows us to contribute our answers to a question that has become infinitely more pressing than when Smiley first wrote of it. To invigorate the critical study of nonfiction, to reexamine the role of the rhetoric of synecdoche in the construction of such nonfiction, and to revise the critical trajectory that dismisses nationalism and its affects, we must explore how texts attempt to answer that question: "What is America?"

Weak Nationalisms

Narratives of weak nationalism challenge the story we tell about nationalism. It is a story of particular moments. In the period after the Second World War, it is a story of sudden flashes of hot nationalism. In the 1950s, McCarthyism came to the forefront as did the John Birch Society, which promulgated a purely capitalist nationalism anchored in white supremacy. In the sixties, national consensus was fractured by the war in Vietnam and stoked by the crisis of the Civil Rights movement, spilling over into the seventies with the rise of minority nationalisms. In the eighties, neoconservatism brought with it a resurgence of exceptionalist nationalism. In the nineties, it was theorized that the collapse of the Soviet Union would lead to "the end of history" along economic and nationalist lines: a "new world order" that would inevitably be liberal and cosmopolitan. Then 9/11 occurred, and a surge of nationalist feeling was harnessed by the Bush II administration, in defense of global terrorism, to justify an encroachment on civil liberties of a type previously unseen in the history of the country. And though the Obama administration was first seen as a moment in history in which racial divides were no longer important, the nationalisms promulgated in the fifties resurged as resentful whites sought a haven from a world that was no longer theirs.

Yet something more complex—and less intense—was going on in the background. These less intense moments are the focus of this book. The increasing heat of the Cold War denied the legitimacy of complex, moody nationalisms like the one captured in Simone de Beauvoir's *America Day by Day*. The foments of strong nationalism throughout the sixties pushed John Steinbeck from a curious, if not voyeuristic embrace of the nation in *Travels with Charley* to a more embittered discontent: the nation was no longer a source of pleasure but was, in *America and Americans*, a source of frustration. Even when strong nationalism proved socially unacceptable during the seventies, Charles Kuralt's *On the Road* portraits captured weak nationalism's dramas and its hopeful resolutions of national dilemmas. The strong affects of Reagan-era nationalism birthed Sarah Vowell's incredulity toward exceptionalist regimes, feelings that complicate her depiction of American history in *The Wordy*

Shipmates and of American contemporary life in *Take the Cannoli*. Even in its strong surges of nationalism, there are always weak nationalisms in the background. It is a background that has proven difficult for critics to interpret. Michael Billig has noted that even in the world of political science, the use of the word "nationalism" "always seems to locate nationalism on the periphery": not at the center of political life or even in the banality of everyday life, but in fringe movements, extremity, and violence.[21] As Billig argues in political science, I argue that literary and cultural criticism has placed the nation as peripheral to our interpretive concern. The work of this book is to take what has been cast to the periphery and place it front and center. Studying how authors write of America defamiliarizes our typical critical practice and, in doing so, sheds light on an object that has been so peripheral to critics that it has disappeared from our vision altogether.

Texts that ask the question "What is America?" have been avoided by critics, partially out of fear that to answer the question would be to simplify it, reducing the scope of the question to an ideological response. At the same time, this question has been reflected on by critics only to the extent that an answer perpetuates criticism's hermeneutics, which tends to suspiciously see such narratives as exemplars of nationalism in the pejorative sense of the word. Indeed, what may at first seem strange about my archive is its relative lack of chauvinist, exceptionalist narratives. But this is strange only because critics focus on the strong affects of hot nationalism. On the one hand, critics are prone to seeing such narratives as innately and inherently insidious. As Gayatri Spivak has understatedly written, what "nationalism conjures is not a positive affect."[22] Similarly, Michael Ignatieff has written, "The repressed has returned, and its name is nationalism."[23] In statements like these, critics presume that all nationalisms are pernicious, and in doing so, they limit their scope of inquiry, making other variants of nationalism and their archives invisible. On the other hand, critics are prone to seeing such narratives as innately insidious because of the strong affects associated with the activity of criticism: the hermeneutics of suspicion.[24] Critics are suspicious that the nation is ultimately a fiction or, worse, a coercive reality from which only negative affect can emerge. Yet a panoply of affects goes into the writing of the nation, including the affects that are the focus of this book, affects which can be described as weak or banal. As Billig has described it, "Banal nationalism operates with prosaic, routine words, which take nations for granted, and which, in doing so, inhabit them. Small words, rather than grand memorable phrases, offer constant, but barely conscious, reminders of the homeland, making 'our' national identity unforgettable."[25] This book seeks to remedy criticism's tendency to presume that all nationalisms are innately "hot" by reminding critics that such narratives contain a variety of affects, and that reading such narratives requires a more sophisticated awareness of the dynamic role of affect that goes beyond the potentially dismissive categories of the "repressed" or the "negative." Through weak nationalism, we see how nationalism proves to be more than "simple answers to complex problems and nationalist solutions to endemic social and economic difficulties."[26] To write about America does not necessarily entail the corrective, disciplinary qualities we ascribe to strong nationalism. Nationalism, we have realized in the election of Trump, is far more complex than the ways we used the word prior to his election. All the more pressing, then, is that we understand nationalism fully, in all its emotional intensities.

Yet it is difficult to read the affects of weak nationalism, because reading affect—of any variety—is more complex than the hermeneutics of suspicion will allow. As an organizing schema, "the net [of] 'nationalism' . . . seems to be used primarily for catching exotic, rare and often violent specimens," Billig writes.[27] The nation often comes to attention only in displays of the strong affects of hot nationalism. "The term 'nationalist' seems to exert a magnetic pull upon the critical adjective 'extreme' in the forcefield of common semantics."[28] It has become common sense for critics that nationalism has pejorative connotations, as "dangerously irrational, surplus and alien," a site of discrimination, extremism, and violence.[29] Surveying a variety of scholarship on nationalism, Billig found that "the words 'fanatical' and 'irrational' attach themselves to 'nationalism'" to the point that these words have become synonymous with nationalism itself.[30] Such language saturates mainstream discourse as well: my own search of several American newspapers found adjectives like "risky," "crude," "retrograde," and "destructive" preceded the word "nationalism." Similarly, words that frequently follow "nationalism" included "rises," "incites," "spreads" and "swells." Occasionally, there were calls for a "responsible," "reasonable," or even an "enlightened" nationalism.

As Billig notes, this vocabulary works to insulate and distance intellectuals—in his case social scientists and in mine literary and cultural critics—from nationalism. When nationalism is characterized as "alien," critics "are assumed to belong to a reasonable world, a point-zero of nationalism."[31] This assumption creates an us/them dichotomy (much like the dichotomy that both incites and limits Smiley's essay) which discourages "us" from the study of nationalism. This dichotomy tacitly discourages the study of affects as well, paralleling the divide between the rational critic and the emotional nationalist, because the "emotional bonds" of nationalism prove "the problem and the threat" for the rational critic to critique and avoid.[32] After all, nationalism can surge only if it has waned previously, and critical attention, often framed as a cautionary narrative, points at strong nationalism as a danger to be avoided. Yet this focus only further perpetuates a binary opposition between reason and emotion as an us/them dichotomy of its own, and ultimately condenses what are multiple variants of nationalism into one. In other words, criticism has proven overly reliant on narratives of strong nationalism to define nationalism itself.

But there is another side to nationalism that allows for an exploration of an archive such as the one of this book, one that reveals an affective richness through its weak affects that does not require recourse to our popular and critical understanding of nationalism as a pejorative. Far from its chauvinist, exceptionalist counterparts, weak nationalism is a reminder of the ordinariness of national affects. And it is its ordinariness that gives weak nationalism its power. As Jon Fox and Cynthia Miller-Idriss write, "Flags thus don't have to be saluted or waved to work their national magic. The near complete assimilation of nationhood into the realm of the ordinary—not its sporadic or spectacular invocations—testifies to its prosaic power."[33] This is not to say that the nation becomes invisible, or that its citizens unreflectively presume its presence. Rather, weak nationalism reminds us that "people recognize, interpret and align themselves with pressing issues in explicitly national terms. But most of the time, the nation is not something ordinary people talk *about*; rather, it's something they talk *with*."[34] Nationalism blends into the foreground to such an extent that one presumes its presence without necessarily seeing it there. Yet like Tomkins's claim that weak affects provide strength to one's affective schema, weak nationalism provides a strength to its practitioners that, while difficult to articulate, should not be underestimated. As Claire Sutherland writes, "The nation is at its most potent when it becomes banal, a taken-for-granted source of loyalty and belonging."[35]

With weak nationalism in mind, we better understand Benedict Anderson's dictum that "communities are to be distinguished, not by their falsity/genuineness, but by the style in which they are imagined."[36] In this book, I study these texts for the affective style in which the nation is imagined, eschewing the claims of falsity or genuineness, which frequently appear in the critical response to the texts in this archive. The word "imagined" in this sense does not mean, as critics presume it to mean, imaginary or "true fictions" but rather an identification of the self as a part of a community that is affective and affecting. As Anderson describes this, "it is *imagined* because the members of even the smallest nation will never know most of their fellow-members, meet them, or even hear of them, yet in the minds of each lives the image of their communion."[37] The "image of their communion" is an issue of affect: as Tomkins writes, communion is one of the primary vehicles of feelings of enjoyment and joy.[38] There is something about the nation that incites interpretation: these narratives are driven by such an incitement through the description of parts that represent the national whole. Through weak nationalism, we witness how "the scraps, patches, and rags of daily life must be repeatedly turned into the signs of a national culture" in a way that is both "pedagogical" and "performative."[39] After all, there is no single narrative that will ever suffice to describe a nation; there is no sole way to imagine a community. Thus it proves more fruitful to understand how such imaginings are performed to better understand the trope and affects they rely on, rather than to judge their falsity or genuineness. That weak nationalism is often structured around the affects of synecdochical reading does not make these texts banal. Rather, it demonstrates the full range of affects that contribute to the ongoing work of composing the nation. But to fully appreciate that range requires us to look for weak nationalism in a particular—and often peculiar—archive of texts.

Nonfiction and Nonfictions of the Nation

The nation is an index of narratives: it exists only insofar as there are narratives that seek to describe it. Yet critics have often interpreted the nation's reliance on narrative to mean that all narratives of the nation are fictional. James Clifford describes a similar dismissal in the field of ethnography: "Interpretive social scientists have recently come to view good ethnographies as 'true fictions,' but usually at the cost of weakening the oxymoron, reducing it to the banal claim that all truths are constructed."[40] In criticism we see something similar at work when critics dismiss the nation without investigating it: the recurring hint of their doing so is their dismissal of the text under examination as banal. To dismiss these texts as banal is to avoid performing a meaningful criticism of them, as much as it is to deny these texts their rhetorical and affective richness. Above all, to dismiss these texts as "true fictions" is to ignore an otherwise startling realization: the United States is both a fiction and a nonfiction. Just as the nation is an index of narrative, the nation is an amalgam of data and representation, of fact and technique. Literary and cultural critics must realize, as Clifford does in ethnography, that we too often weaken the oxymoron: our insistence that narratives of the nation are "true fictions" has hampered our understanding of how the genre negotiates both sides of its construction.

Further, the study of nonfiction suffers from dual hostilities: not quite literature, not quite journalism, the genre is seen by both as a "narrative imperfection," which has led to its critical marginalization.[41] Even the name of the genre, "nonfiction," Robert Root Jr. has argued, encourages an undervaluation of its importance: "we can't define it by breaking down its etymology. Unlike 'nonsense,' for example, or 'nonchalant' or 'nondescript,' 'nonfiction' has yet to reach that same level of invisibility . . . that nonfiction is not just not-fiction anymore—that it's something positive and self-defining in its own right."[42] The category of nonfiction perpetually reminds us of what it is lacking, what it is not. It remains tethered to fiction rather than seen as a genre worthy of an inquiry of its own. This is especially paradoxical because, as Root notes, "nonfiction is really the first genre, not in terms of preeminence but in terms of primacy. You can't decide to make a literary rendition of reality—with rhyme schemes and meter or imaginary characters and situations and dialogue—unless you have a way to report and record reality in the first place."[43] Yet nonfiction has been relegated as a genre by critics and authors alike. John C. Hartsock attributes this undervaluation to the "triumph of science in World War II" in which "positivist assumptions had all but defeated subjectivity as a legitimate cognitive stance from which to interpret the world," but he also notes that the rise of the New Criticism "could not bode well for a discourse . . . which openly acknowledged its phenomenological origins, or its means of production."[44] Similarly, Thomas Hill Schaub has noted how the rise of formalism and the New York Intellectuals "exerted a paralyzing effect" on all prose genres.[45] "Their seemingly opposed demands for social relevance and formal technique actually endorsed a view of reality—both elitist and politically debilitated—which writers did not share . . . since such a view defined only what seemed no longer possible (politically relevant art) or defined a formal 'container' into which a fiction writer must pour his or her content."[46]

Intriguingly, this critical vacuum created by both the New Critics and the New York Intellectuals raised a question that only nonfiction could answer. Even Lionel Trilling complained that a nonfiction book like David Riesman's *Individualism Reconsidered* gave him "the sense of the actuality of our society" in a way that no novel was "able to suggest."[47]

But Trilling himself remained painfully aware that the novel was seen as the mode that established one as a writer. Not only did the novel have—and still does have—dominion in the critical world, it does in the literary world too: to be a writer is to be the writer of novels.[48] Tom Wolfe once characterized writing a novel as the equivalent of the "American Dream": for authors "the Novel was no mere literary form. It was a psychological phenomenon. It was a cortical fever."[49] The supposed inferiority of nonfiction proved to be useful even to those who would be seen as its innovators. At the same time, Wolfe insisted that nonfiction was—and is still—seen as lacking a vitality that the New Journalists saw themselves bringing to the genre. Wolfe himself insisted that "most nonfiction writers, without knowing it, wrote in . . . a calm, cultivated and, in fact, genteel voice. The idea was that the narrator's own voice should be like the off-white or putty-colored walls . . . a 'neutral background' against which bits of color would stand out."[50] As such, nonfiction was known for its "pale beige tone" delivered by "'the journalist,' a pedestrian mind, a phlegmatic spirit, a faded personality."[51]

Wolfe's characterization of nonfiction as a site of the banal is disingenuous, but it enables him to place his New Journalism in the position of recuperating nonfiction from its drab past. Its past practitioners are, as Smiley might write, "unteachable": they are phlegmatic and out of date; they are genteel; they are weak. Wolfe's recuperation is also one premised on a promise of intense affect: not the "pale" or "pedestrian" affects of journalists or "faded personalities" but affects that are neither calm nor neutral. In this way, Wolfe not so subtly played on prevalent critical assumptions about nonfiction in fashioning his alternative to it. His point is to see the New Journalism as a site of innovation. Yet nonfiction was innovative and intense before the New Journalism—and well after it, too. My archive shows the emotional complexity of nonfiction, not a beige tone but one that represents a complex spectrum of affects. The texts that I study are not calm third-person narratives, nor do they proclaim a genteel omniscience, nor are they rehearsals of pedestrian fact. They are first-person narratives, transcripts of their personal engagement with the subject of the nation. Nonfictions of nationalism may not be the New Journalism, but they solicit our attention in a unique way: they invite the personal in their construction of the national. If we identify as fellow Americans, we may find ourselves agreeing or disagreeing, offering, at least to ourselves, similarly affecting narratives that complement or correct the reading of the nation before our eyes. As Vivian Gornick writes, the author of nonfiction has no place to hide, which is all the more true when the subject of their writing is one that others experience in their everyday lives. "The persona in a nonfiction narrative is an unsurrogated one. Here the writer must identify openly with those very same defenses and embarrassments that the novelist or the poet is once removed from. It's like lying down on the couch in public."[52] The analogy of the couch suggests that the nonfiction text serves not as neutral background on which affects occur but as the generator of affect itself. It suggests a transferential space and therapeutic alliance in which another trusts another to connect and assist in the interpretation of the experience. In effect, the text comes to construct an imagined community.

Yet the critical history of nonfiction encourages us to continue treating it as if it were a fiction rather than to give attention to the affects that flow through it. The effect is to preclude a criticism of nationalism in general and to make invisible an entire archive, in my case, of texts that should eagerly remind us how "the 'American temper' or 'ethos' is continually reinvented, constructed and reconstructed. . . . It is 'hidden in plain sight.'"[53] This is not to assuage the power of such narratives to be fictions, nor to underestimate their ability to universalize and render others invisible.[54] Throughout this book, I am as interested, as most Americanists are, in the textual moments in which, as Donald Pease lucidly describes, national identity is realized overtly as an "artifact rather than as a tacit assumption."[55] The tacit nature of this assumption is often evident only when the national narrative becomes hot or breaks down, or when we realize we do not fit into it, rather than when we commune with it and feel so much a part of it that we authorize ourselves to speak for it, to see it in the relationship between ourselves and the whole, the narrative and rhetorical space that encourages a construction of a "we" in the first place. To appreciate weak nationalism, one must look at alternate archives, even if, as Berlant writes, those archives seem to use "the silliest, most banal and erratic logic imaginable to describe important things, like what constitutes intimate relations, political personhood, and national life."[56] If nationalism relies on the use of banalities to assert its importance, it follows that what may seem simple or banal is actually complex and rich because the affects that emerge from such banalities are rich with meaning. The type of nonfiction I study in this book does not have the opportunity to hide its interest in the nation. It is directly and unsubtly about America as the authors see it. It depicts the nation it sees and attempts to persuade readers to their vision. It encourages an immediacy of experience through its synecdochical logic that connects the writer's vision with its audience. Further, its mode is affective. The texts I study engage with affect plainly on the page, without artifice. They do so using traditional modes of nonfiction—the travelogue, the essay collection, the television documentary, the radio essay—without resorting to avant-garde experimentation. What makes these texts interesting is their unmediated, tactile, sensuous engagement with the emotions they portray in their depiction of the nation. These seemingly banal texts and their reliance on synecdoche remind us of the power of affect's ability to function, as Catherine Lutz has argued, as "an index of social relationship rather than a sign of a personal state" exclusively.[57] It is the relative ease through which any banal object or event can be considered affectively "American" that proves to be the nation's most fascinating feature. But how does one read this archive in a way that makes this index evident, that makes the affects of weak nationalism more apparent? What has been described as the "affective turn" in literary and cultural studies offers a way to critically read this archive to illuminate weak nationalism without recourse to the tactics of strong affect and its dichotomous conclusions.

Reading Affects: Closely, but without Suspicion

Affect theory notes the distinctions between affect, emotion, and mood. Given that this book examines how these categories operate to read and construct a common object, the nation, my definition of affect is one that aspires to be unifying, while not necessarily unified, in its deployment. The nation is, after all, a complex articulation of affects, moods, and emotions, and their individuations. With this definition in mind, I use the word "affect" in this book to indicate that which provokes the incitement to read. Affect is the "incitement" to interpret an object.[58] For my purposes, the incitement to read can be an affect in the traditional sense: the irreducible yet promiscuous and potentially autotelic intensities, positive or negative, that occur in response to stimuli.[59] Or the incitement to read can be an emotion: the "ideological attempt to make sense of some affective problems" that have become clustered together and through which we see the relationship, the boundaries and surfaces, between subject and object.[60] Or the incitement to read can be a mood: the impress and atmosphere of "individual and collective feelings ... the slow changing conditions" that "open up an area within which something can be represented."[61] It is not that I disagree with the distinctions of these three categories. But to overly separate them is to lose the unifying similarities and subtle differences in how they construct an object. The authors I study are affected in their own unique ways, whether by an affect or an emotion or a mood: a part has provoked the incitement to read, leading them to write texts that seek to describe the whole object, to describe what America is. And while I do not want to reduce affect to interpretation alone, I assert that interpretation does not take place apart from affect.[62] As the incitement to read, affect colors the object being read in a way that transforms the object itself as much as it involves "a transformation of one's way of being in the world, in a way that determines what matters to one."[63] Often, in the rush of affect, it is not always possible to discern whether the affect is attaching to an object or happening in it. This indiscernibility is particularly intriguing when the object of the affect is the nation, something that seems simultaneously part of the self and much more than oneself, as affects connect the personal to the national. Through synecdoche, the incitement to read demonstrates an attachment to an object, one in which the object is something more than the object, as a part connected to the whole.

This is why I describe the authors whose texts I explore in this book as "affected" readers in an imagined community: it is through their affects, and the synecdochical reading those affects incite, that they come to imagine the nation as an imagined community and themselves as, even if momentarily, a contributor and part of it.

If my definition of affect seems too loose, it may be because some affect theorists have drawn the definition—and the distinction between affect, emotion, and mood—too tight, such that entire vectors of affect theory "could never be easily or fully reconciled."[64] To me, the separation of affect theory into vectors or domains is useful but risks a disservice to texts such as the ones I study in this book, as it could perpetuate their invisibility. It also risks a disservice to affect theory itself, as such distinctions often attempt to cleanly separate affect from other categories such as emotion and mood to assert the primacy of one over the others.[65] We miss something when we draw our distinctions so tidily: we miss something about affect itself, which is unifying but not necessarily unified in its genesis and transmission.

Indeed, what I find productive about affect theory is the untidiness inherent in the shifts from affect to emotion to mood. "Affect," write Gregory J. Seigworth and Melissa Gregg, "arises in the midst of in-between-ness."[66] Affect is that which is between, which may be why Seigworth's and Gregg's *Affect Theory Reader* lists eight different modes of affect theory, with the proviso that the eight modes described are not "fully comprehensive" and there are overlaps between each.[67] The titles of influential texts in affect theory reveal these overlaps as well. *Affect-Imagery-Consciousness*; *The Cultural Politics of Emotion*; *Ugly Feelings*: these titles demonstrate the configuration of affect theory as a theory of overlaps. Even the words "affect" and "emotion" and "feeling" perpetually cross boundaries between noun and verb. These overlaps richly resonate within these influential texts of affect theory as well. Sara Ahmed, in *The Cultural Politics of Emotion*, encourages readers to "feel your way" through the politics of emotion.[68] Ngai describes *Ugly Feelings* as a book that "studies the aesthetics of negative emotion."[69] Affect; emotion; mood: each term is embedded in—and messily reliant on—the other. For Ngai, these terms point out the untidy, transitory moments from one to the other, "the passages whereby affects acquire the semantic density and narrative complexity of emotions, and emotions conversely denature into affects."[70] Affect theory is a way of revealing these moments of reading by reading the emotional energy between part and whole.

Affect, as I have defined it, is the incitement to read. Affect theory, then, is not only the theorization of affects but the reading of incitements as well, which enables theorization in the first place. The consequences of tidily distinguishing between affect, emotion, and mood have much higher stakes than Ngai's reflection that "the difference between emotion and affect is still intended to solve the same basic and fundamentally descriptive problem" of psychoanalytic diagnosis, of distinguishing between self and other.[71] That affects can generate emotions that can generate moods suggests that we must read differently than traditional academic practices of reading allow.[72] What proves frustrating about the affects is their potential to not always produce signification or representation, much less offer a consistent, reasoned reading along the lines that most critics would prefer.[73] Ultimately, to pursue the study of affect, critics need to see their incitements as not satisfied with clean, clinical distinctions, or as incitements that apply the hermeneutics of suspicion alone. (I explore criticism's enduring suspicion, of the nation in particular, at greater length in this book's conclusion.) Rather, the reading of affect is one that reads for the incitement to read: in this book, an incitement that appears in the synecdochical leap from part to whole. Each incitement has its own unique way of reading the object, each with its own logic. What is needed is a way to read these affects and index them, which will require a different sort of reading, something like the more affectively aware criticism I call for in the conclusion to this book, that is more unifying than unified, one that sees its object—in this book, the nation—perhaps more clearly by exploring the affective work in the distances between parts and wholes, much like observing the nation through "the billboards that mark the system of interstate highways, county roads, and city streets that is the United States."[74] What is needed is an analysis of nationalism that "requires less knee-jerk antagonism and more understanding of the affections and ideals that make Americans want to be part of something larger than their local identifications."[75]

Reading for the affective space between part and whole requires a renewed focus on what constitutes the act of close reading. In a way that contemporary critique cannot account for, reading for the between requires us to scan the horizon of a text rather than go mining for its ideology. What makes the texts I study in this book unique is that reading them suspiciously for the purposes of discovering symptoms of ideology is futile: their ideologies, their nationalisms, are on their surfaces, as are their affects, which these texts wear on their figurative sleeves. For texts like these, critics must reconfigure what constitutes a close reading, adjusting their interpretive optometry. I would characterize the style of reading I perform throughout this book as close but not suspicious. I am interested in how a text captures an affect, but I am not interested in reducing that capture to diagnosis: in effect, I do not feel compelled to engage in a "*scrutiny* of an object in order to decode certain *defects* or *flaws* that are not readily or automatically apparent to a nonspecialist perspective."[76] Such diagnostic power comes from "hypervigilance on the part of the critic," a desire to strike an object like a target.[77] Yet there is something excessive about hypervigilance that lends itself to strong affect. If nationalism teaches us anything, it is that for as much as we wish to define it, it is all-encompassing, idiosyncratic, and malleable. The texts that I examine here can be easily dismissed if we apply only strong affect toward them: Beauvoir's *America Day by Day* may seem incoherent; Steinbeck's descriptions of the nation in *Travels with Charley* and *America and Americans* may seem too general; Charles Kuralt's *On the Road* may come off as benign if not hokey; Sarah Vowell's work may appear too self-serving. For the most part, the great eruptive moments of nationalism seem to not concern them. Yet what they reveal are the ways in which nonfiction captures the steady and continuous business of describing the nation. These texts, in turn, show us something important about the work of criticism, that if we are reliant on suspicion alone, even when the object is something that we are most suspicious of, we will not see whole archives of material. In nationalism's wide expanse, the hermeneutics of suspicion gives us no traction. What is needed instead is a form of analysis that gives nuance to "contradictions or qualitative differences" without reducing them to ideology.[78]

Have we avoided the affects of nonfiction—and nationalism—because they conjure the opposite of what criticism—and critics—are supposed to do? As Stephen Best and Sharon Marcus outline in their theory of "surface reading," what drives critics to texts, and to particular canons of texts, is that they facilitate "an image of the critic as wresting meaning from a resisting text," which in turn presents "professional literary criticism as a strenuous and heroic endeavor, one more akin to activism and labor than to leisure."[79] It seems that for most critics, neither nonfiction nor nationalism elicits such "strenuous" interpretations. Yet this is only because what constitutes a reading is an activity that will go to any degree to validate its labor. For this reason, in this book I am not interested in an "uncovering" of texts that interprets affect as an unmasking of a latent history or politics. In such a framework, affects are taken not as affects but as suspicions of other modes of making meaning. And unfortunately, in such a framework, affects are digestibly symptomatized such that they are reduced to aesthetics, which are inevitably reduced to the political.

Indeed, what we find in the hermeneutics of suspicion is a bypassing of the text's affects for the sake of the critic's. Take for instance the oft-maligned phrase "the waning of affect" formulated by Frederic Jameson, who posited that "the liberation, in contemporary society, from the older anomie of the centered subject may also mean not merely a liberation from anxiety but a liberation from every other kind of feeling as well, since there is no longer a self present to do the feeling. This is not to say that the cultural products of the postmodern era are utterly devoid of feeling, but rather that such feelings . . . are now free-floating and impersonal."[80] Critics have misappropriated Jameson's "waning of affect" to mean the absence of affect. Jameson's binary opposition between modernist anomie and postmodern impersonality, centered and decentered, hides, as most structuralist readings do, the point of intersection between supposed oppositions. It is not that affect has waned in the contemporary; rather, it is that contemporary aesthetics found cultural cachet in obscuring affect itself, as Pop Art found through seriality and, as I will explore through the work of Sarah Vowell, Generation X found through tactics of quirkiness, "smartness," and irony. The self, and its affective intensities, are still present in these contemporary aesthetic practices, but their expression of intensity has become secondary to intellectualized displays of incredulity. Jameson's binary opposition between Munch and Warhol proves the point: Warhol can only have an aesthetic effect, regardless of its intensity, if the viewer "gets" the aesthetic smartness of Warhol's seriality and his projection of popular culture onto serious art or the avant-garde. Its cultural cachet is its deliberately crafted emotionlessness, which is not the same as the absence of emotion altogether. Such emotionlessness, or depthlessness, should not be read only as a symptom of the cultural logic of late capitalism in which "the surrender to various forms of market ideology" by the political left "has been imperceptible but alarmingly universal."[81] Rather, such work should be read as an aesthetic practice of a late capitalism that evokes affects of a different type than those prevalent in modernist art.[82] The representation of affect may shift over time: Munch's *The Scream* may capture a representation of an intense affect, yet it is a representation, heightened to achieve maximum affective intensity, while Warhol's *Marilyn* series does not, because it is based more on the cool play of the issues of representation than on representation itself. The waning of affect is an affect, manipulated in the same ways as any other representation of affective intensity.

In this light, ideological analyses like Jameson's "waning of affect" seem a melodramatic byproduct of the hermeneutics of suspicion, the effect of "digging down" through an archive of canonical works of art to reveal the "concealed" predominance of late capitalism rather than a genuine exploration of postmodernist affect.[83] Affects are concealed in plain sight, yet the hermeneutics of suspicion sets what is in plain sight aside to perform the supposedly and purely affectively strenuous, diligent, and ultimately hypervigilant work of criticism. Of course, critics have an emotional investment in making such a claim: the critic interprets that art wanes in affect, all the while delighting in the activist intensity of his affects of suspicion.

Affect is more than a symptom. The affects of nationalism, even in their weakest form, are always more than symptoms of ideology. They never merely affirm an ideology without reflection; rather, they negotiate it, challenge it, incorporate it, transform it into a unique vision of the nation. Such affects, even weak affects, are worth studying on their own, for their own purpose. As incitements to read, they reveal the insufficiency of mainstream critical practice toward both nationalism and nonfiction. Weak nationalism insists that critics expand their preconceptions of nationalism to see it in its variety of forms, and insists that critics expand their archives to closely, but not suspiciously, attend to the rhetorical work that occurs within them. Above all, weak nationalism insists that we read differently than we do at present, to set aside the melodramatic posturing through which our work is affectively registered as appropriately critical, and to reimagine the critical act as one that does not rely on wresting meaning from texts but one that feels its surfaces for their construction of meaning. One way to do so, as I do in this book, is to closely read the affective valences of synecdoche.

Reading Synecdoche

The trope of synecdoche is the prevalent modus operandi of nationalism. Synecdoche—the trope of substituting part for wholes—is both produced by affect and affect-producing. Indeed, synecdoches produce affects with such efficiency that they are often overlooked until they go awry, such as in moments of hot nationalism. Synecdoches always do more than make the connection between part and whole: they are also, as Diane Rubenstein notes, figures of "integration suggestive of a qualitative relation. The example 'He was all heart' does not designate a part of the body (literally) as much as it designates a quality (empathy, compassion)."[84] It is this qualitative relation that the texts I study in this book most clearly manifest in how they construct national qualities from figures. In their doing so, they attempt to answer a question that can be answered not directly but only through a relation between the particular and the abstract. To answer the "What is America?" question is to understand the figurative relationship between the personal and the national, the individual and the community.[85] It is to posit a relationship between part and whole. The United States is an actual, political, legal, economic entity. Yet "America," insofar as it exists, does so in the transferential, affective space of synecdoche, in the space between part and whole.

It is precisely because synecdoches traverse the literal and the figural—and refuse to be exclusively either—that makes them so provoking. Synecdoches point toward something we see that is greater than what is actually seen.[86] Synecdoche, in particular, articulates the network of relations affectively, drawing out the qualitative relationships embedded in the objects that are interpreted to be part of that network. But literary critics in particular find themselves mired in the evaluation of the qualitative rather than understanding the qualitative as the generation of affect. It should be of notice that when rhetorician Kenneth Burke defined synecdoche in *A Grammar of Motives*, he chose the United States as the example par excellence. "[N]ote that a reduction is a *representation*. If I reduce the contours of the United States, for instance, to the terms of a relief map, I have within these limits 'represented' the United States."[87] Burke later characterized nationhood as a synecdochical relationship as well:

> A similar synecdochic form is present in all theories of political representation, where some part of the social body (either traditionally established, or elected, or coming into authority by revolution) is held to be 'representative' of the society of the whole. . . . And though there are many disagreements within a society as to what part should represent the whole and how this representation should be accomplished, in a complex civilization any act of representation automatically implies a synecdochic relationship (insofar as the act is, or is held to be, "truly representative").[88]

Synecdoches are reductions that allow for representation to take place. In other words, they imagine the large by reducing it to the small, the universal to the particular. And as Burke notes, such representation is inherently political, not only in terms of political representation itself but in the debates it conjures, the extent to which any synecdoche is "truly representative" of the whole it seeks to represent.

Critics have proven suspicious of synecdoche because of the qualitative dimension that it raises. This suspicion is most directly evident in the correspondence between Kenneth Burke and one of the cofounders of New Criticism, John Crowe Ransom. When Burke wrote to Ransom about the subject of synecdoche, Ransom responded by writing, "I hate the vulgarity of rhetoric. . . . People are entitled to the plain truth, the plainer, the better."[89] This is an astonishing comment given New Criticism's interest in the "close reading"—along with allegory and irony—of ambiguity.[90] For Ransom, there is a "vulgarity" to synecdoche that places it outside the orbit of apolitical literariness that the New Critics and other formalists so highly prized. The word "vulgar" is telling: synecdoche is not intellectual but popular, not educated but the trope of the unteachable.[91] Criticism's suspicion of nonfiction and its affects parallels criticism's suspicion of synecdoche. Spivak's and Ignatieff's dismissal of nationalism as "conjuring" and "repressed" are similar to Ransom's dismissal of synecdoche as "vulgar." Both perpetuate a divide between the academic and the popular, encoded as a divide between reason and emotion. And in his own way, Ransom is echoing a tradition in rhetorical criticism from Quintilian through Hobbes and Locke, in which synecdoche is seen as unnecessary ornamentation for that which should be "plain" and "true."[92] Much like the impulse to distinguish imagined communities through degrees of falsity or genuineness that haunts the study of nationalism, this tradition seeks to rein in the qualitative and affective dimension of synecdoche—in order to evaluate the falsity or genuineness in the "truly representative"—that Burke discovered as he was developing his theory of tropes. For while Ransom saw it as vulgar, Burke confided to him that he had "come to believe" that synecdoche is "Trope No. 1," writing that "with Platonizing efficiency I began to see synecdoches everywhere."[93] That Burke came to see the trope "everywhere" points toward how synecdoche offers an explanation of the world as much as an incitement to read it. The extent to which synecdoche had become "Trope No. 1" is evident in Burke's definition of what constituted it: it was not only part for whole but "whole for the part, container for the contained, sign for the thing signified, material for the thing made . . . cause for effect, effect for cause, genus for species, species for genus, etc.," as well as "before for after, implicit for explicit, temporal sequence for logical sequence, name for narrative, disease for cure, hero for villain, active for passive."[94] Synecdoche inductively activates an expansive network of associations in such a way that synecdoches can be seen everywhere.

But with such expansion, the issue of the "truly representative" begs the question of the stability of tropes altogether.[95] When "cause" can synecdochically represent "effect" and "effect" can synecdochically represent "cause," critics may feel trapped in synecdoche's potential for circular thinking. Synecdoches are "neither definitive nor absolute; they suspend sentence and make every formulation a probation."[96] I suspect what frustrates critics most about synecdoche is that despite our best critical efforts to reign in the trope by defining it, to adopt it to a method replete with logics and fallacies, we cannot fully discipline synecdoche's inductive, qualitative, and affective potentialities.

For me, synecdoche provides the way to read the rhetoric that makes visible not only the connection between part and whole but also the affects in the space between part and whole that compose and make synecdoche—and the incitement to construct them—visible in the first place. It is in the relationship between part and whole that reveals, regardless of affect, emotion, or mood, that the incitement to read has "an irreducible systematicity which must be taken into account in any analysis of it."[97] My approach has been highly influenced by Ahmed's "sociality of emotions" that examines the way in which "emotions are not 'in' either the individual or the social, but produce the very surfaces and boundaries that allow the individual and the social to be delineated as if they are objects."[98] As strongly as they originate inside us, affects are vexing because they are social processes and need to be recognized socially for interpretation, for others to understand us, and for us to understand ourselves. As unpredictable as they seem, "emotions create the very effect of surfaces and boundaries that allow us to distinguish an inside and an outside in the first place. So emotions are not simply something 'I' or 'we' have. Rather, it is through emotions, or how we respond to objects and others, that surfaces and boundaries are made."[99] This is why I write that affects occur in the space between part and whole. To evoke the language of literary criticism, affects reveal the "metonymic proximity between signs."[100] Throughout this book, I study this metonymic proximity through reading synecdoche for the way in which "the work of emotion involves the 'sticking' of signs to bodies."[101] At the same time, affects are sticky, and while stickiness helps to provide traction, affects also run the risk of getting "us" stuck, gluing objects into positions, into narratives, that we can neither detach ourselves from nor see alternatives to. Strong affects in particular tend to stick to everything in their path, such that they ignore evidence that would reduce their monopolizing, or find evidence for them in ways that ultimately undermine them. No wonder then that Ngai has written that emotions are "unusually knotted or condensed 'interpretations of predicaments.'"[102] They are also interpretive predicaments, as Eva Illouz has written: "emotions are cultural meanings and social relationships that are very compressed together. . . . It is this compact compression which confers upon them their energetic and hence their pre-reflexive, often semi-conscious character. Emotions are deeply internalized and unreflexive aspects of action, but not because they do not contain enough culture and society in them, but rather because they have too much."[103]

"Too much" means that even weak affects are dense and rich with meaning. In their affective compression, synecdoches induce feeling: they induct, inductively. They conscript us by their seeing larger principles from small examples, inciting an interpretation that promises we can make similar inductions. In their elasticity, a space for imagination is established. David Lodge writes that synecdoche is "produced by deleting one or more items from a natural combination, but not the items it would be most natural to omit," challenging the "naturalness" of language and reminding critics of the power of figurative language.[104] Yet the affective power of synecdoche is probably what made it "Trope

No. 1" for Kenneth Burke: the trope's persuasive capacity to conscript us into groups we had never thought ourselves members of before; or to push us away from one identification and inspire us to construct new identifications of our own description.

Synecdoche, then, is itself an affective turn—a turn with certain risks involved. As Michel de Certeau wrote, "synecdoche makes more dense: it amplifies the detail and miniaturizes the whole."[105] The efficiency of synecdoche to make the world understandable, however, comes at a cost. Between amplification and miniaturization, there is always instability in the synecdochical process. Affects risk misdirection, overwhelming the rhetorical tactics that generate them in the first place. Returning to Tomkins, synecdoches, by making weak theories of affect visible, risk turning weak theories into strong theories of affect. And the nation, as an object, invites such moments of risk. Weak nationalism, as Sutherland notes, "keeps the embers of nationalism glowing."[106] To understand such narratives for the synecdochical construction of their affects allows us to see how the embers of nationalism can wax and wane, shift suddenly from warm to hot, from weak to strong. And yet for such risk, it provides many rewards and promises that one's affects have a meaning and a place among other citizens.[107] Criticism, in prioritizing the quantitative over the qualitative, too often sidesteps the openness of affects (which is key to their weakness) in favor of a hermeneutics of suspicion that sees affect as delusion—of being in the bush for too long—or as interpellation—how we are taught to cope yet persist when the facts of the world get us down—or as vulgar rhetoric—the antithesis of what merits close reading—without fully appreciating, as affect theory does, its value as the "languages and logics of calculation that people use to live their lives."[108] Hegemonic it can be, but that does not negate the impressive productivity of its narratives and its narrative potential to offer writers and readers a shared moment of affect. Of course, as Priscilla Wald writes, "An official story of 'a people' invariably lags behind the seismic demographic changes and corresponding untold stories that ultimately compel each revision."[109] While the official story lags behind, it is also perpetually modified, appropriated, and revised: parts that, in turn, recast and rejuvenate the story of the nation.

And even if we find its synecdochical discourse to be hackneyed, it nevertheless persists in our culture. As Wendy L. Wall notes, the Cold War project of consensus and unity—the search for a definitive American Way of Life—has persisted well after its height of rhetorical power: "phrases coined or popularized . . . 'free enterprise,' the 'Judeo-Christian tradition' and the 'American Way' remain staples of US political and cultural discourse."[110] Such synecdoches have been appropriated by both the left and the right, in moments of both strong and weak affect, as keywords to justify their political programs, even if such programs seldom point to the centrist vision behind the origin of such phrases. At the same time, the attempt to impose consensus and unity through synecdoche reminds us how the trope can be used to conceal the frayed politics of the present. Through its interplay of parts and wholes, weak nationalism envisions the nation as a universal that all participate in. At the same time, this conception of the nation can come at the expense of something: an intense affect that is lessened; a politics that is weakened. Indeed, weak nationalism can work to minimize legitimate critiques of the nation. Its synecdochical strategies and universalizing guise can obscure and co-opt discontent. In its appeal to the whole, it can sidestep the thorny politics of parts. Take, for example, the universalizing impulse behind the recent "All Lives Matter" movement. As Judith Butler has commented, the movement "misunderstand[s] the problem, but not because their message is untrue."[111] By this, Butler means that while "it is true that all lives matter, it is equally true that not all lives are understood to matter."[112] The synecdochical leap of the movement, and its presumed universalism, fundamentally obscures the political charge of the "Black Lives Matter" movement, namely, that throughout American history and in the present, African American lives have not "mattered": as Butler puts it, "that black people have not yet been included in the idea of 'all lives'" itself.[113] The movement presumes that all lives already matter, even as contemporary events, including those that birthed the Black Lives Matter movement, remind us time and time again that what counts as "life" in America is highly racialized. The All Lives Matter movement thus offers an example of how weak nationalism's universalizing strategy frequently dismisses the legitimacy of activist discontent as a mere local phenomenon—as a part—that is unrepresentative of the whole it claims to represent. And it too frequently skirts the issue of minority representation in the name of a broader consensus, one that in the worst case perpetuates the invisibility of minorities in its synecdochical depiction of the nation. Its vision of the nation frequently ignores the intense political work that needs to be done to truly bring the vision it depicts to all.

Thus the affects that synecdoches of weak nationalism evoke remind us of the expansiveness of the nation as a concept, the complex and potentially contradictory ways in which we deploy it, and the limitations of our ability to read it. The rhetoric of the nation always extends beyond both its historical origins and contemporary uses, and refuses to comply with our critical methodologies. The texts I study in this book remind us not only of the dynamics of weak nationalism but ultimately of critical reading's biases toward nationalism, nonfiction, affect, and synecdoche. Thus to study these texts closely but without suspicion opens many doors, not only for the texts themselves but also for what I hope will be a greater discussion of the complexities of nationalism, a respect for a genre whose history is marked with neglect, a turn in criticism that engages with affects both weak and strong, and a rhetoric that is far from vulgar but rather makes prominent the intelligence of the affects.

In the chapters that follow, I examine how affected readers synecdochically interpret objects that they come to see as representing the nation, and thus participate in the imagined community of the United States. I read their texts for their affects: their origins, their deployments, their effects on the objects that incite the incitement to read. I begin each chapter with an overview of the critical response—or lack of critical response—to these texts in order to account for how other critics see texts as banal or otherwise unworthy of serious inquiry, before parsing the affects that structure the texts themselves. The first chapter of this book, "Moodiness: The Everyday America of Beauvoir's *America Day by Day*," studies the French philosopher's 1948 travelogue as an example of what I call everyday reading, a way of reading that is far from the pronouncement and maintenance of a consistent methodology but is an affective practice that resists our urge to quantify it. Doing so allows me to explore how Beauvoir's analysis of the United States is held together by both sense and sensuousness. For me, the "moodiness" in *America* is indicative of an open and intense response to the flux of everyday life and its sensoria, the narrative energy that comes from the everyday—and even when critical—enjoyment of responding to the nation.

The second chapter examines the changing nature of John Steinbeck's curiosity toward America in his last two books, *Travels with Charley: In Search of America* and *America and Americans*. For Steinbeck, such curiosity is personal and libidinal, allowing him to connect with a nation he fears he does not know anymore, one that, as he describes in *Travels*, becomes a broader representation of himself. His fascination with the part-whole relationship, between macrocosm and microcosm, is so intense that it leads him to invent the nation through the analysis of the garbage left behind in a hotel room. I juxtapose this with the waning of his curiosity in *Americans*, in which synecdoches of the United States seem to fuel Steinbeck's discontent toward a rapidly changing America rather than a continued curiosity for the nation. Steinbeck's reading of the nation seems forced because it is bound up in his attempts to contain the nation under the synecdochical assertion that all American problems stem from one single cause that he cannot precisely define.

The third chapter studies the affect of hopefulness and its cultural context in the popularly acclaimed but critically panned *On the Road with Charles Kuralt* segments that often concluded the CBS *Evening News* from the late sixties to the early eighties. While some in the news industry found these segments to be a waste of precious broadcast time and others argued that they were bastions of myth during a time of disillusionment, I argue that Kuralt's segments illuminate how synecdoche generates hopefulness in a time of national hopelessness. *Road* was popular because it offered a hopeful portrait of the nation, in juxtaposition to the sobriety of the evening news, a diffuse, warm feeling that reinforced the goodness of the nation and its promising future. Yet the affect of hopefulness performs the emotional work of hope without ever encroaching on the radicalism of hope itself: the segments never point toward the politics required to realize individual or national hopes. This becomes evident—and problematic—in Kuralt's scripting of hopefulness, which synecdochically streamlines his subject's narratives in ways that obscure national dilemmas to perpetuate hopefulness's warm feelings.

This book's final chapter, "Incredulity: Reading Sarah Vowell," focuses on the work of an author most popularly known for her contributions to the radio series *This American Life*. I trace how synecdoches of the nation constructed in Vowell's work are Generation X engagements with what Jean-François Lyotard describes as incredulity—a disbelief in a metanarrative that is not a total disbelief in that metanarrative. I explore how Vowell's often quirky (and frequently rueful) synecdochical readings of the nation are indicative of a generational reaction to Reagan-era affects of Cold War triumphalism through which Vowell aspires to fashion herself by being opposed to it. Yet in the discourse of incredulity, what is critique is also an appreciation, if not an admiration: the synecdoches that frame Vowell's incredulous affects remain anchored in her credulity toward the tenets of triumphalist metanarratives. Though she cannot entirely rid herself of it, her desire is to believe in America. Yet when provoked, the "cool" of Vowell's incredulous nationalism erupts into a credulity for the narratives she purports to oppose. Here the problem of how triumphalism, particularly its redeployment after 9/11, has conscripted the nation as a site of intense affects that benefit neoconservative politics becomes evident. If it is possible for an affective intensity toward the nation to be reclaimed without the valences of triumphalism, it may not be through incredulous nationalism's contrarian tactics.

My conclusion shifts from a reading of texts to a reading of criticism itself. Considering what has become known as "the limits of critique," I examine why the issue of weak nationalism has been so invisible to literary and cultural critics. Nationalism is innately present in the work of American literary and cultural critics, yet critics construct themselves—and an imagined community of their own—around a suspicion of nationalism that I argue limits the horizon of inquiry. I explore this limited horizon through canonical—the work and career of Lionel Trilling—as well as contemporary criticism. My goal is not to dismiss these critics, nor to postulate a "postcriticism" that would only perpetuate the affective intensities embedded in the hermeneutics of suspicion, but to suggest a more affectively aware criticism, one that engages with affects such as those of weak nationalism with dexterity and depth, a criticism that possesses a plurality of affects, which may make visible new paths of inquiry and make visible new archives through which such inquiry can be pursued. The price of our critical limitation is evident not only in the invisibility of archives like the archive of this book but also in the critical invisibility toward nationalism at a time in which the study of nationalism and its affects is all the more pressing.

The urgency of defining "America" persists in nonfiction today. And that urgency has increased as hot nationalism has not only surged but come to occupy the White House and Washington DC: the very synecdoches that represent us as Americans. What weak nationalism reminds us of in moments like these is that nationalism need not be this way. Rather, there are endless varieties of weak nationalism, and though they may use the same rhetoric, each has its own affective trajectory. Much like the texts I study in this book, we too are affected readers in the imagined community of the nation. Each of us has a theory of America, and while most of us would never identify ourselves as nationalists, our theories of America push and pull us toward objects that we read as parts of the whole that we feel is the nation. Weak nationalism, as I show throughout this book, reveals the dynamism of such theories of the nation: their synecdochical underpinnings, their manifold affective intensities, and above all, in the very richness of its weaknesses, nationalism's persistent and paradoxical vitality.

1 MOODINESS

The Everyday America of Beauvoir's *America Day by Day*

The American critical response to Simone de Beauvoir's 1948 travelogue, *America Day by Day*, has a curious lineage. It is connected, in part, to the American critical response to existentialism at the time of its publication. As George Cotkin surveyed in *Existential America*, responses to the book reveal a critical tension: for some, existentialism was "hard talk and intellect," while for others, it was a fashionable vogue "to be ogled and wondered at [rather] than be taken seriously."[1] Those who associated existentialism with hard talk found *America* to be lacking. Elaine Marks wrote in the *French Review* that "our author is too often seduced by generalizations not invalid, but rather banal."[2] In the *New York Times*, Henri Peyre wrote "there is much she has failed to observe. And much that she observed was banal . . . a disappointment to the demanding reader."[3]

Banal: the word that is the most derisive synonym of everyday life; the most derisive word to describe texts that attempt to answer the question "What is America?"; the most derisive word to indicate the critical disappointment that Beauvoir did not see America through the "demanding," intellectual lenses these critics had anticipated. Further, those who were more dismissive of existentialism found the book to be not only banal but insidious. Whereas Marks found Beauvoir's "generalizations not invalid," Diana Trilling concluded in her review, which I return to at the end of this chapter, that the travelogue was nothing more than "a mere bald, flat job of nasty political propaganda."[4] On its publication in the United States in 1953, Mary McCarthy borrowed an analogy from the book to write that Beauvoir's descriptions of America were "all wrong, schematized, rationalized, like a scale model under glass."[5] This critical dismissal, this insistence that Beauvoir was "wrong" about America has remained with the book, persisting well after the vogue of existentialism waned. Later critics have repeated McCarthy's critique, writing that "ultimately, Beauvoir fails to comprehend America because her prescribed notions of American culture establish a glass wall between her self and her experience."[6] The "scale model under glass" or the "glass wall between her self and her experience": these analogies construct a barrier to "right" understanding that is invisible to the "wrong" observer—but visible to the "right" critic. The American critics see the nation for what it is; Beauvoir cannot.

Yet Beauvoir expresses at the beginning of *America* her desire to "break through the glass wall" between herself and others, to "see the world truly, without restraints."[7] As she tours the United States, Beauvoir is routinely vexed by the glass walls, or floors, of major tourist sites, including the Grand Canyon, which in her opinion, substitute for "a direct view, which would be raw and violent."[8] And it is not entirely clear what the "right" critics have found: while Mark Dunphy has traced the similarities between Beauvoir and Beat poetics for their shared distaste in the mainstream of the time, Tamara Teale found the paradoxes and ambiguities in Beauvoir's writing to be the sign of a rushed traveler who "attempted to grab the richest experience without working for it, without studying and planning," as if the nation can be understood only through laborious preparation and the execution of diligent ratiocination.[9] Given such a lack of critical praise, combined with weak sales, it may be unsurprising that *America* was not republished in the United States until 1999, with a new translation by Carol Cosman.

I begin this book with what may seem an unusual choice: a text that purports to describe America that is not written by an American author. Of course, non-Americans have affects about the nation, which has been the subject for many French writers from Tocqueville to Baudrillard. Yet Beauvoir's writing of the nation seems especially rich for its emotional honesty, what I call its moodiness, which critics from McCarthy to Totten have had difficulty detecting because they seem caught up in making a judgment of falsity or genuineness, the sort of judgment Benedict Anderson so strongly eschewed in *Imagined Communities*. When Beauvoir's text is examined through the lenses of both everyday life theory and affect theory, what critics saw and continue to see as generalizing, as banal, is in fact a text rich with meaning, though not "meaning" in the form that critics expect.

At work in the American critical response to *America* is a strategy that Toril Moi finds to be paradigmatic of the criticism of Beauvoir's work in general, one in which "by discrediting her status as a speaker, they intend to preclude any further discussion of what she actually says."[10] As the criticism of the travelogue shows, much of this discrediting is performed through using the everyday in a pejorative sense: the everyday as unintellectual; the everyday as banal. In this way, the lineage of the critical response to *America* is also paradigmatic of the critical discomfort for everyday life, which, as Joe Moran writes, has emerged as a "subject of intellectual inquiry" in a "slightly begrudging, tangential way" over the last century.[11] But what makes everyday life seem tangential is its very centrality: "what is most difficult to discover" about the everyday, according to Maurice Blanchot, is that "the everyday, then, is ourselves, ordinarily."[12] The ordinariness of everyday life is what makes it difficult to discover, especially for critics whose careers are premised on the ability to demonstrate their own sort of "hard talk" through the critical readings of texts. This is not to besmirch Beauvoir's critics— nor the endeavor of criticism itself—but to suggest that the lineage of the American critical response to *America* has often, in dismissing its everydayness as banal, undemanding, or wrong, produced "critical" readings of the text that often ignore the fundamental, central role of moodiness in the composition of everyday life.

This chapter reexamines *America* by envisioning what has been seen by critics as a weakness, instead, as a considerable strength.[13] In this spirit, I reexamine *America* as a contribution to the study of affects, a moody text that demonstrates the role of everyday life in the construction of national narratives. Everyday life theory reminds us, as Ben Highmore writes, that the everyday is not a "sleight of hand," a tactic of dismissal, but a "problematic, a contested and opaque terrain, where meanings are not to be found ready-made" and self-evident.[14] Accordingly, in this chapter, I examine how Beauvoir constructs America, day by day: how she makes meaning of the nation, and the nation that emerges from that making of meaning. I explore what I call Beauvoir's everyday reading of America, a way of reading that is not bound by consistency nor stringency but is driven by an arsenal of personal and cultural experiences that offer Beauvoir meaning through their sensual, emotional, and intellectual resonances. Such everyday reading inevitably shapes Beauvoir's perceptions of America, and reveals much about Beauvoir's perspective as a French intellectual visiting the nation for the first time.

To read *America* through the lens of mood in everyday life is not to deny its potential to be enlightening: as Rubenstein notes, "critics too often approach travel writing as a narrative supplement or contextualization for theoretical work done elsewhere."[15] Indeed, my reading of Beauvoir's travelogue suggests that there is much theoretical work performed through Beauvoir's everyday reading of America, evidenced in the everyday nation constructed from her reading. As everyday reading, *America* reveals the connection between mood and the narrative construction of the nation's everyday life. Michael Taussig writes that everyday life is "caught *in media res* working on, making anew, amalgamating, acting and reacting" to the world the subject encounters.[16] And because everyday life is always in the midst of things, we may better see the everyday nation which emerges from it as a conceptual site that is always, as Bhabha writes, "half-made because it is in the process of being made" as it is "caught . . . in the act of 'composing' its powerful image."[17] While it may seem unusual to begin a book about the affects of nationalism with a chapter focused on a preeminent French philosopher, doing so provides an example of the "in medias res" of everyday life that informs Beauvoir's perception of America, the nation she imagines by composing her image of the United States.

As an outsider looking in at the nation, Beauvoir explicitly demonstrates the rhetorical tactics, the narrative strategies employed by the authors in my archive. The directness of her reading, and the intense response it generates, captures an immediacy of experience in a register unmediated by the need to explain oneself to fellow insiders. Looking in, Beauvoir sees synecdoches of America in ways that are defamiliarizing, rich, and startling to American audiences, who presume they know their country well. *America* demonstrates how one writer, in the midst of things, makes sense of the nation she is visiting, how she engages with it, and in writing about it, how she composes a narrative of reactions and amalgamations—comparisons, synecdoches, and analogies—that construct an everyday America of her own. This should not only remind us of how the nation is, like everyday life, a contested and opaque terrain but should also encourage critics to explore with more generosity the panoply of styles in which the nation is imagined, of which Beauvoir's everyday reading is one of many, as well as the crucial role of mood in formulating such narratives. Similarly, by considering the role of mood in everyday life, we can come to see Beauvoir's travelogue as a point of entry for a larger reimagining of what it means to construct the nation: not correctly nor officially, not for the purpose of political persuasion nor exclusion, but rather through the processes of making meaning that are undertaken every day by those who participate in the imagined community of the nation, even if only while traveling through it for a brief period.

In this chapter, I examine Beauvoir's everyday reading of America: how her observations of drugstores, bowling alleys, college cafeterias, and the urban grid lead her to interpret everyday American life. I read her everyday readings through multiple lenses, attempting to balance Beauvoir's intellectual and cultural background with the dynamism of her sensual, affectively charged responses to the everyday life she observes. In other words, I attempt to account for Beauvoir's moodiness. I attempt to read Beauvoir with a generosity that has not yet been afforded by American critics, one that understands Beauvoir's moodiness as the incitement to read, and the product of that incitement being a type of writing that critics have not yet appreciated. My reading of Beauvoir is markedly different from, as I explore later in this chapter, the hostile and microscopically intense scorn of American critics, best represented in Diana Trilling's review of the book. Trilling's review of Beauvoir, for me, reflects the role of tone in moodiness: how mood's totalization of its object is evidenced through the tone of the reading produced by it, and how critics respond to Beauvoir's tone with a critical tone of their own, one that, in Trilling's case, is more of an eruption of a developing Cold War hot nationalism as much as it is literary criticism. Moodiness thus reminds us of the importance of mood itself. Moods are difficult to account for, and perhaps therefore all the more easy for critics to dismiss. But to understand the moodiness of a text like Beauvoir's is to reveal the intensely varied incitements that emerge in texts which seek to describe the nation.

Moods and Moodiness

Theorists of affect have long been fascinated by the encompassing and inescapable nature of mood, for mood is the landscape from which emotions and affects emerge in the first place. The word for mood in German, *stimmung*, captures both mood itself and the concept of tuning, the attunement to the world one has when one is in a mood. For Martin Heidegger, such attunements are the "'*how*' according to which one is in such and such a way."[18] Moods encompass us and cast light on the objects we see in accordance with our mood. Moods are thus the "presupposition," the landscape in which our "thinking, doing, and acting" take place, the "'medium' within which they first happen.[19] As such, moods "assail us . . . and in this sense mood is also total, or totalizing. Moods do not shed light on some one thing in particular, but on a whole environment."[20] Moods may be typically described "as ambient, vague, diffuse, hazy and intangible" yet "a mood lingers, tarries, settles in, accumulates, sticks around."[21] Because mood assails us, "mood . . . is not optional, but a prerequisite for any kind of intellectual engagement."[22] Moods make possible the objects we see and shapes how we see them: for Heidegger, mood is the only way in which we can see them. Because moods persist, moods thus have a role in "modulating thought, acknowledging a dynamic and interactive relationship between reason and emotion."[23] And in the reading of objects that moods assail us with, in thinking about those objects while we are in a mood, we give substance and sustenance to our moods. As Felski and Fraiman write, "the process is reciprocal and dynamic; styles of thinking, in their turn, also promote and sustain moods."[24]

Going farther, one could say that moods are synecdochical, a whole that infuses the reading of parts in a totalizing way, turning parts into an affective ensemble. That mood infuses reason and emotion, that mood is reciprocal and intangible, may also explain why "our mood often seems larger than we are, its location difficult to ascertain or pin down."[25] Highmore and Jenny Bourne Taylor have noted that because "mood is made up of individual and collective feelings, organic and inorganic elements, as well as contingent, historical and slow changing conditions," mood comes to incorporate "the entire situation as well as the 'players' in it."[26] Moods are a whole of which we feel a part, which may be why the texts I study in this book seem to seek out a national mood while describing it from an individual perspective. In our cognizance, or incognizance, toward a mood, we position ourselves as players in it and deploy synecdoches that attach objects—and ourselves—to a mood.

There is a certain boldness in doing so. In the English language, the history of the word "mood" evokes three synonyms: "mind," "heart," and "courage."[27] The word's history repeatedly cautions of mood's potential to lead to arrogance. The word "mood" points toward an excess that can fog one's mind, can betray one's heart. Mood walks the fine line between reason and emotion, between giving us our bearings in the world and our being overbearing in that world. While mood may give the courage, the incitement to interpret the world, the convictions of one's mood has the potential to render one overly confident in what their moods tell them. Such "courage" comes from the totalizing effect mood has on one's perception of objects, which is displayed in the tone of the pronouncements of these perceptions.

Perhaps the promises and perils of mood help to explain what we talk about when we talk about moodiness: we describe, in a pejorative sense, the out-of-place mood of another. Moodiness is the fluctuation of mood, a reminder of its contingency when mood is otherwise presumed to be slow-changing and subtle. When someone is "moody," their affects run counter to the mood of others, or of moods in general: such affective friction is often understood as a latent expression of frustration or anger. The moody person is not in the mood, meaning that the mood is not felt inside one. Yet moodiness may alert us to the potential for seeing things otherwise. Moodiness is synonymous with feeling "withdrawn" from a socially predominant mood. Yet such friction and withdrawnness can be productive in ways that point beyond the pejorative use of the word, as being withdrawn places one outside the norm and thus able to see what is normal to us in a more insightful way. The moody person is not in the mood but outside of it and looking in, seeing something of those in the mood that only the moody person can describe. Because "mood is the form that attention takes," moodiness is the sign of that attention taking form, of the moody person's awareness of an investment in an object, and the desire to understand how others—and themselves—are affected by it.[28]

Felski and Fraiman write that "mood is like the weather."[29] If that is the case, moodiness is the shifts in the affective weather that evoke an ongoing reading of its objects. Moodiness may point then toward the moment in which we sense some turbulence in the weather, feel caught in the sway of mood, and adjust our interpretive bearings. Heidegger understood such turbulence as "the movement of falling" away from an authentic encounter with the world and into the "nullity of inauthentic everydayness," yet he also understood the potential expansiveness of the term, as the turbulence of thrownness is "neither 'a fact that is finished' nor a Fact that is settled."[30] Moodiness is a tentative space where moods— and its meanings—are neither finished nor settled. Similarly, if a mood is a "phenomenon which functions methodologically," then moodiness is the point at which mood comes to function like a methodology.[31] Like the moody outsider looking in, the readings that come from our moodiness may be tentative and temporary, uneven or uninformed, but they reassure us that there is something of value to read, and of our ability to read it. To see the readings that emerge from moodiness as exclusively leading toward "inauthentic everydayness" does much to deny the other possibilities of moodiness, much less everydayness. To see the moody person as caught in the sway of mood suggests that their understanding of the object is in transition. This may explain why Moi writes of Beauvoir that "at its best her writing lets her affects—joy, anxiety, depression—flow freely through language; at its worst it becomes a lifeless simulacrum of representation in which the only affect conveyed to the reader is that of boredom."[32] Moodiness registers in language the flow from affect to affect, the transition from anxiety to confidence, from disinterest to interest. The moodiness of Beauvoir's reading of the nation sometimes results in a fascinating appliqué of existentialism onto America—and sometimes seems unreflective in its sensuous enthusiasm for the nation. Her reading sometimes defamiliarizes and thus refreshes the potential for an authentic engagement with the complexities of the nation—and sometimes reinforces European stereotypes of Americans. Her reading offers a possibility that sometimes allows for a fuller examination of its object—and sometimes dismisses those objects with resignation. Moodiness registers the dynamism of our response to being thrown into a world that we sense and seek to understand. Thus moodiness tells us much about mood. If mood is an atmosphere, it is one that we can decipher only through feeling moody toward it, as we "first immerse ourselves" in a mood that "attunes us through and through" in how we see objects.[33] The "through and through" of moodiness is important here, for attunement occurs not smoothly or cohesively but, like an instrument being tuned, gradually and repeatedly. We come to be in a mood over time, as moods saturate the objects we see. Similarly, we may resist a mood in some ways and not in others. We can become critical, or intellectual, toward the moods we perceive in the sway of resisting them. Our intellectual stance toward an object is a type of critical moodiness toward an object, after all.

It is through our moodiness that we indicate how we are touched by the world, and "only when we are touched . . . we feel what matters to us."[34] Moodiness may reflect the moment in which we "do our best to exert agency in relation" to a mood.[35] Moodiness may show us the moment of focusing, the lens of mood as it adjusts its sight on an object. "Only when we have been 'tuned in' to the world in a certain way can we be 'turned on' to the things and people around us. Moods enable us to focus our attention and orient ourselves."[36] In moodiness, our attention may be focusing but not fully focused; it may be orienting but not oriented. Moodiness is captured, then, in what I will call everyday reading, a way of reading that is not bound by the strictures of full focus or firm orientation or rigorous analysis. In the sway of mood, the moody person's sense of the objects in their purview shift, making connections between objects that were not visible before, while the connections that were visible before disappear. Everyday reading captures the attentiveness—and inattentiveness—of reading that occurs when moods shift. Moodiness shows us the moment in which objects connect with affects, in which parts connect with a whole. Moodiness shows those moments of fusion in both their deliberate and haphazard fusing, in which reason and emotion are intertwined and spark the incitement to read.

Beauvoir's travelogue is fascinating because of its moodiness, which defamiliarizes the objects which compose the nation. Her reading of America captures alternate possibilities of national moods and the understanding of the nation itself. Of course, "we all only have access to the moods we find around us, the moods into which we have been educated, and the moods that have been shaped or determined by the concrete historical context in which we coexist."[37] Beauvoir came to America equipped with a unique arsenal of moods. As I explore below, Beauvoir's moodiness comes in part from her education, specifically, the education she received at the École Normale Supérieure, or ENS, which is reflected in the process and tone of her reading of the nation. But because Beauvoir came equipped with a different arsenal of moods is not to say that Beauvoir's moods are false or lacking genuineness, as her American critics claim. Rather, it is the moodiness she brings to the nation that enlivens it, the way she encounters the objects of the nation, sees synecdoches where they were previously unseen, and describes those synecdoches with a tone of directness and force that reflect the mind, heart, and courage of Beauvoir's everyday reading. It is a strength that "her ironic accents, the way she attacks her phrases, the energy she brings to the structuring of her narrative, the intensity of her imagery—these and other elements ceaselessly fluctuate across a spectrum" of affective responses.[38] Beauvoir's moodiness captures a nation we sense but not yet see, and which we may only be able to see by taking Beauvoir's moodiness seriously. I will leave it to the philosophers to study Heidegger's and Beauvoir's competing existential philosophies. But I would argue that the everyday reading Beauvoir performs in *America* reveals a negotiation of mood in which moodiness, as an incitement to read is neither inauthentic nor null, and far from banal.

Everyday Reading, Reading Everyday America

As if anticipating those who would argue she was "wrong" about America, Beauvoir never claimed to be "right" in her understanding of the nation. From the book's beginning, she makes clear that the four months she spent in the United States, where she "traveled for pleasure and wherever I happened to be invited"—she was on a lecture tour—did not allow enough time for "a serious study, which would be presumptuous of me to attempt."[39] Noting that she was neither able to visit factories nor meet political elites, Beauvoir focused on what she could see: the landscape as she traveled the country, the occasional monument and "tourist trap" she was escorted to, the personalities of the intellectuals she met along the way. Most important, she further writes, "Indeed, often I never arrived at a fixed viewpoint" of the United States, "and it is the whole collection of my indecisions, additions, and corrections that constitutes my opinion."[40] Beauvoir encourages readers to read each journal entry—each day—as a part, while keeping in mind that each part contributes to the whole collection, her portrait of the nation, which is more dynamic than the parts alone. In fact, the travelogue form of the book is meant to accentuate "the chronological order of my amazement, my admiration, my indignation, my hesitation, and my mistakes."[41] The conclusion to the preface is precise: "This is what I saw and how I saw it. I have not tried to say more."[42] In so clearly defining her project, she may have done so to a fault. One suspects that in writing that she did not try to say more—"right" or "wrong"—Beauvoir understood that she would be misconstrued.

But, regardless of the chance she would be misconstrued, there was something about America that incited her to write about it. In a letter to Nelson Algren, Beauvoir wrote:

> I should not like this travel to be lost; I must keep something of it, with words if nothing else is possible. I shall speak of America, but about myself, too; I should like to describe the whole experience of "myself-in-America" altogether; what means arrival and departure and passing by, and the attempt to look at things, to get something of them and so on. And at the same time I'll try to get the things themselves.[43]

Hyphenated, and in quotation marks too, the phrase "myself-in-America" is telling: the hyphens inseparably fuse Beauvoir to her subject. As Beauvoir told Algren, she sought to describe "the whole experience," the spectrum of moods that one experiences as one arrives and departs, how one looks at objects as they pass by her purview. She looks not only at those parts but also at the whole, as it coheres for her, a traveler in a foreign land, speaking for the nation she sees, and for herself as well. To take her letter to Algren as a frame complementary to the preface, the book becomes, as she writes, a reading that tries "to get something" of the nation and its objects, an "attempt to look at things," but not perform a definitive reading. As such, to demand methodological rigor or exacting description is to miss the point. Thus, if critics are to go beyond claims of falsity or genuineness, we need to appreciate the intellect and insight the text offers in a different way, one that not only acknowledges the synecdochical structure of the book but also appreciates the moodiness inherent in the construction of a whole from individual parts.

The nation, as Beauvoir approaches it, requires an alternative mode not only of writing but also of reading. This is why I characterize Beauvoir's reading of the nation as everyday reading: a way of reading that is far from the pronouncement and maintenance of a consistent methodology but a contingent practice that resists our urge to quantify it. To borrow from Certeau, in everyday life, the reader drifts across the object being read with wandering eyes, expecting, appropriating, and improvising meaning.[44] In doing so, the everyday reader "poaches on it, is transported into it, pluralizes himself in it like the internal rumblings of one's body."[45] This is how we take what we see and make it our own. Our doing so "includes much that is not sense so much as sensuousness, an embodied and somewhat automatic 'knowledge' . . . that is imageric and sensate rather than ideational."[46] The dynamism of everyday reading makes it hard to explain to ourselves and others because it makes sense to us. Everyday reading captures how sense is endlessly made and remade. A definitive interpretation of everyday reading, while convenient, would be falsely reassuring.

Beauvoir's first descriptions of America are, indeed, sense combined with sensuousness. She feels the nation through the heat of the hall as she clears customs at LaGuardia Airport. "People have warned me, 'It's always too hot in America.' This dulling heat, then, is America; and this orange juice handed to me by a young woman with shiny hair and a practiced smile is also America."[47] The sensation of heat may be wishful thinking (or perhaps wishful feeling), since she has been warned about it: not of any particular place in the nation, but of the nation as a whole. Seeing the orange juice and smile of the hostess as "American," Beauvoir expresses the overwhelming potential for signification: are there "American" signifiers everywhere in this nation? If the heat is American, then what isn't? Reacting to such overwhelming sensation (and signification), Beauvoir concludes that America "will have to be discovered slowly; it will not let you devour it like a big piece of candy."[48] The comparison of the nation to candy is telling, as it connects the sensual to the intellectual: the sensual love of candy to the intellectual's love of knowledge.

The interplay of sense and sensation in everyday reading is dynamic and at times contradictory, but always surprising. As Penelope Deutscher has noted, while Beauvoir could be faulted for sounding uncritical about the nation—comparing it to a big piece of candy, for example—at the same time, everyday reading can lead to "some kind of social analysis," from which a philosophical or critical project can emerge.[49] It is not that Beauvoir sees only what she wants to: in fact, she is often suspicious of the things she has been told to see. Even as she is aware, in her walks throughout New York City, that "I encounter another contrast with each step, and they are all different," at the same time, she finds that the descriptions she has heard of the city are both "hollow" and accurate.[50] As she walks through the Bowery, she remembers, "People have told me something more precise: 'On the Bowery on Sundays, the drunks sleep on the sidewalks.' Here is the Bowery; the drunks are sleeping on the sidewalks. This is just what the words meant, and their precision disconcerts me."[51] Precision may be disconcerting to Beauvoir because it denies the incitement to read: if what you see matches up with what you have been told you will see, then there is not much more to say.

This frustrates Beauvoir. As Moi writes, there is a connection between Beauvoir's moodiness and "the incitement to interpretation" throughout her corpus.[52] "Moodiness" should not be taken as a disabling "feminine" stance in opposition to a moodless "masculine." Rather, Beauvoir's frustration, as an expression of moodiness, reveals a transition in her reading of an object, which obligates her to read the object again and interpret it anew. Such moodiness is indicative of an open and intense response to the flux of everyday life and its sensoria, the narrative energy that comes from everyday life, and the enjoyment of responding to it: as Lars Svendsen writes, "moods open up an area within which something can be represented."[53] And as Jean-Paul Sartre described her to Madeline Gobeil, Beauvoir was a person who "thinks about what confronts her . . . without any detour."[54] If the direct confrontation of mood itself—often taken as a sign of moodiness—incites her writing, that incitement registers a tone that has no detour either, but takes aim at its object with force. The immediacy and intensity of Beauvoir's reading of the nation comes from the very texture of her writing—her thinking and her feeling the nation. That texture reveals an honesty that Moi describes as Beauvoir's inability to conceal "the slightest oscillation in her belief of the power of language to signify."[55] Her frustration that her reading of the Bowery matches what she has been told about the object yields disconcertment because her reading is in concert with others. It might be said that in the Bowery, she is too much in the mood of others. And so Beauvoir feels frustrated because she is aware she has nothing to add to a reading of the Bowery. She acknowledges that frustration without detour and with some dissatisfaction, and adjusts her affective bearings so that what seems empty becomes filled with meaning. Moodiness therefore shows how mood, as Felski and Fraiman write, "paves the way for ideas, helping to determine what will matter to us (or not). A state of curiosity, wonder, irritation, or optimism animates us to pursue a certain path of inquiry."[56] As the atmosphere that encourages certain affects and discourages others, as the atmosphere that unlocks some interpretive doors and locks shut others, mood is the affective compass that guides the paths of inquiry, fuels interpretations, and evokes tonalities in those interpretations that reflect the incitement to make meaning from that which is read.

One can trace the contours of Beauvoir's moodiness through her fascination with the American drugstore. They are exotic to her because "I was not really able to imagine them."[57] In her fascination, she at first sees a totality: the diversity of items available for sale seem related, so related that they merge into each other. "The glossy paperback books, the tubes of toothpaste, and the boxes of candies all have the same colors: one has the vague impression that reading these books will leave a sweet taste in your mouth, and that the candy will have stories to tell."[58] But the wonder of such synesthesia is quickly restrained as she continues: "Here the creams are creamy, the soaps are soapy: this honesty is a forgotten luxury."[59] Yet again, like her walk through the Bowery, the direct correspondence between sense and sensation seems to leave little more to interpret and so the "forgotten luxury" of such "honesty" is not luxurious long before she becomes disconcerted again. "And then one soon perceives that beneath their multicolored paper wrappers, all the chocolates have the same peanut taste, and all the best-sellers tell the same story. So why choose one over the other? In this useless profusion, there's an aftertaste of deception."[60] Sense and sensation intertwine: deception is an aftertaste that emerges from the now discounted perception of honesty. Following her suspicion to its conclusion, Beauvoir writes that in America, there are "a thousand possibilities, but they're all the same. In this way, the American citizen can squander his obligatory domestic freedom without perceiving that this life itself is not free."[61]

Though this encounter takes place in one day and within one paragraph, Beauvoir's reading of the drugstore provides a guide to the readings she performs throughout *America*. What begins as a synesthesia that will have stories to tell quickly becomes a narrative of intellectual—and existential—condemnation. If Beauvoir's conclusion seems forced—as McCarthy would see it as "schematized" or "rationalized"—it is because of how the everydayness of the drugstore fits, for Beauvoir, into a theoretical schema she knows well, an existential one. And because moods affect us in a totalizing way, because moods assail us, the moodiness that comes from their assailment infuses and affects the tone of the prose that emerges from such moodiness. In this way, the previously unimaginable drugstore becomes, through fluctuations from delight to disdain, from honesty to deception, a simulacrum of freedom. Enticement of the senses generates the incitement of interpretation, which checks Beauvoir's senses and allows for an interpretation of American life. The nation is no longer what she has been told to expect, much less what she senses; instead, it is an interpretation, an argument of her own making. Is it warranted to judge the presence or absence of the conditions for an authentic existential choice in America based on a visit to a drugstore? Likely not. Yet the fear that there may not be more to describe—the sensuality of the heat, the soapiness of the soap, or the tubes of toothpaste—vanishes under the sobriety of such weighty interpretations, which for the intellectual provides a different pleasure than the senses alone. In these moments of moodiness, something about America, sensual and intellectual, emerges that is worth writing about—and we can see why America provoked Beauvoir to write.

Of course, the "forgotten luxury" has been forgotten for a reason: the poor to nonexistent supply and quality of goods in France in the immediate aftermath of the Second World War. The sensational and ideational cannot be sheared from the cultural and the political. But their inseparability should not presume their synthesis. It should be expected—to an extent—even as Beauvoir remains suspicious of the "wisdom" she receives from her friends, that Beauvoir reads everyday American scenes through what she presumes to be French equivalents. They can lead her to see spectacle where there is none, drama in commonplaces. Both fascination and despair are evident in her characterization of American bowling, which she observes in Queens. Beauvoir writes:

> I remember a set of ninepins in the alley of a French village one afternoon on [Bastille Day]. The uneven ground provided traps for the players. Gardens, cafés with music and dancing, table shaded by plane trees, all of this is replaced in America by these large air-conditioned halls where, with no laughter or discussion, people throw standardized balls into precisely measured lanes. Into the gears of this machinery they've inserted one human being, the pin-boy. You see only his feet and hands when he sets the pins back up again, and he quickly withdraws so as not to get hit by the heavy wooden mass. The rhythm of these appearances is regulated like the movement of a prison. The game is so popular that the lanes are booked days in advance. It's monotonous to watch.[62]

Travelers are at liberty to compare apples to oranges. Beauvoir's association of bowling with ninepins on Bastille Day connects the game to a holiday. The American equivalent does not possess a similar resonance; as a result, the everyday sport of bowling appears even less special to Beauvoir, inevitably less human by comparison. As such, bowling becomes an indictment of mechanization and commercialization. Removed from the gardens and cafés, with their music and dancing, the bowling hall becomes "standardized" and "measured," lacking "laughter" or "discussion." Compared so, the bowling alley is a prison, and Beauvoir further infers from the popularity of the game—"booked days in advance"—that these bowling Americans enjoy their imprisonment.

The comparisons are incongruous: a holiday to the everyday, the extraordinary to the ordinary. Such comparisons lend themselves to binary thinking: American standardization and mechanization versus French idiosyncrasy and humanity. In making these comparisons,

Beauvoir is certainly not alone: it was a presumption for French critics to see the United States "as much as a missed opportunity, a god that failed, or a dream that did not come true, as it is a demonic monstrosity or a spiritual nightmare."[63] And it may be that the construction of such binaries facilitates the moodiness of the text, as they in turn "justif[y] the extreme polarization of the judgments passed upon [the nation]."[64] Yet Beauvoir's perceptions of the nation were not unipolar: they changed as her reading changed. In this instance, the reader of the bowling alley has apparently forgotten what she wrote the week before: "Likewise, the American citizen does not submit passively to the propaganda of the smile. . . . It is really he who freely presents himself as cordial, trusting, and generous. . . . Whatever I think of American ideologies, I will always have a warm sympathy for taxi drivers, newspaper vendors, shoe-shine boys, and all those people whose daily gestures suggest that men could be allies."[65] Of course, these very same people could enjoy bowling, and Beauvoir's appreciation of them—and concern for them—appears, disappears, and reappears throughout the book.

While Beauvoir remains aware throughout *America* that individuals are not synecdoches of their nation, the incitement to interpret is irresistible. For Moi, Beauvoir's rhetorical tendencies are cultural: it is not just that Beauvoir "writes like a man . . . but like a highly specific group of men, the French *normaliens*" of the École Normale Supérieure.[66] Inasmuch as we learn to read by writing, Beauvoir mastered a rhetoric that enacts "the very arrogance and snobbery cultivated by the ENS . . . the highly condescending rhetorical structures typical of French elite teachers in relation to their students."[67] The tone of Beauvoir's training at the ENS is reflected through the affective tonality of her writing. Its emphasis on writing with "polemical forcefulness" both amplifies (rhetorically) and diminishes (substantively) her reading of the nation.[68] Tone is not in Beauvoir the "soft impressionism" that most literary critics have deemed tone to be, but a direct, in-your-face intensity that is fused with the critical act itself.[69] What Beauvoir sees—and does not see—in America is connected to the rhetoric she mastered, which structures the tone of her reading in ways that the English use of the word "mood" warns of: the potential for arrogance. Her characterizations of America have force because they risk condescension; they reveal something about the nation as Beauvoir walks the precipice between the polemical and the intellectual. In the context of the everyday reading of the nation, rhetoric and substance are fused in ways that reflect how tone is the compressed assessments of the complexity of the nation, though we often read it for something else altogether, the "compressed assessments of complex 'situations,' for indicating the *total* web of relations" that Beauvoir experiences in America.[70] Beauvoir's tone may sound arrogant because of her desire to understand the "whole experience" of America, perhaps itself a sign of arrogance, which when combined with her intellectual training, obligates her to read the parts she sees in ways that compress her assessments into a whole with a tone of definitiveness. Like the students of the ENS, we feel lectured about something that we, as Americans, have knowledge of as well.

Such forcefulness may be driven by either sincere commitment or plain stubbornness—or both. The complexities of condescension—not only between teacher and student—are evident in Beauvoir's visit to Oberlin College:

> We drink milk in a dreary cafeteria, and we chat. Most of the intellectuals I met in New York amazed me with the abstention from social and political questions, but these young people amaze me more. I know very well that there is no political life in America, but at their age it's normal to try to create one. No. Even among themselves they don't talk about social problems; they hardly talk about intellectual concerns either, they say. 'What do you talk about?' I ask. They shrug their heads, nothing. More specifically, sports or college organizations. These are the chief distractions offered to the students. They elect presidents and committees; they thrash around and think they are acting.[71]

Oberlin may not be Manhattan—the cafeteria is not the café—but it is also not, to Beauvoir's vexation, the ENS. The "chat" seems neither heated nor critical: the relationship between American student and French professor is dissimilar. Much to her credit, Beauvoir appears to have forgotten her role at Oberlin: the visiting, distinguished foreign intellectual, and she is generous in her presumption that undergraduates are fellow intellectuals. But the degree of familiarity and comfort required—the mood—for the conversation Beauvoir wants to have is not yet present. Beauvoir anticipates a wellspring of comments, but her question is a poor one and, if anything, generates intimidation: its lack of specificity can only lead to an unspecific answer. When asked "What do you talk about," what else can one do but shrug? Even then, the examples of college politics that are available to students—clubs, sports, and the like—seem to pale in comparison with Beauvoir's sense of "politics." Perhaps the everyday is the site of poorly asked questions, too, but the lack of an answer to her question regardless only reinforces her opinion that "there is no political life in America."[72]

It is little wonder then that Beauvoir feels disconcerted in her conversations with Americans: "When I offer them some actual details, I feel like I'm shocking them."[73] She is surprised at their surprise: "Others are surprised that we really had to do without pineapples and oranges during the war; they even hesitate to believe it. Yet they did without many things themselves."[74] That Americans have forgotten the past so quickly—a recent past for the United States that was the present in France—leads Beauvoir to write:

> If Americans have so little sense of nuances, it isn't that they're incapable of grasping them—after all, American reality itself is sufficiently nuanced—but that they would be troubled by them. To accept nuances is to accept ambiguity of judgment, argument, and hesitation; such complex situations force you to think. They want to lead their lives by geometry, not wisdom. Geometry is taught, whereas wisdom is discovered, and only the first offers the refreshing certainties that a conscientious person needs. So they choose to believe in a geometric world where every right angle is set against another, like their buildings and their streets.[75]

Harsh as this assessment is, Beauvoir arrives at her conclusion gradually. At first, she leaves the door open: we are capable; American reality is "sufficiently nuanced." But that door does not remain open for long, for Americans do not wish to be affected by nuance. Even worse, they don't want to be forced to think, and finally, they do not want to think at all. Conscientious, yes; but wise, no. For Beauvoir, this incapability is evident not just ethically but geometrically: Americans have chosen not to think and instead "believe in a geometric world." The urban grid is interpreted as a synecdoche of the American mind.

This use of synecdoche demonstrates how Beauvoir poaches a rhetorical technique, turning it into a tactic for everyday reading that makes the unfamiliar understandable. Everyday life is abundant with synecdoche because, as Certeau notes, "synecdoche makes more dense: it amplifies the detail and miniaturizes the whole."[76] However, tone's ability to amplify rhetoric at the cost of diminishing substance is much like synecdoche's ability to amplify detail at the cost of miniaturizing the whole. Between amplification and miniaturization, there is always instability in the synecdochical process. Synecdoches wobble; they collapse on inspection. But in everyday life we read onward, without great concern that our everyday reading collapses into itself. So as much as it aspires for polemical forcefulness, a desperation forms in this passage: the argument thins as it validates itself, the analogy to geometry seems as general as any attempt to describe "American reality." The tone of the interpretation sounds definitive but at the expense of losing the very "nuance" it values. Certainly, Americans are more than their streets.

Has Beauvoir contradicted herself? One feels that if this were someone else's work and she the reader, Beauvoir would point out a contradiction. Yet, in everyday reading, contradiction is not, in effect, contradictory because as everyday reading it is an "argument" that establishes its own definitiveness along the way. Everyday life is a space marked by "uneven attention."[77] As a representation of such "uneven attention," everyday reading poses a challenge because it is not always logical, rational, uniform, or even "intellectual." The moodiness of everyday reading is unifying but not necessarily unified in its articulation or transmission: it is a world of partially read objects and poached rhetorics, of improvised connections and unreflective assumptions, of unsubstantiated polemics and untenable theses.

Yet, even in its uneven attention, the blindness of everyday reading still generates insight, because the nation that emerges from everyday reading is as fraught as the reading itself, multitudinous and contradictory. (This may explain Teale's surprising concession at the end of her article that "Beauvoir was far more balanced in her views than I have been willing to admit.")[78] As she concluded her lecture tour, Beauvoir's final reflections on the nation are—she would feel vindicated years later—ones that would soon be reflected in American sociology: the "organization man," a member of the "lonely crowd." Beauvoir's everyday American:

> He goes up and down from one floor to the other by elevator; he travels around by subway, speaks on the telephone, writes on a typewriter, sweeps up with a vacuum cleaner. Interposed between food and his stomach are factories that make canned goods, refrigerators, and electric stoves. Between his sexual desires and their satisfaction, there is a whole set of precepts and hygienic practices. Society hems him in from childhood. He learns to look outside himself, at others, for a model of behavior; this is what we call "American conformism."[79]

Beauvoir observed a nation in the grips of conformity, a conformity birthed from the Second World War's political project of unity. Conformity and unity were not only effects of the world war; they were a political project by design, a fusion of public and private interests that sought cohesion by rewriting symbols of difference. As Wall notes, both the government-sponsored War Advertising Council and private corporations indulged in advertising national unity through a discourse of "harmonious business-labor relations, and the prowess and ingenuity of American business."[80] This unity campaign would evolve into a commercially sponsored postwar celebration of consumption. In the aftermath of the war, Americans may have come to think that everyday devices—the elevator, the telephone, the vacuum cleaner—make for better living, but Beauvoir saw them as obstacles to understanding the world, and ultimately ourselves. As she tries to articulate this belief, the interplay of sense and sensation proves to be a difficult one to negotiate. Her observations of the nation lead Beauvoir to analogize: "In Hegelian terms, one can say that the negation of the subject leads to the triumph of understanding over Spirit—that is, the triumph of abstraction. And that's why in this country, which seems so doggedly turned toward the concrete, the word "abstraction" has come so often to my lips. . . . They miss the thing itself and attain only concepts."[81]

Drawing on what she knows—and feels—to explain what she sees, the dynamic relationship between sense and sensation becomes evident to Beauvoir. She is aware that true understanding cannot be analytical alone, that "it is not enough to cognize the world abstractly without engaging and attempting to change that world."[82] Yet in this passage, Beauvoir seems compelled to negotiate what she perceives as the American tendency toward abstraction. Here, the impulse to change the world is complicated by the very urge to explain it in the way she knows it, in this case, through Hegel. To explain American abstraction, she must be abstract, which separates sense from sensation. This may be why the sense of "abstraction" comes to her lips, but from where that sense comes, she does not say. She may not speak it, but the emphasis is not on the throat, nor the mouth, but the lips, the visible, sensual flesh that shapes its speaking. It is not that Beauvoir is contradicting herself. With abstraction on her lips, sense is irreconcilable with sensation. America leaves Beauvoir, at times, tongue-tied.

From beginning to end, in *America*, Beauvoir is aware that her reading of the nation does not always capture the complexity of her feelings toward it. As she tries to clarify this insecurity to her readers, she asks herself, "If, as I reflect on these things, I again find so much to criticize, why do I feel, despite everything, so sad to leave?"[83] She writes that there are "different things, perhaps, but just as depressing" in France, that "our ways of being unhappy, of being unauthentic are different from those of Americans—that's all."[84] In writing those words, she must admit, "The judgments I've made on Americans during this trip are not pronounced with any sense of superiority."[85] Beauvoir concludes, "To 'like' America, to 'dislike' it—these words have no meaning. It is a battlefield, and you can only become passionate about the battle it is waging with itself, in which the stakes are beyond measure."[86] A battlefield it is perhaps, but in reframing it as a civil war, the "battle it is waging with itself," it is no longer her battle to fight. While it is tempting to read the conclusion of *America* as some sort of defeat, as a writer returning home, from the perspective of an existentialist philosopher, it is the most honest to give.[87] Alexander Ruch makes this point clear: that "Beauvoir's only authentic response to this realization that she is not willing to stake her life in this world . . . is to move on."[88]

America ends with Beauvoir's arrival at Orly. She sees Paris with American eyes:

> On the dreary streets that lead toward Paris, people are poorly dressed; the women have undyed, untidy hair; the men have gray faces and look humiliated. The vegetables in the market are stunted. There's no taxi stand at the Invalides; at the edge of the sidewalk the travelers become irritated and begin to quarrel with themselves. It's gray outside. Paris seems numbed; the streets are dark and morose, the shop windows laughable. Over there in the night, a vast continent is sparkling.[89]

Paris lacks the "sparkling" sensations of America. It is as if she has forgotten, prior to leaving for America, that she was "poorly dressed, badly nourished, living in squalid hotel rooms on the Left Bank before moving, in 1948, to a leaky room in a rundown building near Notre Dame."[90] A traveler becomes habituated to the place they have traveled to, which makes home a different one than before. The streets are "dreary," its people "untidy" and "gray," matching the "gray outside," which describes the weather as much as the mood of Paris. Forgetting years of shortages, the vegetables now look "stunted," the slowly recovering economy is evident in the "laughable" shop windows. At the same time, one also romanticizes home while abroad, which inevitably makes returning home seem "numbed" by comparison. Neither the "dark and morose" streets nor the quarreling travelers at the Invalides match up with the gardens and cafés that give ninepins the dignity that is so lacking in American bowling. Acclimated to the everyday in America, France seems extraordinary. The last sentence of the book captures Beauvoir's realization that "I'm going to have to become reacquainted with France and climb back into my own skin."[91] It will take time for everyday France to become her everyday again.

Hot Nationalism, or Defending the Nation through Correct Spelling

As I outlined at the beginning of this chapter, the critical response to *America* was mixed at best. It often took a nativist, chauvinist form, pointing out the supposedly alien nature of Beauvoir's perspective, mocking her moodiness as symptoms of her foreignness, of her not "being in the mood," and therefore not "being in the know" of the nation, thereby simultaneously discrediting both the affective and intellectual caliber of her observations. There is an awkwardness, for example, in the review of the book by *Time* magazine, whose anonymous author goes to great lengths to never name Beauvoir as an intellectual: instead, she is referred to as "Author de Beauvoir," "Diarist de Beauvoir," and "Tourist de Beauvoir" whose "baggage was overweight in preconceived notions."[92] Attempting to read the book thematically instead of chronologically, the *Time* review erases the flux of Beauvoir's everyday reading, making it clear that Beauvoir is not American by making her sound alien: ("Like many foreigners . . . Tourist de Beauvoir hated racialism and loved orange juice").[93] The *Time* review constructs connections that are not linked in the text. The invention of such connections runs amuck, leading the *Time* reviewer to conclude that *America* is "a mixed salad of surface impressions, often crisp and pungent, more often hand-me-down gossip and soggy *ad hoc* generalizations, mostly unripe."[94] The reviewer, having taken Beauvoir's ideas as out of season, rewrites the purpose of the book so that its insights are unrecognizable—and unpalatable.

Gordon Hutner has written of a moment in the late forties in which "a kind of novel meant to help citizens learn how to behave amid new social fluidities . . . a primer in nation making" with instructions replete in "dramatic intensity" came to the fore only briefly before it was "squashed by anticommunist jingoism."[95] Not only does Beauvoir capture in nonfiction the same pressing question—what is the character of American life?—but the critical reception of her work gives us a guide of that squashing in action. Perhaps no better example of this misreading is

Diana Trilling's reaction to *America*. The tone of Trilling's review of the book is so adamant, so driven by strong affects, that it attacks not only the content of the travelogue but its surface as well, as if pointing out the spelling errors introduced by Beauvoir's translator is evidence of her anti-Americanism. Trilling's reading—or misreading—of Beauvoir shows how affectively intense the response to moody narratives and their totalizing tonalities can be, and how such strong affects work to deny the complexity of moods themselves, to expel as "un-American" narratives from the index of narratives that constitute the nation. Thus Trilling's review of the book shows how hot nationalism totalizes the objects it seeks to expel, as well as the tonality of the criticism it performs to expel it.

Trilling's review of the book, tucked into the 1953 *Avon Book of Modern Writing*, edited by *Partisan Review* allies William Phillips and Philip Rahv, at first deems the book "a singularly dull affair," yet escalates quickly into describing it as "disingenuous of sovereign proportions."[96] Trilling's treatment of the text—and its author—makes Peyre's description of the book as "a disappointment to the demanding reader" reasonable by comparison.[97] For Trilling, the structure of the text is a ruse intended to hide "its hostility to America," an attempt to humanize "a mere bald, flat job of nasty political propaganda."[98] It is evident that Trilling has already decided that Beauvoir is not intellectual; but it is that Beauvoir is considered to be an intellectual that sparks a ferocity in Trilling that seems to know no bounds. It is revealing that Trilling devotes a twenty-sentence paragraph in her review to pointing out typos, not in the American edition, which had yet to be released, but in the United Kingdom edition, which Americans would likely never see: "The Grand Central Station in New York Mme. de Beauvoir calls the Central Station. The Hispanic Museum she calls the Spanish Library. The name of the architect Kiesler she gives as Kisler. The painter Max Ernst Mme. de Beauvoir calls Marx Ernst. The name of Dashiell Hammett she gives as Dashiel Hammet."[99]

And so on. Trilling reassures us in a footnote, "I have checked the English edition against the French. Although the translation is poor, it cannot be blamed for the errors I list."[100] And, just in case it occurs to us that typos like these are not catastrophic "errors," Trilling counters that "it should be kept in mind that I am not citing from the work of any ordinary tourist, but from the work of a trained scholar."[101] Clearly, Trilling suggests, intellectuals who misspell are not intellectuals at all; for her the misspellings show Beauvoir's "lack of respect in which she held the subject of her investigations, a lack of respect integral with her animus."[102] Animus, indeed; for in fixing her spelling, Trilling's review fixes with certainty her intense affects toward Beauvoir's writing. Spell-checking can serve as criticism only if there is nothing of content to criticize.

But why is Trilling so fixated on Beauvoir's spelling—in actuality, Beauvoir's translator's spelling? In part it is because Trilling's fascination with the surface of Beauvoir's writing provides a way to establish a totalizing, critical tone over Beauvoir's writing. As Ngai reminds us, tone is the "text's affective bearing," which is picked up by critics who then "generalize, totalize, and abstract the 'world' of the literary object."[103] For Ngai, this makes tone "particularly conducive to the analysis of ideology" through which critics respond to texts and envision literary periods through which those texts are interpreted.[104] Once Trilling has established a critical tone toward Beauvoir's work, she is able to demonstrate that her misspellings are surface-level flaws, symptomatic of a larger, ideological flaw. And she is able to account for Beauvoir's tone through those misspellings, a tone that she sees as hostile and disrespectful toward America. Thus Trilling is able to say, with a tone that is intellectually forceful, that she does not like Beauvoir's tone.

Yet "tone's generality and abstractness should not distract us from the fact that it is always 'about' something."[105] Tone begets tone, and particularly in the case of literary criticism, once a tone has been established, it is seductive to read the text for its tone alone, rather than for its tonal complexity, much like one reads a text for a consistent mood rather than its moodiness. In this case, Trilling's tone is not only formed in response to Beauvoir's but is also reflective of the tone of hot nationalism, the hostility toward an outsider looking in, of describing the country the nationalist is supposed to know better than any other. The defamiliarized perspective of an outsider looking in at the nation can easily activate a hot nationalist response. Nationalism, as Bhabha notes, is pedagogical and performative.[106] Hot nationalism is predicated on an intense reaction to what nationalists perceive as a misuse or misreading of their objects and the narratives that emerge from such misreadings. Hot nationalism is the eruptive moment in which such a response is triggered and comes to the surface in a way that seeks out and attempts to "correct" the misreading, the inappropriate "slide between figures" that the outsider has performed in their reading of the nation.[107] In its most virulent form, hot nationalism may well be the "mobilization of hate as a passionate attachment closely tied to love."[108] But it need not be so virulent: it can take minor forms, such as the expression of correction, like Trilling's correction of Beauvoir's typos. What is felt, regardless, is hot nationalism's tone: the preachy, pedagogic, totalizing tone that is hurled at the other who is deemed wrong for incorrectly interpreting the national object. The hot nationalist's veracity of tone indicates their confidence of correctness—and love of country—that exposes the outsider's supposed misreading as animus toward the nation. Any reading that does not conform totally to the strong nationalist's view is characterized as nasty political propaganda. To paraphrase Ngai's study of tone, hot nationalism's affects generate a lot of noise in its encounter with the other.[109] Hot nationalism shouts that even minor things like typos are in actuality betrayals, it screams over whatever the evidence is to bring others to agree with its interpretation of falsity. It is also a noise for its own sake, not only to bandage the injury to the national body that the hot nationalist perceives, even when no damage exists, but also to rouse and induce new followers. Hot nationalism seeks to repair what it perceives has broken down with a "dramatic psychology of the emotions."[110] In the loudness of its tone, hot nationalism dramatically shouts over weak nationalism to demonstrate its strength and, in doing so, demonstrates itself as a "strong" theory of affect that is as totalizing as it is monopolizing, seeking to alter the mood of inquiry—and thus the potential for inquiry itself. But like strong theories of affect, hot nationalism is inflexibly unstable. While weak nationalism defamiliarizes, expands the index of narratives that constitute the nation, hot nationalism desires to correct the ungainliness of such expansion, to correct and edit out of the national narrative that which it does not believe fits it. Perhaps Trilling's hostility toward Beauvoir—and her typos—is unsurprising after all, as at the level of minutiae it does what hot nationalism does more broadly. Its tone is hot nationalism at the level of the literary critic's milieu, where the politics are so vicious because the stakes are so small.

But Trilling's hostility—her mood toward Beauvoir—has both personal and political dimensions. (Though they were oceans apart, Beauvoir and Trilling were, in a way, in the same boat. Both women were, unfortunately, perceived as "second" to the men in their lives, a double bind that, to quote Moi on Beauvoir, may have made both women "victim and perpetuator of symbolic violence" in their deployment of polemical forcefulness.)[111] It may have been important for Trilling to preclude discussion of *America* because the book includes descriptions of Beauvoir's encounters with the *Partisan Review* crowd, which suffered from mutual ideological misunderstandings, in addition to basic issues of conversing in mutually foreign languages. Finding herself with its staff at a dinner party, Beauvoir admits to being "a little bewildered; I'm not familiar with their journal, I don't know what they're implying or what their values are, and through the virulence of their attacks, I can't make out what points we have in common or what underlying disagreements separate us."[112] In other words, Beauvoir could not infer from the group's virulent tone the politics they sought to champion (and certainly Beauvoir's unfamiliarity with the journal would slight the egos of its editors and contributors). From Trilling's perspective, it must have been easier to dismiss Beauvoir rather than to explain why she may not have been familiar with a journal that its crowd considered to be preeminent. And Trilling's sense of Beauvoir's politics was no doubt influenced by her own evolving political trajectory: Beauvoir may have represented an earlier self who had not yet overcome the naiveties of socialism. "The trouble with intellectuals like her is that they cannot identify politics with mind," Trilling writes. "They leave their usual intellectual criteria at home when they step into the political arena because almost by definition politics means to them power without mind."[113] Trilling's insistence that Beauvoir practices a politics "without mind" points to not only an intellectual dismissal, a synecdochical dismissal of Beauvoir's intellect, but a political one as well, anchored in the binary opposition of reason and emotion: Beauvoir is at fault because she is emotional. In this way, Beauvoir's everyday feelings toward the United States (and her translator's misspellings) in *America* are interpreted by Trilling as systematic and symptomatic of a wholehearted support of Stalin.[114] (In the midst of the second Red Scare, this is a claim that could stick with ease.) Because for Trilling, an intellectual "can dislike the United States in itself, as he might dislike England in itself or France in itself," but it becomes "one thing to dislike the United States in itself and quite another to dislike it *vis à vis* Soviet Russia, for Soviet Russia spells death to everything that constitutes his life as a thinking person."[115] Beauvoir's inability to see this, Trilling writes in the last sentence of her review, does not disqualify a person from politics; rather, "it merely disqualifies him as an intellectual."[116]

In examining Trilling's review and the lineage of American critical responses to *America*, there is a systemic disregard of the travelogue's moodiness, a disregard that erases the everyday reading it undertakes to dismiss Beauvoir as a foreigner, as nonintellectual, or both. *America* became caught in what Frederick M. Dolan calls "Cold War metaphysics," the equivalent of a "looking-glass war" in which "the antagonists could never be certain that the enemy was not one of their own, reflected back to them in an uncanny register."[117] The defamiliarizing effect of Beauvoir's moodiness produced in critics such an uncanny read that she was dismissed as seeing imperfectly through distorted lenses, as if she were seeing the nation through enemy eyes. If McCarthy accused Beauvoir of looking at America like it were a "scale model under glass," Trilling's accusations of Beauvoir reflect the extent to which Trilling was in the grip of "Cold War metaphysics," "tormented by fears of an evil demon capable of creating false images, but equally possessed of the conviction that doubt can be resolved, clarification achieved, immediacy regained."[118] Thus as hot as her review of Beauvoir is, Trilling still presumes, like a good Cold War warrior, that her analysis is ultimately corrective. Trilling's review is particularly instructive of hot nationalism in how it does not deal with the text at an intellectual level: it stays on the surface, obsessed with typos and labeling, rather than making a serious rebuke of the book and its author. It is also dismisses the travelogue's moodiness, how the book and its author approach directly the experience of narrating a nation, as emotional in the pejorative sense, emotions that cannot be, according to the hot nationalist, intellectual. Yet the reviews of *America* are more like the book than its critics may want to believe. If the book captures Beauvoir's everyday reading of the United States and its "uneven attention," its critical response in the United States captures the tones of everyday "uneven attention" we give to outsiders who write about our lives. One could argue that the reviews of *America* are just as "everyday" as the text itself, if not more so: replete with mischaracterizations, intimidating theses, excessively quantitative gestures, easily conjured dismissals, quickly conjectured conclusions—and some name-calling. In the personal, visceral reaction of the critics, Beauvoir would inevitably be proven wrong in writing, "To 'like' America, to 'dislike' it—these words have no meaning."[119] In fact, they have much meaning, not only for those who live in it but for those whose critical authority depends on their delineation of it, the corrective tone they display to suppress the voices of others, and the hot nationalist sentiments that such critical authority encourages. In its simultaneous diligence and adamancy, through its pedagogical tone, the critical response demonstrates how ordinarily—and vehemently—one may react to the everyday being described by an outsider, critically or otherwise, to the nation one imagines, one constructs, and in which one feels the need to believe.

Conclusion

From her arrival in New York City, with its dulling heat and smiling hostess, to her return to Paris, where she will endeavor to "climb back into her own skin," Beauvoir captures the dynamic interplay of sense and sensation throughout *America*. Thus she reveals her own process of composing a nation through what I have called everyday reading, a plural practice that blends observation with emotion, perception with mood. The drugstores, bowling alleys, college cafeterias, the urban grid: for Beauvoir, these are representative of American life, and come to be so by her opportunity to engage in an everyday reading of those sites that display her moodiness, her energy toward interpreting the nation. The text that emerges from such everyday reading is not necessarily banal—or "wrong"—but, to return to Certeau, captures the reading of the nation as it is experienced in everyday life, its meaning expected, appropriated, and improvised along the way, in the midst of things.[120] Because of this everyday reading, *America* is an encounter with the nation that captures how the nation itself is "half-made because it is in the process of being made."[121] The plural ways in which Beauvoir composes her reading of everyday America bespeaks the ongoing, necessarily plural work of narratives of the nation.

Indeed, as Benedict Anderson wrote, it is the very plurality of narratives that allows for such communities to be imagined in the first place. The feeling of "deep, horizontal comradeship" that is associated with the nation occurs in the convergence of boundaries.[122] In *America*, we see such convergences at work in the comparisons, synecdoches, and analogies that constitute Beauvoir's reading, as she walks through the Bowery, compares bowling to ninepins, sees college life as a synecdoche of American politics or the urban grid as a synecdoche of the American mind, and analogizes the "organization man" through Hegel, we witness Beauvoir expecting, appropriating, and improvising meaning from what she observes in the nation. These textual convergences broaden the horizon of what the nation may mean, through one writer's perspective, an engagement in the nation through a comradeship that critics did not anticipate nor appreciate. Perhaps they could not anticipate it: after all, it would be difficult to acknowledge the work of everyday reading if we did not also acknowledge the centrality of everyday life in the making of these narratives, an acknowledgement that has indeed, much like the study of everyday life itself, proven for critics "most difficult to discover."[123] And it would be difficult for critics to acknowledge the role of moodiness when mood is relegated to an inauthentic everydayness, or consigned to the binary opposition between emotion and reason, or obscured if not buried under the tone of hot nationalism—or the tone of criticism—itself.

Everyday life is the most difficult to discover because critics so seldom look at it, much less look at travelogues, much less examine texts that aspire to answer the question "What is America?" Perhaps critics have underestimated *America* because it is not written in a privileged genre of literary criticism. As Timothy Brennan writes, it is the novel, as a form, that prevents the "chaotic splintering" of the nation by "objectifying the nation's composite nature," thus providing a framework to turn the nation into a linear, coherent narrative.[124] Whereas the reading of novels unifies elements into a whole to minimize splintering, everyday reading does so through unifying for its own sake, not necessarily to produce a text that is unified. The directness, the immediacy of Beauvoir's travelogue runs counter to the distant, studied contemplation that is encouraged by the critical reading of novels. Which is not to say that critical reading and everyday reading are polar opposites: it is to say instead that everyday readings are more conscious of their moodiness than those who study novels are willing to give credit. In this chapter, I have sought to demonstrate that examining Beauvoir's travelogue as everyday reading allows for a flexibility that can strengthen our understanding of texts like *America* without imprisoning them in a definitive and "studied contemplation," allowing moody, affected texts like Beauvoir's to be examined without condemning them, as its American critical response has, to degrees of "correctness."[125] To read texts like Beauvoir's as everyday reading, to hear their voices this way, allows for the imagining of a nation that is not a homeland in need of the security of right and wrong. Rather, the nation becomes a home that we make our own, in which we make and remake ourselves, day by day.

2 CURIOSITY AND ITS DISCONTENTS

Steinbeck's *Travels with Charley* and *America and Americans*

While it is tempting to dismiss American criticism of Beauvoir's *America* as the work of the chauvinistic nativism of hot nationalism, it is noteworthy that the texts in my archive, even those written by their fellow Americans, have also received little critical praise. An acclaimed, quintessentially "American" author like John Steinbeck was not immune to such dismissals. Of *Travels with Charley*, the narrative of Steinbeck's journey across the continental United States with his pet poodle, Orville Prescott wrote in the *New York Times* that the book "is lightweight fare and contains nothing much of significance about the present state of the nation."[1] *Time* claimed that *Travels* was "one of the most dullest [*sic*] travelogues ever to acquire the respectability of a hard cover," concluding that "Steinbeck's attempt at rediscovery reveals nothing more remarkable than a sure gift for the obvious observation."[2] *America and Americans*, an essay collection and the last of his books published during his lifetime, was described as "whimsical, superficial, idle observations . . . disappointing," while the *New York Times Book Review* called it "at best the intelligent ramblings of a first-rate reporter," jibing at the book's larger claim, "We're a great people, warts and all, and what else is new?"[3]

And much like the critical silence that surrounds Beauvoir's *America*, these dismissals have persisted as a silence in Steinbeck criticism. Some of this silence is historical: both *Travels*, published in 1962, and *Americans*, published in 1966, fall outside Steinbeck criticism's focus on what has been deemed, as one essay collection is titled, "his years of greatness," which critics place between 1936 and 1939. Only recently has Steinbeck's later work elicited scholarly attention. Jay Parini has noted of *Travels* that its tone is "tremendously contemporary, almost poststructuralist."[4] All the same, Susan Shillinglaw and Jackson J. Benson note that, particularly in *Americans*, in his "struggle to contain the present," Steinbeck "could not find an adequate form or a convincing tone to contain his discontent."[5] Yet Steinbeck's nonfiction, produced outside his supposed "years of greatness," reveals a personal and unmediated intimacy toward the nation. By the late 1950s, Steinbeck was unsure whether he knew the nation anymore and was curious to know it again, yet once he reencountered America through his travels, it evoked in him a profound discontent. Thus his nonfiction reveals the complexity of Steinbeck's attempt to capture his own voice in his writing about America. At the same time, Steinbeck's nonfiction shows the complexity of his struggle with form and tone that are not only personal struggles but national ones. Steinbeck's nonfiction is reflective of an exhaustion of synecdoche as a way to construct the nation, representative of an exhaustion of Cold War–era narrative conventions and the tropes that structured those narratives. The struggles of Steinbeck's nonfiction reflect an impasse that would fully emerge in the late sixties, when answers to the question "What is America?" constructed through synecdoche could no longer represent the nation, given the discontents of the period.

The drives that propel Steinbeck to answer to the question "What is America?" are at the core of this chapter. As the playwright Arthur Miller told Benson, in the years after he wrote *East of Eden*, Steinbeck "was trying to find a community in the United States that would feed him, toward which he could react in a feeling way rather than merely as an observer or a commentator."[6] While other critics who saw Steinbeck as having passed his years of greatness could dismiss an observation like Miller's, affect theory uncovers statements like them as part of its archive: Steinbeck was looking for a nation to be affected by; a nation to affect. And so he turned away from the imagined communities of his fiction to the imagined community of the nation. Of course, to construct a community through an imagined world of fiction is much different from constructing one out of the realities of the nation: Steinbeck's turn to nonfiction shows the difficulty of finding the community one imagines, as much as the difficulty of representing it. Steinbeck readily admits in *Travels* that he runs into "literary difficulty" as he attempts to read synecdochically the garbage left behind in an unmade hotel room as representative of America.[7] Attempting to distill the nation out of its disparate elements, Steinbeck looks at the nation—and perhaps the nation he has constructed—and admits in *Americans* that "the whole thing is crazy."[8] Steinbeck's literary difficulties, his inability to find the right form or tone, are demonstrative of the difficulty of composing a nation through synecdoche.

In both *Travels* and *Americans*, Steinbeck attempts to imagine the nation. His "feeling way" of doing so incites his interpretation of the nation, which registers in the affect, tone, and form of his prose. In *Travels*, Steinbeck reads the nation microscopically, as a curious puzzle of parts that can be fit into wholes. *Travels* offers a prototype for such a synecdochical reading, in which Steinbeck's curiosity, his interest and excitement for making parts fit into wholes, manifest in his reading of the detritus of an unmade hotel room as a representation of the nation. In *Americans*, this process repeats but on a much broader and seemingly less persuasive scale, as he reads parts—football teams, gang life, the structure of corporations—as if to contain these unwieldy parts within a national whole. Reading macroscopically, his discontent with the nation becomes more pronounced, his examples less convincing. As Steinbeck struggles with composing a container to fit these disparate and contradictory elements, his work to contain that which cannot be contained becomes all the more apparent. The nation is no longer a novelty that a curious Steinbeck takes pleasure in exploring but instead becomes an apocalypse that a discontented Steinbeck finds little pleasure in attempting to redeem.

His curiosity about the nation in *Travels*, his discontents articulated in *Americans*: these affects index Steinbeck's response to a changing America as he aspires to fashion an imagined community in prose. Steinbeck's search for affect parallels his search for America. To react in a "feeling way" is not only to react with feeling; it is also a "way," a method that invents a community to feel. Having feelings for one's imagined community articulates one's place in that community, enabling a method that allows for the construction of a narrative in which the personal fits into the national, through which parts fit into wholes. Steinbeck's need for a feeling way to understand America is a reminder that the nation is an imagined community through which intense, personal affects are mobilized as methods for understanding it. In this way, both *Travels* and *Americans* go beyond the mythos of "his years of greatness" to ask fundamental questions about how affects are mobilized in the attempt to understand one's imagined community. For Steinbeck, the understanding of the nation is certainly personal, spurring him, in *Travels*, to connect with a nation he fears he no longer knows, one in which America becomes, synecdochically, a "macrocosm of microcosm me."[9] This fascination is equally evident in *Americans*, though its discontent is more prominent as Steinbeck synecdochically constructs a narrative container that will prove his assertion that all American problems are "manifestations of a single cause."[10] Steinbeck's discontented rhetoric pushes synecdoche to its extreme, to the extent that the whole, the "single cause," cannot be derived from its parts: indeed, Steinbeck never explicitly identifies that single cause in *Americans*. That he never identifies that single cause indicates synecdoche's exhaustion as a strategy for explaining the nation. The container can no longer explain what it contains: there is no single cause to describe the tumults of the sixties, no single answer to the question he aspires to answer: "What is America?"

Accordingly, my reading of *Travels* focuses on how Steinbeck pursues his curiosity to generate a synecdochical narrative of America. It is a reading that is psychoanalytic in method, though I also rely on theorists of narrative and the observations of ethnographers to draw out the fine line between objectivity and subjectivity that Steinbeck's narrative makes evident. My reading of *Americans* focuses on how Steinbeck's discontent is fashioned by a wide, generalizing reading that seeks to contain a turbulent nation. I draw on Alan Nadel's description of the period's "containment culture" to examine how Steinbeck's attempts to generate a narrative in which "dual natures" are made into "straight stories" of the nation, in which his narrative difficulties in containing the nation are paralleled by the construction of a nation on the verge of implosion.[11] Thus, in *Travels* and *Americans*, we see both curiosity and discontent fluctuate between weak and strong affects through Steinbeck's synecdochical rhetoric, and see how these affects evoke the weak nationalism that may bring about a critical response that Ngai has described as the "merely interesting" or, at worst, that accuses Steinbeck of presenting that which is self-evident or banal, a rejection of Steinbeck's increasing nationalism.[12] Steinbeck's synecdochical rhetoric also illuminates the connection between curiosity and discontent in the imagining of the nation. As much as curiosity rouses strong affects, there is something about curiosity that seems by its very nature to result in discontent. Perhaps this is because, in narratives that seek to describe the nation, curiosity, as much as it is spurred by discontent, creates discontents of its own.

Curiosity and Culture

The word "curious" comes from the Latin *cūriōsus*, meaning "to care": to have curiosity is to apply care.[13] Its obsolete meanings include the demonstration of concern and the feeling of anxiety. Curiosity is, of course, a mode of care: perhaps a reaction to anxiety, a demonstration of concern for an object by attending to its intricacies, and by doing so, restoring its value. Tomkins considered curiosity, as part of the spectrum of interest-excitement, to be the "affect which has been most seriously neglected."[14] For Tomkins, interest is produced by novelty. The stimulus for novelty is such that it excites one's attention but not so novel that it surprises or startles: to be interested or excited is not the same as to be surprised or startled. Tomkins also found that "an enduring discontent or at least the absence of complete seduction by the familiar is a necessary condition for the pursuit of the novel."[15] To be curious, one must be discontent. Curiosity and discontent are thus intertwined, embedded like parts and wholes, in each other. The curious writer is not completely seduced by the object they are curious about, in order to see the novelty in it. Or an enduring discontent may lead the curious writer to examine an object again and again in hope that it will bring about at least a temporary contentment. In other words, what makes the object interesting is not so much the object but the curious writer's approach to it: the interpretive and affective work that turns the object into a novelty, a curiosity. The production of that novelty; however, brings the curious writer, as much as his object, into question. The affective roots of that production—the attempt to seduce, or become contented with the object—also reveals the desire to be seduced or contented by the object. And because curiosity and discontent are embedded in each other, the rhetoric of curiosity can sound much like the rhetoric of discontent: the rhetoric of curiosity is almost always tinged with the sadness that the object has not totally seduced the writer; the rhetoric of discontent is almost always tinged with a yearning for the object to seduce the writer. In their embeddedness, these affects may come to sound like each other, such that their tones are scarcely different. Yet the difference is a difference of synecdoche: of part for whole, or whole for part. Whereas Steinbeck's curiosity in *Travels* leads him to invent parts that he claims represent the whole, in *Americans*, his discontent leads him to invent a whole that he claims represents the nation's parts. The result is that while Steinbeck curiously overreads the nation in *Travels*, he discontentedly underreads it in *Americans*. Particularly in *Americans*, Steinbeck's discontent does not propel his curiosity about the nation but articulates only his discontent.

Barbara Benedict writes that curiosity is the "ambition to go beyond."[16] Such ambition, for Benedict, not only is manifested in the study of objects found to be strange by mainstream culture but also reflects a frame of mind that finds value and takes pleasure in strangeness for its own sake. "Curious things or people have a great but hazardous value; their value is hazardous because they confuse distinctions between the abstract and material and they have the potential to usurp common culture with idiosyncratic concerns."[17] The pleasure in strangeness can easily mutate into the pleasure of seeking the strange in the familiar. Just as the curious may confuse the abstract with the material, they may also confuse the part with the whole, obsessing over the part's intricacy of minutiae to the extent that they no longer see the whole. On the one hand, curiosity is private and personal, an interior motivation that, because it is not always visible, may induce suspicion. On the other hand, it is through being curious that individuals transform—and as members of an imagined community, fashion—themselves. "Curiosity indicates strangeness, desire, and rejection: the longing to know something that has already been identified as other, the loss or transformation of self in a projection outward toward another identity."[18] In this way, Benedict sees curiosity as "the expression of the contest between individual and public truth," as the curious person sees strangeness where others do not see it, takes interest in the strangeness of their culture, and in doing so, becomes strange themselves.[19] Curiosity is a defamiliarizing affect that makes both the curious person and the subject of their curiosities unfamiliar. The curious person is perpetually at risk of transgressing cultural norms in their "thirst for information, the quest to penetrate forbidden areas, the insistence on personal witnessing" of curiosities.[20] Indeed, as Steinbeck shows in *Travels*, his thirst for information requires the penetration of what is forbidden, which he converts into a representation of the entire nation that, temporarily and problematically, sates his curiosity. The desire to know the other, and the way in which that desire is framed, reveals the extent to which the curious person is "curious" themselves. Curiosity, then, is the matter of degree that questions the relationship between self and other, private and public, subject and object.

This matter of degree ultimately reveals what Alberto Manguel describes as curiosity's "double meaning."[21] In his archive of the word, Manguel quotes the Renaissance lexicographer Covarrubias, who writes that curiosity is both "positive, because the curious person treats things diligently; and negative, because the person labors to scrutinize things that are most hidden and reserved, and do not matter."[22] Those who are curious are subject to curiosity's double meaning: they may only recognize moments of excess indirectly, because their affective and narrative energies are focused on the curious object. Their curiosity can often leave incurious persons puzzled: a curious but ultimately weak nationalism may particularly vex readers—consider the reviewer who asked of *Americans* "What else is new?"—who expect diligent treatment and get instead the scrutiny of minutiae or the pontification of generalities.[23] But to read for curiosity is to read a narrator and narrative that is negotiating the word's double meaning, in ways that are as shaped by narrative as they are the affective impulses that motivate the reading in the first place.

Steinbeck's search for America reveals the reciprocal relationship between curiosity and discontent. The curious writer is not only discontented with what they see but also anxious that what they see is without substance, is without content. Steinbeck begins *Travels* by expressing both levels of discontent: knowing America only from reading its newspapers while living in Long Island, he finds that he "could not tell the small diagnostic truths which are the foundations of the larger truth" of the nation.[24] His curiosity is driven by a perceived insufficiency, a discontent that his perspective is based on the information of others rather than his direct experience. But curiosity can also leave one discontented with the novelties they find. The curious writer may find that what he believes to be an intricate puzzle, a representation of the nation, is only mildly interesting to others, or worse, only mildly interesting to himself. Steinbeck begins *Americans* by dejectedly noting that his book cannot "pretend to be objective truth . . . of course it is opinion, conjecture and speculation. What else could it be?"[25] And there is always the risk that the curious writer is so driven by discontent that they build a puzzle from the wrong pieces, forcing content into a frame that the curious person wants to see—and would be contented with—but is not actually there, or perhaps worse, as Covarrubias describes, does not matter. Perhaps this is why Steinbeck repeatedly refers to America in *Travels* as a "monster land" that he cannot tame, a "monster symbol" that evokes uncertainty—and curiosity's archaic meaning of anxiety.[26]

The double meaning of curiosity, the stimulus the affect provides, recalls issues of narrative and discourse: the desire to tell a story, to articulate a method for doing so. For Steinbeck, that method is primarily synecdochical. This method reveals much about the elasticity of the trope: how synecdoches can construct an imagined community, expand an interpretive horizon, as much as they can seem to be "merely interesting," merely descriptive, unexpansive diagnoses of the nation. As Manguel notes, much of our skepticism of curious people comes from those who are curious about things that we are not, or are curious in ways that make no sense to us, what Benedict has described as curiosity's "unstructured empiricism."[27] Ngai notes too that narratives produced by curiosity often omit what made its author curious in the first place: the merely interesting result seems unique only in a "yet-to-be-conceptualized way from a general expectation or norm whose exact concept may itself be missing."[28] The text produced by curiosity—or discontent—triggers a discourse of legitimacy, "as to throw the spotlight entirely on the question of its own legitimation."[29] Curiosity is the perfect vehicle for weak nationalism, for it propels the finding of evidence that does not set nationalism ablaze but rather evidence that "keeps the embers of nationalism glowing."[30] The curious writer sees the nation from the perspective of an "avid reader of all signs," then interprets those signs as fascinating facets of the nation, even if doing so risks creating synecdoches that prove to be monstrous, unwieldy, and potentially illegitimate.[31] And discontent incites interpretation that is interested no longer in nuances but in generalities that contain those nuances, even if the discontented writer is aware, perhaps bitterly so, that he is producing without full legitimacy a "set of generalities" to be "canceled out by another generality."[32] In this way, Steinbeck's curiosity—and the discontent that propels it—says much about the role of curiosity in the formulation of nationalism: how one keeps the embers of the nation glowing with new material while the other keeps the embers glowing through its scorn.

To historicize the immediate past of *Travels* is to reveal the role of curiosity in the period in which the text was produced. The fifties and early sixties are reflective of a culture with a self-conscious fascination with knowledge and knowing to the extent that, as David A. Hollinger describes, even the most technical of texts like the Kinsey reports on human sexuality could be, and indeed were, best sellers. "Librarians were obliged to catalogue them in the science section," Hollinger writes, but "at home, however, individuals found good reasons to shelve these fascinating tomes next to David Riesman's *The Lonely Crowd*, Gunnar Myrdal's *American Dilemma*, and Henry Nash Smith's *Virgin Land*."[33] Perhaps what made these technical texts so popular was their response to national curiosities—sex, class, race, culture—that assured readers they were not alone but part of a macrocosm, even in the most private parts of their individual lives. That individuals were parts of a broader and unified whole was presumed in the major "strong readings of society" offered by psychologists, sociologists, and others, texts that examined the "pressures of society on the self" such as William H. Whyte's *The Organization Man*.[34] But the objective methods that produced such research also perpetuated a discourse that, as Hollinger points out, "confused the local with the universal" in their "claims about or on behalf of all humankind for which the salient referent was later said to be a fragment of that elusive whole."[35] Such confusion is evident in these strong readings that frequently conflate the nation with states, states with counties, counties with cities, cities with communities, and communities with individuals. It is a misconception driven by synecdoche: in the case of texts that offered such strong readings, a synecdoche derived by sampling. In depicting whole domains—sex, class, race, culture—from parts, these strong readings offered a portrait of the nation that was to some degree illusory: nonfiction texts that were at least, in part, fiction. And these texts were recognized as such within a few years of their publication, given the epic social and cultural shifts of the sixties. Yet such strong readings encouraged the curiosity of a writer like Steinbeck to engage in strong readings of his own, to know the nation again through synecdoches of his own making. Yet curiosity's double meaning also reveals the double meaning of the word "knowledge" that the curious person seeks to gain, a meaning that is both sexual and mental, and perhaps, as Freud illuminates, mental because it is, in the extreme, sexually charged. Such strong readings may satisfy because they transgress through their knowledge, offering their readers a pleasure in the insights such readings expose. Much like how the Kinsey reports shed light on the nation's desires to audiences who were coming to terms with their own, to see parts in the whole of the nation is to see a national body that evokes desire: its own combination of curiosity and discontent.

To understand Steinbeck's search for a "feeling way" to imagine the United States is to understand not only the mode of that "way"—the strong readings of the nation produced at the time—but also the motives and pleasures of finding that way through curiosity and discontent. (As Tomkins writes, "much of the motivational power of the drive system is borrowed from the affect system.")[36] Epistemophilia, one of Freud's lesser-studied theories, offers insight into the double meaning of curiosity and the sources of curiosity's discontents. At its core, epistemophilia is the effort—conscious or not—to siphon the pleasurable sensations attained from physical stimulation and convert them into a pleasure that can only be attained through mental cogitation. In his characterization of Leonardo da Vinci, Freud comments that Leonardo "had merely converted his passion into a thirst for knowledge; he then applied himself to investigation with the persistence, constancy and penetration which is derived from passion"; and that once mental exercise had achieved a sort of climax, once "knowledge had been won," the satisfied Leonardo would discard his project, completed or not, and move on to another project, repeating the process.[37] In this characterization, Freud transforms Leonardo into a researcher whose thirst for knowledge is the sublimated performance of passion.[38] Yet the persistent, penetrative researcher is also a detached observer, as Freud writes that "a man who has won his way to a state of knowledge cannot properly be said to love and hate; he remains beyond love and hatred. He has investigated instead of loving."[39] Knowledge does not seem to bring about the same rewards as genuine passion, for once knowledge is won, the passion for that knowledge is no more. If "the absence of complete seduction by the familiar is a necessary condition for the pursuit of the novel," then once the object has been seduced, it no longer provokes the novelty that led to its curiosity.[40] To connect Freud with Tomkins, satiation is itself a discontent. The epistemophile's thirst for knowledge is never quenched by their mastery of a subject: it only brings about discontent, a thirst for more knowledge elsewhere. Epistemophilia illustrates how curiosity, in its extremes, supplies itself with an endless dissatisfaction, a perpetual discontent.

In examining both *Travels* and *Americans* simultaneously, it can be observed how Steinbeck's curiosity changed into discontent, influenced not only by the frustrations inherent in his potentially epistemophilic motivations in knowing the nation, but also by major cultural changes in the nation within the span of a few years. If *Travels* was fostered by a nation fascinated with a universalizing type of knowledge, the production and dissemination of strong readings of American society, such universalizing narratives quickly became insufficient to explain the dynamism and tumults of the nation in the mid and late sixties. *Americans* seems all the more generalizing and exaggerated because its mode remains dependent on a strong reading that universalizes a nation that was coming to identify more with its diversities than its unity. In both texts, Steinbeck's "feeling way" of reading the nation allows him to define the parameters of a strong reading of American national identity in terms of his affects: his curiosity and intimacy toward the nation in *Travels*, his discontent in *Americans*. Thus texts like *Travels* and *Americans* show how nonfictions of the nation and the synecdochical rhetoric that structures them are driven by affect, and how curiosity and discontent are embedded in a rhetoric that buttresses and complicates the discovery, observation, and explanation of what is America.

The Incitement to Report

The sociological and psychological tomes that would become best sellers in the fifties were successors to the rise of polling and surveying techniques developed decades before. As Sarah E. Igo notes, polls about national opinion evoked intense personal responses. "Citizens' sense of the national mood" as it was depicted in polls "gave them their bearings, situating them within their own imagined public," while it simultaneously concerned "those who had been accustomed to gleaning opinion from their local communities and networks. . . . It could be alienating to discover that their specific public opinion community appeared to be so out of step with the larger one."[41] In effect, nationwide polls gave Americans details that made their imagined community more concrete—a sense of majority opinion on an issue, or a register of a response to a national event—from which individuals could fashion themselves as a majority or a minority within that community. Polls helped people position themselves, and occasionally swayed them to conform or resist the "majority" of Americans the polls constructed. In particular, the simplified poll data distributed in newspapers and magazines were "exhibited as if the public spoke in one voice."[42] Of course polls, like strong readings, simplify synecdochically: a sample is presumed to represent a whole. It is this simplifying—as well as the assurances provided by such simplifications—that seems to have spurred in Steinbeck an incitement to read the nation as more complex than the one he saw being presented in mainstream discourse.

The incitement for *Travels* is Steinbeck's curiosity to know the nation, driven by his discontent of such comforting analyses. As he traveled the continental United States in a pickup truck with camper top, named after Don Quixote's horse (Rocinante), and accompanied by his pet poodle (Charley) during the 1960 election season, Steinbeck writes of his double-edged envy for those who offer "strong" readings of the nation:

> I've always admired those reporters who can descend on an area, talk to key people, ask key questions, take samplings of opinions and then set down an orderly report very much like a road map. I envy this technique and at the same time do not trust it as a mirror of reality. I feel that there are too many realities. What I set down here is true until someone else passes that way and rearranges the world in his own style. In literary criticism the critic has no choice but to make over the victim of his attention into something the size and shape of himself.[43]

Steinbeck's discontent is double-edged: he does not trust the reporters, even as his distrust leads him to align himself with those he is anathema to: literary critics who victimize texts by turning them into "something the size and shape of himself." But such discontent is the genesis of his journey. *Travels* begins with Steinbeck's admission that he no longer "knows" his own country:

> I discovered that I did not know my own country. I, an American writer, writing about America, was working from memory, and the memory is at best a faulty, warpy reservoir. I had not heard the speech of America, smelled the grass and trees and sewage, seen its hills and water, its color and quality of light. I knew the changes only from books and newspapers. But more than this, I had not felt the country for twenty-five years. In short I was writing about something I did not know about, and it seems to me that in a so-called writer this is criminal.[44]

There is a bit of pathos in this. At the time of its composition, Steinbeck lived in America, on Long Island, and he frequently traveled to other parts of the country. But these are only parts of America. To recall the archaic meanings of the word, Steinbeck's curiosity is incited, in part, because of his anxiety that he no longer knows the country he cares so much about and has come to be identified with, synecdochically, as an "American writer"; not only a composer of the nation but a representative of it as well. Perhaps his reputation as an "American" writer further incited his desire to see the whole country, and not just to see it, but to know it by feeling it; not just to know and feel what is acceptable about the country—to smell the grass—but know and feel what is transgressive or unacceptable about the nation—its sewage—lest he be branded as a transgressor, a "criminal" writer, no longer representative of the nation. (As if the nation were a body, Steinbeck wants to observe what the nation ingests as well as what it excretes.) Newspapers provide him with information, but they cannot provide the sort of bodily sensations—the feelings—he wishes to experience in his travels. Thus Steinbeck presents a schema that Peter Brooks has theorized as a common epistemophilic trope: "the body often presents us with a fall from language, a return to an infantile presymbolic space in which primal drives reassert their force."[45] To know the nation through the language of others is not the same as to feel it, but to feel the nation oneself brings both feeling and knowing, absolving himself of the criminal feeling of being a writer who no longer knows his country. Through his sensations of hearing, smelling, and seeing, Steinbeck is assured that he will come to know the nation again by feeling it. His curiosity will yield insight that will yield knowledge: he will once again be an "American writer," "writing about America." Brooks describes the conflation of sight as knowledge with elegance: "*voir* is *savoir*."[46]

Steinbeck's goal, then, is to understand the entirety of the nation, to know it through seeing, smelling, and feeling parts of it, because, he writes, "Otherwise I could not tell the small diagnostic truths which are the foundations of the larger truth."[47] Steinbeck's purpose in knowing the nation is so that he can construct a synecdoche of it. Yet once on the road, he is quickly bombarded by the issues of his project, the unfeasibility of his task: "suddenly the United States became huge beyond belief and impossible ever to cross. I wondered how the hell I'd got myself mixed up in a project that couldn't be carried out. . . . It is like starting to write a novel."[48] Here, Steinbeck's curiosity for the nation merges with the method he is most accustomed to using to resolve that which is impossible to cross: the writing of a novel, a unified object that will contain the splintered narratives within it. The inability to carry out the project only motivates his curiosity further. Much like the novel, the nation becomes for Steinbeck what Judith Roof has argued is the primary motivator for narrative, that "perhaps the end is always in the beginning and a story's satisfaction consists in going on anyway."[49] Travel and narrative are similarly entangled, yet narrative, unlike travel, requires an ending. As Roof claims, "the whole story takes pleasure in the fact of an end, in the possibility of an end toward which the story goes, its specter there as a promise, a reaffirmation of the mastery we think we have from the beginning."[50] While Steinbeck may feel overwhelmed because traveling the country is like starting to write a novel, his statement also reveals a desire to contain the nation as if it were a novel, an imagined community of his own design; to organize the nation as if it were a story, a story of which he is the sole author. To do so is to give the nation a coherence that it otherwise lacks, a coherence reliant on the synecdochical, organizational powers of narrative that "constantly reproduces the phantom of a whole, articulated system, even where the concept of a system is a product of narrative, where the idea that there are such things as parts and wholes is already an effect of narrative organizing."[51] For Steinbeck, narrative can give life to the nation and its complexities. But the narrative that emerges from the curiosity for such complexities may bring about even more discontents, because such curiosity may be more of a reflection of the self, and the self's interior motives, than it is the nation.

"Macrocosm of Microcosm Me"
Throughout *Travels*, Steinbeck dons the guise of a reporter, interviewing individuals from whom he can derive a sense of the nation. Given the precipitous election season during which the book was composed, the bulk of these interviews are attempts to discern politics, often unsuccessfully. There are also interviews with individuals whom Steinbeck envisions as a "new class" of Americans: truckers, mobile home owners, nuclear submarine lieutenants. His interviews with this "new class" feel staged. On what Steinbeck sees as a new "culture" of mobile home owners:

> "What is the usual income bracket of the mobiles?"
>
> "That is variable but a goodly number are in the ten-thousand to twenty-thousand dollar class."
>
> "Has job uncertainty anything to do with the rapid increase in the units?"
>
> "Well perhaps there may be some of that. Who knows what is in store tomorrow? . . ."
>
> "How are they purchased?"
>
> "On time, just like an automobile. It's like paying rent."[52]

Such question-and-answer sessions quickly lose their appeal: Steinbeck fires off questions as if he were a census taker, having difficulty deriving the "foundations of the larger truth" from them.[53] This difficulty stems from his perspective that mobile home owners are a distinct culture. Perhaps because mobile homes are new to him, he approaches their denizens like an ethnographer taking field notes about a foreign tribe, taking novelty in noting that these "dwellers" "gather in groups of like to like."[54] When he tries to survey this foreign culture, the informants respond with questions of their own:

> "One of our most treasured feelings concerns roots, growing up rooted in some soil or some community."
> "How many people today have what you are talking about? . . ."
> "Don't you miss some kind of permanence?"
> "Who's got permanence?"[55]

Steinbeck's conclusion, dryly, is that "permanence is neither achieved nor desired" by the "mobile people."[56] What he seems to have missed is that his interviewees sense the heavy-handed rhetoric of Steinbeck's line of inquiry, and that perhaps what is "one of our most treasured feelings" for him is not a treasured feeling for them. Steinbeck has also missed that when approached directly about their feelings of nationalism, "many people find it difficult to talk about the things that are most obvious to them. . . . Direct questions about national identity often produce consternation: scrunched foreheads, quizzical looks, hemming and hawing and even evasiveness."[57] The questions his informants ask him show their puzzlement: their way of life is obvious to them, but not to Steinbeck, who, in his curiosity, has donned the guise of an ethnographer fascinated by what he sees as a new America. (Steinbeck enthuses for several paragraphs about the amenities of mobile homes, noting his astonishment that a dinner he had in one of them was in an "immaculate kitchen, walled in plastic tile, with stainless-steel sinks and ovens and stoves flush with the wall.")[58] But the curious writer can go on about the minutiae that he is fascinated by, forgetting that his own camper-truck has similar amenities, and is a smaller variant of the homes of the "mobile people."

Ultimately, such question-and-answer sessions are as unsatisfying to Steinbeck as they are unimpressive to his informants. Their staged feeling may be due to their form, structured as a formal process of question and answer, of the type a pollster or sociologist might perform. And they lack the pathos of the search Steinbeck has placed in his project: instead of finding the foundations for a "larger truth," they lead to reticent informants whose responses do not satisfy his curiosity. Or they reveal a pathos that Steinbeck does not want to find: his witnessing of a group of "cheerleaders" in New Orleans protesting the integration of a local school leads him to conclude that their actions "left New Orleans misrepresented to the world."[59] Where Steinbeck's curiosity is most sated is in private reminiscence: observing the beauty of the national parks, writing after a long day of driving the emerging interstate highway system, moments in which the nation's "unity lies in the mind."[60] That national unity, for Steinbeck, is mental, is a reminder of curiosity's power to see things where they may not be seen, and a reminder that the nation resides only in the inward moments in which "the minds of each lives the image of their communion."[61] And it is a reminder that such seeing is often taken up out of an overwhelming desire to see a whole, even from the most scattered of parts.

The reticence of his informants encourages Steinbeck to construct the nation internally, to make evident the nation that he sees that his informants do not. Without others to supply the information he needs in his search for America, he turns inward. The intensities of Steinbeck's curiosity in *Travels* reach an epistemophilic extreme when he stops in Chicago to await the arrival of his wife. When he later reflects on this stop, he at first claims it is only "a break in my journey, a resumption of my name and happy marital status."[62] But he also reflects that while waiting in Chicago, "I ran into literary difficulty. . . . Chicago broke my continuity."[63] A pause in the journey, a break in continuity, a confession that most writers would edit away. The pet poodle Charley, his "bond between strangers," has been taken to be groomed.[64] For the moment, Steinbeck is alone; he has no subjects to interview, no animal to act as bait to generate a narrative about America.

What is the curious writer to do? For the only time in *Travels*, Steinbeck invents characters to scrutinize; concomitantly, nowhere else in the book does Steinbeck demonstrate the extent of his curiosity about what is America to the degree found during his stay in Chicago. In this moment, Steinbeck demonstrates that one need not travel to produce a travel narrative: the trip is as mental as it is physical, ultimately embodied in a curiosity that only requires objects to decipher. Perhaps Chicago breaks his "continuity" because it reveals the narrative process Steinbeck utilizes to understand America, displaying the epistemophilic extremes of his curiosity. These extremes may be only tacit elsewhere: even after his dull question-and-answer sessions with informants, he states, "I cannot write hot on an event. It has to ferment."[65] This fermenting indicates the brooding nature of epistemophilia, the formative moments between observation representation, *voir* and *savoir*. For not only is evidence fermented in this epistemophilic moment, that fermentation signals a shift—from research to text—that pulls the event and its characters out of its original context and into the realm of his desire to construct the "whole" nation. As Clifford describes it, such a process of writing creates "fields of synecdoches in which parts are related to wholes, and by which the whole—which we often call culture—is constructed."[66] Similarly, Roof states that "characters absorb and represent the ideological weight of narrative transformations, acting as synecdoches of ideological positioning."[67] Connecting Clifford to Roof, the synecdoches of culture synchronize with synecdoches of character in order for narratives of the nation to cohere, and these parts (characterization, scenery, ideology) are conflated into pleasurable wholes that mask the latent instability of the nation as a text. The characters that emerge in this moment become representatives not only of the nation but also of Steinbeck's ability to grasp the "whole" nation. But their masking of the text's instability is partial: Steinbeck's "break in continuity" reveals how these characters also represent the limitations of his curiosity and expose the literary difficulties of his discontent in the indecipherability of the nation, even from a single scene of his own construction. This is the scene where primal drives are reasserted, the textual location of what Lauren Berlant calls the "fantasy-work of national identity" takes place.[68] It is this moment in *Travels* where Steinbeck's epistemophilia is most condensed.

Once Steinbeck is at the hotel, he discovers that the room he has reserved is still occupied, and is offered a recently vacated, unmade room to rest in until his is ready. "The room had not been touched since its former occupant had left. I sank into a comfortable chair to pull off my boots and even got one of them off before I began to notice things and then more things and more. In a surprisingly short time I forgot about the bath and the sleep and found myself deeply involved with Lonesome Harry."[69] Scanning the unmade room for artifacts of its previous occupant, Steinbeck finds himself constructing a character of that occupant, a representative American of Steinbeck's own invention. Just as his mission is to "feel" the country, he similarly finds a mission to "feel" Harry's presence, quickly becoming "deeply involved" with him. The phrase "deeply involved" is especially revealing, for it connotes a sense of participation and intimacy in his relations with Harry. It foreshadows the imposition of Steinbeck's desire to manufacture a situation that reflects the mission he has set out to accomplish: to know the country. By writing that "I began to notice things and then more things and more," Steinbeck emphasizes his own heightened reaction, his interest shifting to excitement, his emerging epistemophilia, which exoticizes and eroticizes the unmade room. The use and repetition of the word "things" and the building up of both ambiguity and tension by using the word "more" indicate the appearance of something indiscernible, something that elicits his curiosity, to be discerned and incorporated into his mission. (The word "thing" will come to plague Steinbeck in both *Travels* and *Americans*: it is the part he desires to connect with the American whole, yet ultimately cannot specify, which spurs his curiosity and eventually, in its vagueness, his discontent.) The sentence's polysyndeton heightens this tension, so that the "things"— the objects themselves—quickly lose their importance and are replaced with a "more," a mere modifier at the end of the sentence. Steinbeck's desire is not only to know the "things" but to know "more." What has been discovered loses precedence: what proves essential is that there is "more" for him to feel curious about. Here, the epistemophilic tendency to discard objects as soon as they are mastered is heightened as

Steinbeck relishes the possibility that there will be even more to tell about the nation through the unmade room.

Steinbeck has noticed something but, much like the curious writer fascinated with minutiae, has yet to tell the reader what is noticed. The dramatic structure of this sentence mimics the excitement of the epistemophilic process, step by step, furthered by a pivoting between part and whole. His "deep involvement" with Lonesome Harry leads Steinbeck to reflect that "an animal resting or passing by leaves crushed grass, foot-prints, and perhaps droppings, but a human occupying a room for one night prints his character, his biography, his recent history, and sometimes his future plans and hopes."[70] Steinbeck's claim that the room is representative of mankind allows him, much like in his reading of the "mobile people," to position himself as an ethnographer describing an entire culture through the analysis of parts (footprints, character, biography) that will subsequently support his characterization of the nation that emerges from them. But unlike the "mobile people" he studied previously, the inhabitants of the unmade room have left it: there are no people to interview, no one to respond to Steinbeck's theories of the nation with reticence. Steinbeck is by himself. The world he makes of these parts then, much like curiosity, blurs the line between investigator and investigated, between self and the other. But only much later will Steinbeck acknowledge that the synecdochical construction of the nation is also a construction of his curiosity, that "this monster of a land, this mightiest of nations, this spawn of the future, turns out to be the macrocosm of microcosm me."[71]

Steinbeck's overt admission that he is "an incorrigible Peeping Tom" seems an encouragement to inspect the unmade room as a body to be deciphered and enjoyed. "I could feel that recently departed guest in the bits and pieces of himself he had left behind," he writes.[72] And *voir* being *savoir*, Steinbeck states that the guest "is as real to me as anyone I ever met, and more real than many."[73] These bits and pieces are brought to life by Steinbeck's comparison of them to living people: they become representative. But the only way this guest can be more real than anyone he has ever met is if he has constructed him: as such, his constructions are closer to him, "more real than many" people he knows, parts of himself projected onto the room, and subsequently, the nation. He might say he sees a person, or a nation, but what he sees most is himself. The border between fiction and nonfiction, narrator and narrative, subject and object continues to blur.

How can Lonesome Harry be real when Steinbeck creates him out of what he has left behind? To make Harry real, Steinbeck evokes a language that indicates his "sensitive contact with the world to be understood, a rapport with its people" and subsequently "a concreteness of perception" that demonstrates his understanding of Americans and thus his credibility as an "American" writer.[74] But to solidify his interpretation, Steinbeck must cloak his own narrative's potential to be fiction. And so he conflates the conventions of his curiosity with the strong readings of society he perceives as more secure than his own, weaves the approach he has taken with "real" people—the mobile home owners and the like—into Lonesome Harry as well. Steinbeck begins this by writing that Harry "is not unique, in fact a member of a fairly large group."[75] To be real, it seems that Harry must be classified as representative, as a synecdoche. As Harry is being assembled out of remnants, he is simultaneously brought to life by being placed in the context of a cultural whole. Steinbeck attempts to make Harry real by making him common, normal, familiar if not similar to ourselves. He is made into the assembly of Steinbeck's assumptions of the "American" character. And making Harry "real" authorizes Steinbeck's writing about him, justifying his epistemophilia, if only long enough to represent in the unmade room that which he sees as a synecdoche of the nation.

Steinbeck proceeds to patch Harry together from the objects he discovers in the room: a laundry strip, crumpled hotel stationery, antacid wrappers, cigarette butts, whiskey bottles. Out of this, he "suspects" Harry commutes to work; Harry's signature on the hotel stationery "seems to indicate that he is not entirely sure of himself in the business world."[76] Patching Harry together further, Steinbeck guesses he is on a "business trip with some traditional pleasures thrown in."[77] In Steinbeck's weighty suggestions, he assumes that Harry has had intercourse during his stay in Chicago. Uncannily, form follows function: the result of the analysis matches the mode of inquiry. (To play on the multiple meanings of the word "knowledge," Steinbeck demonstrates his knowledge of Harry's knowledge.) Not only is his perception of the scene driven by epistemophilia; the construction of the scene itself leads to the interpretation that a sexual act has taken place. Steinbeck has woven the structure of his analysis into the event itself, embedding it in his narrative of a "traditional" American pleasure. "His guest was not C.E. with a contract. She was a brunette and wore very pale lipstick—cigarette butts in the ash tray and the edge of the glass. They drank Jack Daniels', a whole bottle—the empty bottle, six soda bottles, and a tub that had held ice cubes. She used a heavy perfume and did not stay the night—the second pillow was used but not slept on, also no lipstick on discarded tissues."[78] The use of dashes demonstrates the bridge between argument and evidence. They double as a skeleton connecting the object and the reporting of it, a structure for putting together objects to create an explanation of events, a narrative that supplies the definition of the nation. But Steinbeck's original goal to "hear accents" of the national body has been put aside in favor of a narrative that analyzes the intimacy of bodies. The intensity of Steinbeck's curiosity has led to a narrative difficulty in which the microcosm, the inferred, conjectured narrative of the hotel room, cannot speak for the macrocosm, the larger truth of the nation he wishes to reveal. Steinbeck's detective work seems vast, but the result of his detection seems narrow: the nation is more than a one-night stand.

While "Harry" is his choice of the name for the male guest—indeed, he knows his real name from the signature on the hotel stationery he has excavated from the waste bin—he equivocates on the name of Harry's female counterpart. "I like to think her name was Lucille—I don't know why. Maybe because it was and is."[79] Though the male character leaves his signature, Steinbeck withholds it as a sort of chummy gesture. But the underlying motive of doing so is to cover up the power dynamics between Harry and Lucille and its role in this story of the nation. At first, Lucille is a "nervous friend," then she is described as possessing "a fine businesslike quality about her."[80] If Harry is a businessman who lacks confidence in his profession—his signature on the stationery attests to this—then he has been duped by Lucille, whose businesslike quality is framed not as a positive but as a negative reflection of her personality, even though she seems more successful at her work than he ever will be in the world of business. "She . . . did not stay the night—the second pillow was used but not slept on."[81] Only then does Steinbeck opt to name Lucille and allude to her potential profession. Once act and profession are connected, he indulges himself with its wry connotations, writing that "she didn't leave too many things around, as an amateur might."[82] His emphasis on Lucille's professional qualities—his pushing of this point—subsumes what is actually a difficulty for him, that Lucille has left less evidence of herself to scrutinize than Harry has. This only heightens his curiosity more, as demonstrated by the markedly thicker layer of symbolism over her artifacts in his purview: Lucille did not take with her the two roses (love and attachment) supplied by the hotel; she dumped the alcohol into a vase, poisoning any potential for romance (or readings of romance) with it.

In Lucille, Steinbeck's desire to describe the nation through this synecdoche and his frustration at not being able to do so with confidence becomes apparent. In this way, Steinbeck becomes Harry, attempting to seduce a narrative out of remnants in the room much like Harry attempted to seduce Lucille with a narrative of romance. Steinbeck admits to checking the trash, ashtrays, and plants for evidence; he searches under the bed and inside the closet. He expends great effort in creating this scene: he plunders the unmade room for contents to prove an interpretation that justifies his curiosity, one that completes his interpretation of the room as a representation of the nation.

After constructing the scene of the affair—and the nation which emerges from that scene—Steinbeck shifts from analysis to self-reflection. "I wonder what Harry and Lucille talked about. I wonder if she made him less lonesome. Somehow I doubt it. I think both of them did what was expected of them."[83] Through such reflection, Steinbeck returns to a strong reading, not just of Harry and Lucille, but of a culture in which they exist, in which both characters conform in their transgression, doing what is expected of them. From assembling Harry and Lucille to reflecting on a culture they represent—the very culture he has tried to prove exists—Steinbeck finds himself dissatisfied by the results of his curiosity:

> Three things haunted me about Lonesome Harry. First, I don't think he had any fun; second, I think he was really lonesome, maybe in a chronic state; and third, he didn't do a single thing that couldn't be predicted—didn't break a glass or a mirror, committed no outrages, left no physical evidence of joy. I had been hobbling around with one boot off finding out about Harry—he hadn't even forgotten a tie. I felt sad about Harry.[84]

As Steinbeck weaves his curiosity—through Harry and Lucille—into a broader analysis of American culture, there emerges a tone of sadness, if not discontent in the scene he has constructed. It seems that the product of his curiosity is not as gratifying as it should be: too predictable for both the intellectual labor and the physical "hobbling around" he has put into constructing it. That it is not predictable to him indicates that there is still something missing from the scene that he cannot locate, the artifact that definitively completes his analysis. Not that it would have been more helpful if Harry had forgotten a tie. Steinbeck's sadness, his "literary difficulty" is the result of the temporary satiation of curiosity, and the discontent such temporary satiation brings.

The Fantasy-Work of Synecdoche

The essence of Steinbeck's "literary difficulty" is that he does not have enough material to complete his scene in Chicago. In his frantic search for more information, it is obvious that his picturing of America through Harry and Lucille lacks definitiveness, what Roof calls "the new end to the story."[85] The satisfaction of epistemophilia is not enough for his reading to be epistemologically convincing, to show that his writing reflects more than his role as "an incorrigible Peeping Tom," but instead a strong reading of the nation. He must provide some sort of closure to the report he has begun to write, so that he can emerge by the conclusion of the episode not as a voyeur but as a reporter, a narrator of the nation. But in Chicago, he cannot complete his analysis. Its very incompleteness "haunts" him because it undermines the explanatory power of synecdoche in the narrative construction of his search for America as much as it undermines his authority as a quintessential writer of the nation and its narrative.

Steinbeck's curiosity is his literary difficulty. As Paul Rabinow writes, "desire alone does not yield conversation."[86] Epistemophilia is not epistemology. In the unmade hotel room in Chicago, Steinbeck's desire to know the nation for the pleasure in knowing the nation, and the "unstructured empiricism" through which he comes to know it is exposed.[87] Without a supply of informants through which he can craft synecdoches of the nation, he invents them. He feels "sad" about Harry, not because of the banal act he and Lucille have committed but because his efforts to construct a report of America through Harry's misadventures does not satisfy his curiosity. The telos of *Travels* is to do just that, to evoke America through a series of episodes that are supposed to characterize the nation as a whole and, in doing so, allow Steinbeck to know the nation once more. But the claim that Steinbeck evokes in the unmade room is that people have sex without passion, that extramarital sex is just one of the "traditional pleasures" of traveling businessmen, as a way of coping with their inadequacies in the world of capital. It is a transgression that, to Steinbeck, is not a transgression but a synecdoche of the nation. We may infer, supposedly, that sex is ultimately an unsatisfying act, that its participants are more interested in tidying up the messes they make than in the messes themselves. But what is necessarily American about that? There is so much precision and tidiness in his adultery that Harry doesn't even forget a tie. Almost in response to their tidiness, Steinbeck makes a mess in the hope that cleaning it up will reveal more about their motivations, turning garbage into artifacts, in the hope that they will say something definitive about America. Perhaps what "haunts" him about Harry and Lucille is his construction of them, how they reveal his desire to illuminate the "thing" that is the nation through the construction of something from nothing. He has rearranged the hotel room, and his analysis of the nation, to the "size and shape of himself." "America" becomes a burdensome whole on which parts, bits, and pieces are interpreted and substituted for the sake of his curiosity. Synecdoches form the fantasy-work of the nation, and the nation provokes fantasy from its synecdochical narratives.

But such fantasy-work can only yield discontent. It seems that Steinbeck's sadness stems from the realization that there is no definitive end to Harry's story, an ending that will ultimately sate his curiosity. His sadness also reveals a discontent about synecdoche itself, that parts do not always create the whole story—the whole nation—he desires to know. It is also a reflection of the discontent inherent in the curious writer's desire to know the whole story in order to demonstrate mastery over it, in this case, the story of the nation. But the nation cannot be mastered from the top-down gaze of the curious writer because the relationship between self and nation is "always conceived of as a deep, horizontal relationship."[88] While this issue persists throughout the book, the unmade room in Chicago illustrates the difficulties embedded in the desire to write a book about America. This "literary difficulty" unhinges the assumptions and methodologies that flow throughout the book, exposing the drive, the epistemophilia that underlies the interest in knowing the nation. If *Travels* is an attempt to produce knowledge for pleasure's sake, this knowledge is complicated in that curiosity's relief brings no pleasure.

To play with a phrase made famous by the victor of the election under way as Steinbeck wrote *Travels*: it is a matter of asking our country to do something for us. Steinbeck assumes that America will satisfy his curiosity about it, yet throughout *Travels*, it only raises more questions. His curiosity toward the nation, and his attempt to satisfy that curiosity synecdochically, reveals the fantasy-work that seeks to see himself as part of the nation in an intimate, libidinal way. Yet the nation he produces is only a discontenting, unsatisfying microcosm. The extent to which Steinbeck seeks to know his nation reveals the extent to which nations are "imagined because even members of the smallest nation will never know most of their fellow-members."[89] In this moment in *Travels*, Steinbeck performs that work of imagination on the unmade hotel room. Perhaps such imagining is symptomatic of the need for an image of communion, even in the remnants of the garbage left behind by his fellow Americans, in the hopes of being refreshed by the nation's "complete confidence and steady, simultaneous activity."[90] That Steinbeck goes to such extremes to read the nation indicates the nation's tremendous power to keep its citizens enthralled by it, even as they hobble about with one boot off to find more remnants that might ultimately reveal the narrative of the nation.

Such enthrallment—and such sadness—stem from the nation's ability to provoke curiosity, and to provoke narratives that attempt to satisfy that curiosity. Both nation and narrative are similarly "driven by the same questioning impulse, asking who did what, and why, and how, so that we can in turn ask ourselves what it is that we do, and how and why we do it," and in this way, both nation and narrative are "are mirrors of what we believe we don't yet know."[91] Narratives of a nation come with satisfactions as well as vexations: the narrative provides an answer to the questioning impulse but also only temporarily satiates the affective intensity that brought the story into being in the first place, and further vexes in its revealing of what the questioning impulse cannot answer. The objects we find curious eventually reveal the contingency of our curiosity in them. For Steinbeck, the satiation of the unmade room brings sadness: not only that the narrative has reached its conclusion but, in looking at the unmade room, that he has found himself more than the nation he has sought.

The Discontents of *America and Americans*

Travels begins to reveal how Steinbeck struggled with the idea of America. The national issues he had confronted—the Great Depression, the Second World War—through fiction seemed easier to grasp than the realities of the Cold War. His vision of the nation, particularly as the sixties progressed, lurched toward extremes, becoming both pessimistic and patriotic, both cynical and idealistic. These extremes are captured in a letter Steinbeck wrote to Pascal Covici in July 1961. Reflecting on the trip that produced *Travels*, he wrote, "In all my travels I saw very little poverty. I mean the grinding terrifying poorness of the Thirties. That at least was real and tangible. No, it was a sickness, a kind of wasting disease. There were wishes but no wants.... Over and over I thought we lack the pressures that make men strong and the anguish that makes men great.... Through time, the nation has become a discontented land."[92] Steinbeck's view that America was suffering a "wasting disease" that could only be cured by an "anguish that makes men great" captures both his cynicism about midcentury successes as well as the loftiness of his idealism about what could remedy them. The letter also reveals how Steinbeck continued to see the nation through the trope of the body— not as a healthy body but as one wasting away in illness—a nation that can only be understood through synecdochical narrative.

It is the way in which Steinbeck sees a discontented land, the way he writes of American discontent in *Americans*, that says much about the discontent inherent in curiosity. Steinbeck's curiosity was inevitably bound up with his discontent. As he found in *Travels*, his curiosity only revealed himself. At the same time, in having traveled the nation, it became familiar to him: the nation seemed to lose the novelty required to sustain his curiosity. While Steinbeck's discontent is, like his curiosity, the product of a synecdochical reading of the nation, the incitement that propelled his synecdochical constructions changed: no longer interested in curiously exploring the nation, in finding parts to represent an elusive whole, he instead crafted synecdoches that diagnosed the nation, a whole to represent elusive parts. Throughout *Americans*, Steinbeck presumes that parts of the nation speak to a whole; he insists that the paradoxes and problems of the nation are "manifestations of one single cause."[93] This is a change in scope from the "larger truth" of the nation he sought to find in *Travels*: a "larger truth" is metaphorical, but "one single cause" is literal, reflective of a shift in his nationalism. Inferring a whole nation from the parts he describes, Steinbeck finds that midcentury America does not meet his vision of what it should be. Indeed, as he ventures toward the end of the essay collection, the Americans he writes of may be tearing the nation apart. Steinbeck's "discontented land," then, is as much a rhetorical issue—a problem of synecdoche—as it is a narrative issue—the nation that is composed through synecdochical rhetoric.

To understand the extremes of Steinbeck's discontent is to understand the limits of synecdochical rhetoric. On the one hand, his insistence that the whole can be read from parts is an extension of Cold War–era thinking, a reading of objects whose "gaze must be comprehensive, all embracing, synoptic, and range 'in all directions.' Moreover, its gaze must penetrate: it does not simply inspect superficial events but identifies . . . deeper forces expressive of broad historical tendencies or sweeping political projects."[94] In this way, the Cold War actively promoted an epistemophilic reading of objects, even if such a reading proved ludicrous. On the other hand, Steinbeck's discontent reflects the larger problem of an eroding social consensus during the midsixties and the exhaustion of a rhetorical strategy that buttressed that consensus. Steinbeck's inability to contain his discontent may be an issue of synecdoche itself, of how the figure both amplifies the part and miniaturizes the whole, which risks a discontented tone, either when parts fail to represent the imagined whole, or when the imagined whole is forced onto parts that inadequately describe it. Tone may falter due to the inadequacy of the form: synecdoches can, as Nadel writes, generalize "dual natures" into "straight stories," as complex dualities are interpreted as parts that fit into a single, straight whole, rendering static the dynamism of the nation.[95] Synecdoche can undermine itself, raising issues of its legitimacy as it reduces dualities to a single representation. Examining *Americans* for its rhetoric offers insight into how Steinbeck's nationalism was predicated on a certain, increasingly static way of interpreting the nation. In this way, reading *Americans* illustrates the rhetoric at work in narratives of the nation, the contradictions innate to that rhetoric, and the discontents captured through it. It is not that Steinbeck's discontent was unfounded but that the extremities of his discontent were anchored in a presumption that strong readings of parts can represent the whole, a presumption that Steinbeck held to strongly in *Americans* but was by the midsixties increasingly contested.

American Synecdoche

Americans began as a commission by Viking Press president Thomas H. Guinzburg for an introduction to "a picture book with captions."[96]

As Benson writes, Steinbeck "approached the project with the understanding that it would be a short 'commercial' job that he could do in a couple of weeks, but as he became more involved, what had started out in his mind as a sort of 'booklet' was transformed into a collection of essays."[97] That an introduction grew into a booklet, and booklet grew into essay collection, demonstrates Steinbeck's continued difficulties in containing the nation: much like his deep involvement with Lonesome Harry's detritus in *Travels* incited a narrative, in *Americans* Steinbeck became "more involved" in what was supposed to be a booklet, inciting an entire essay collection. (And much like how the narrative Steinbeck constructs of Harry is tenuously an "American" narrative, there is little connection between Steinbeck's narrative and the photographs in *Americans*.) He found himself, as he wrote to John Huston and Gladys Hill, "taking 'the American' apart like a watch to see what makes him tick": in doing so, he found "some very curious things are emerging."[98] As *Travels* shows, curiosity, for Steinbeck, often evokes a body that the epistemophile reads for its supposed transgressions, which are then subsumed synecdochically into a universalizing narrative of the nation. In *Americans*, Steinbeck's approach changed, as demonstrated in the metaphorical shift from body to watch, from man to machine: the curious things that emerge in Steinbeck's study of America consists of parts that work together to produce an orderly, useful whole. The nation is no longer a body that produces pleasure but an instrument with a functional purpose. The nation is a watch that ticks.

Steinbeck's choice of metaphor—and the "curious things" that emerge from that choice of metaphor—also reveals a tension that became evident to him in moments like the Chicago hotel room, but which he removed from *Travels*. In the "L'Envoi" that was its draft conclusion, Steinbeck admitted, by the end of his travels, that "I do know this—the big and mysterious America is bigger than I thought. And more mysterious."[99] The incitement for Steinbeck to write *Americans*, then, may have been the opportunity to explore the "big and mysterious" or "curious" nation in a way that would bolster his confidence that America was exact and provable, that the nation was not only the "sick" body he had described to Covici but, like the parts of the watch he had described to Huston and Hill, could be taken apart, reassembled, and remain functional. But the gulf between these two synecdoches—between the nation as sick body and the nation as a watch that ticks—is a wide and frustrating one. Steinbeck's shift between *Travels* and *Americans* is the shift from one to the other: he seems interested in seeing the nation as possessing not the eccentricities of the body but the orderliness of the watch. Perhaps the discontent that is registered in Steinbeck's tone throughout *Americans* is the author's frustration that never the twain shall meet.

The relationship of the part to the whole is addressed in the beginning of *America and Americans*, as Steinbeck states that while his is "a book of opinions, unashamed and individual," it will offer an "inspection of our whole nation and its citizens."[100] Though his opinions are "unashamed" and "individual," he inspects the "whole nation" because it is the whole of the nation, according to Steinbeck, that makes it distinct. "For I believe that out of the whole body of our past . . . something has emerged that is itself unique in the world: America," a whole that is "complicated, paradoxical, bullheaded, shy, cruel, boisterous, unspeakably dear, and very beautiful."[101] This "whole body," with its complications and paradoxes, has been seldom described: its attendant feelings have "rarely been set down about our whole country."[102] Steinbeck's repeated use of the word "whole" presumes that the nation, while complicated and paradoxical, is ultimately coherent and contained. His repeated emphasis on constructing a whole out of the nation's parts bespeaks the synecdochical rhetoric that is predominant throughout *Americans*. But by the time Steinbeck was writing *Americans*, the consensus behind such strong readings of society was rapidly eroding. As James Patterson writes, the new "era of good feeling" that the *New York Times* predicted in January 1965 was more accurately described by a popular song released that autumn, Barry McGuire's "Eve of Destruction."[103] Identification through consensus began to shift toward the politics of identity, which, as Leerom Medovoi writes, promulgated a "rhetoric of 'liberation'" that would become dominant in the late 1960s.[104] And as Igo notes, "Those taking the measure of the nation in the 1960s and beyond sought to explain the United States less as a singular bundle of beliefs or an easily calculated center point than as a set of contending publics. . . . Pollsters recalibrated their strong majoritarian frame, detecting new significance . . . onto the old singular nation."[105] In light of these shifts, Steinbeck's assumption that parts fit into wholes was a rhetorical position that was quickly losing credibility.

The rhetoric of synecdoche, combined with the turbulence of the midsixties, helps to explain why, as much as Steinbeck wishes to write a different narrative than those who "refer to America as a 'precious inheritance'—our heritage, a gift proffered like a sandwich wrapped in plastic on a plastic tray," he often ends up sounding like the very narratives he is writing against.[106] For as much as he finds the "precious inheritance" narrative to be overly packaged, and for as much as he remains curious about the nation, he inviolably believes in the larger narratives wrapped underneath. The first essay of *Americans* provides for Steinbeck a way to demonstrate that "the motto of the United States, '*E Pluribus Unum*,' is a fact . . . a strange and almost unbelievable truth."[107] The result of "four centuries of work, of bloodshed, of loneliness and fear," Americans became "in little, little time . . . more alike than we were different—a new society; not great, but fitted by our very faults for greatness, *E Pluribus Unum*."[108] Out of many, one: the national motto is one of the most profound statements of representation, a motto that bespeaks the promise of synecdoche. The way in which synecdoche functions as a container for the contained is most evident in Steinbeck's rhetorical maneuver of "not great, but fitted by our very faults for greatness," in which the "new society" is "fitted" by its faults into something greater than itself.[109] The motto parallels Steinbeck's method, making out of many one by fitting parts, in this case national faults, as if they are pieces of a watch, into one successful and ultimately orderly whole. At times, such fitting feels forced. The national motto, of course, is not a fact. Yet Steinbeck attempts to make facts out of mottoes and claims: for example, the claim that the "seeming ethnic anarchy" of early America has, for instance, led to some of the nation's great accomplishments.[110] Steinbeck's contemporary example of this is college football: "Yet in one or two, certainly not more than three generations, each ethnic group has clicked into place in the union without losing the *pluribus*. When we read the lineup of a University of Notre Dame football team, called the 'Fighting Irish,' we do not find it ridiculous that the names are Polish, Slovak, Italian or Fiji, for that matter. They *are* the Fighting Irish."[111]

For Steinbeck, each ethnic group "clicked" into place: the sound a part makes when it is fitted to its proper place in a machine. The various ethnicities of the football team are present in the names of its players but subordinate to the team itself. His example presumes a consensus among its players that they are the "Fighting Irish," that the team will work together under the auspices of its name, a "union" that stands together against the opposition, with the goal of achieving victory. The example presumes too much: that names reflect ethnicity, that ethnic diversity can be subsumed under a team identity, that team identity is a harmonious union. (It also subsumes the history of ethnic tension inherent in the phrase "Fighting Irish.") But it is the parts that Steinbeck employs to represent the whole which have the effect of both exaggerating the part and miniaturizing the whole. America is certainly more than college football. But the rhetoric of this example demonstrates Clifford's claim that writing creates "fields of synecdoches" onto which culture, as the whole, is constructed.[112] In this case, the construction feels forced because it is so abstract, as Steinbeck maps the culture of football onto the culture of the nation. The synecdoche of the nation is thus reliant on the synecdoche of the football team: trope becomes reliant on trope, further distancing representation from reality. As much as synecdoche allows Steinbeck to assert that the nation is "fitted" by its faults for greatness, synecdoches can also function to construct "phantoms of the whole" as they simplify the complexities of the whole for the sake of their "narrative organizing."[113] As such, the synecdoches constructed by discontent in *Americans* aspire to make the phantom of the nation real but do so in a way that reveals how the whole is a phantom, spurring further discontent.

And in his discontent, Steinbeck's nationalism becomes increasingly hotter. His insistence that the national motto is a fact, that football teams represent the ethnic diversity of the nation: Steinbeck's perspective of the nation had become, by *Americans*, astonishingly literal. The hot nationalist does not see the nation figuratively but literally. Hot nationalism attempts to limit figurative language by seeing the nation not as a representation but as reality; in Steinbeck's language, it is a real "thing" with visible proof and presence. Much like Diana Trilling's review of Beauvoir, Steinbeck's literal interpretation of the nation is limited to the surface of the objects, as he is more interested in building a container that reins in the index of narratives that constitute the nation, that will offer proof of the "thing" he sees as the nation, than he is in pursuing the inevitable complexities of the nation. The work of containment that the hot nationalist pursues never totally captures the nation but corrals only the hot nationalist's limited vision of it. The sense of certainty such a container provides is never thorough: the nation cannot be reduced to one person's imagination of it. It can repel objects seen as un-American but in so repelling becomes all the more dependent on them for its own definition. The literal "thing" Steinbeck searches for needs the figural to constitute it: the real needs the phantom. Steinbeck's discontent may emerge from his sense that the nation is a wasting body, but it also emerges from his sense that the nation is something more than that, something more than the "thing" he aspires to describe and thus contain. As *Americans* progresses, searching for patterns that explain the nation, Steinbeck finds himself increasingly discontented with it, perhaps because of his understanding of contemporary events, but perhaps too because the nation is more dynamic than his increasingly literal thinking allows.

Containing America

The shift in Steinbeck's thinking about America during the midsixties is especially apparent in the second essay, "Paradox and Dream." Whereas the Steinbeck of *Travels* found that "paradox crops up too often for comfort . . . it means that certain factors are missing in the equation," the Steinbeck of *Americans* revels in describing them, because he thinks that they will reveal the single cause that will explain the nation.[114] Steinbeck attempts to anchor several conflicting generalities about Americans—that "we spend our time searching for security, and hate it when we get it," that "we are aggressive, and defenseless"—by asserting that such generalities point toward a common American identity.[115] Just as the nation is fitted by its parts for greatness, Steinbeck finds that "Americans seem to live and breathe and function by paradox; but in nothing are we so paradoxical as in our passionate belief in our own myths."[116] Presented this way, the nation's paradoxes prove unparadoxical. The dream of the American home, for example, "is one of the deepest American illusions, which, since they can't be changed, function as cohesive principles to bind the nation together and make it different from all other nations."[117] (Here, Steinbeck seems to have concluded that the home is no sign of permanence.) Illusions are not illusory; rather, as principles, they create communities that "bind" the nation together and make it real. The intensity of Steinbeck's synecdochical thinking becomes apparent as he reads illusions as wholes that make the real nation exceptional. Grafting concreteness onto an abstract rhetoric, Steinbeck goes further, asserting that illusions that make up the American dream are "some kind of genetic tape," so that "the national dream of Americans is a whole pattern of thinking and feeling and may well be a historic memory surprisingly little distorted."[118] The American character, Steinbeck asserts, has DNA, a code that is duplicated, and, considering the other prominent definition of tape, an adhesive that keeps the nation together, allowing for that "whole pattern of thinking and feeling " that is "little distorted" from its original.

Steinbeck's evocation of DNA returns to the trope of nation as body, connecting his attempts to discern the national body from the unmade hotel room in *Travels* to his letter to Covici, in which the national body is described having a "wasting disease." His insistence that the "national dream" is a genetic tape equally insists that, in a microscopic, microcosmic sense, there is a code that makes the body work as a whole. It also places Steinbeck, as in *Travels*, in the position of a detective: this time, not the insecure Peeping Tom but, in *Americans*, the authoritative scientist who can identify and objectively discern the genetic tape. As insistent as

Steinbeck is that there is a "whole pattern," his attempt to link dreams with history, national character with genetic tape, reveals how fervently he wishes to link past with present, to see a whole in parts, even if those parts are not necessarily connected with each other. To see a whole in discordant parts is the risk of synecdochical thinking, that the container cannot represent the medley it contains. Such containment becomes obvious as "dual natures" are eliminated from the "straight stories" of the nation, as illusions turn into principles, as abstractions are presented as national realities.[119] In "Paradox and Dream," instead of examining the parts that might represent the whole, he grafts a whole onto parts to assert that while "no one can define it or point to any one person or group who lives it," the American dream "is very real nevertheless."[120] So much for the exact and provable thing: the more Steinbeck tries to describe America, the less it seems to exist—and the more he insists that it does, indeed, exist. Above all, Steinbeck presumes that his generalizations indicate the general. This presumption encourages him to minimize distortions, to see patterns across time and continuities across communities where they may not exist. Further, it leads Steinbeck to see the origins of the nation far beyond its own history and borders. The American interest in mobile homes returns again to remind him that "the Tartars moved whole villages on wheels, and the diehard gypsies have never left their caravans."[121] The "inventiveness once necessary for survival" in America is evident to him through the teenagers who buy "for a song an ancient junked car, and with parts from other junked cars put together something that would run."[122] (Americans still know how to take parts and make useful wholes.) It may be the effect of such pattern seeking, but for Steinbeck, it interests him "that the youthful gangs in our cities . . . take on noble names, and within their organizations are said to maintain a code of behavior and responsibility towards one another and an obedience to their leaders much like that of the tight-knit chivalric code of feudal Europe; the very activities and attitudes that raise the hand of the law against these gangs would, if the nation needed them, be the diagnostics of heroes. And indeed, they must be heroes to themselves."[123] Seeking to connect the past with the present, Steinbeck errs by generalizing the specifics of both eras. The present becomes banal as Steinbeck's interest in gangs is because of their "noble" names, not the immediate political, social, racial, or ethnic discriminations that birthed them, that "within their organizations are said to maintain" a code of behavior "much like that of" feudal Europe, not the actual deviance or violence gangs both medieval and contemporary performed. Constructed so, these gangs are not dangerous rebels but "youthful" people who are "heroes to themselves" and who could be easily conscripted to serve the nation (though as gangs, they are by definition outside the nation) if it needed them.[124] Examined in this way, the parts continue to contain the whole, not so much through historical accuracy or biological objectivity but, as Benson described it, through Steinbeck's selective and stubborn insistence, "the heat of his certainties and his scorn."[125]

Yet, as much as Steinbeck saw gangs as modern knights, as his letter to Covici demonstrates, he also saw "very little poverty" in his recent tour of the nation, little of the "grinding terrifying poorness of the Thirties."[126] To contain the America he wishes to see, to construct the whole of the parts he describes, Steinbeck's sense of history is highly selective, sacrificing, as Certeau suggests synecdoches do, depth for breadth. Much of this may have to do with what Steinbeck believes is past. As the latter essays reveal, Steinbeck believes that many American dilemmas have been resolved or are close to being resolved. For him, "there is no question that Negroes will get their equality—at law; not as soon as they should, but sooner than pessimists would believe" in part because African Americans "now have access to the wealth and to the ability to distribute it; businessmen all over the country have finally come to see what is bad for Negroes is eventually bad for business, and so for America."[127] Similarly, "today, instead of the old, highly visible capitalist we have the corporation," which Steinbeck finds to be "stranger" than the tycoons who now, "far from boasting of their wealth . . . live almost like fugitives, secret and shy."[128] Corporations are now run by "shareholders" who "became increasingly a cross-section of lively Americans."[129] As if still frustrated by Lonesome Harry, Steinbeck seems more discontented with the "Corporation Man" whose "position in the pyramid of management is exactly defined by the size of his salary and bonuses" than he is with those who "were rich and proud of it," who "gloried in showing the world how rich they were.... In the latter part of the last century these vital, boisterous figures were at once our curse and ornament." The "rich and proud" have, for him, "disappeared."[130] There is, of course, a leap in time between the Gilded Age and the Cold War as much as there is a leap between medieval knights and gangs, or Americans and Tartars, all leaps that Steinbeck should have noticed. That he bypasses these complexities indicates not only a lack of curiosity but the depths of his discontent.

This simplification also shows how Steinbeck's discontent is similar to, but ultimately distinct from, the larger discontents of the period. Steinbeck's thinking—and its limits, as seen in his commentary on race and economics—is predicated on a model of Cold War consensus, one that emphasized "individual freedoms, rights and opportunities" and deemphasized "majoritarian democracy or egalitarian economic values."[131] As Wall notes, while consensus was a valuable means for fighting "anti-Semitism, national origin quotas, and de jure racial segregation," it also "made efforts to address institutionalized economic inequality politically difficult, if not untenable."[132] And Steinbeck shared a concern with many Cold War warriors about the increasing conflation of equality with middle class mediocrity, as David Farber describes it, the idea that "equality was simply the right of every American to push a shopping cart and to decide what brought happiness."[133] Yet Steinbeck's insistence that the nation is a whole is dependent, along with the rise of strong readings, on the advent and appeal of mass-marketers which were instrumental in developing the campaigns that constructed a mass public, and who advertised and sold a cohesive national culture to be consumed.[134] (Steinbeck's discontent is so intense he has forgotten that he was commissioned to write a coffee-table picture book, a "commercial job" that would be marketed to a mass audience.) Of course, it is much easier to be discontented with the mainstream than it is to be contented with oneself. It is telling, then, that Steinbeck's moral disagreement becomes evident in the essay titled "The Pursuit of Happiness," which focuses on children and seniors, in which he finds yet another "strange" element of the nation. "Americans did not always fear, hate, and adore their children: in our early days a child spent its helpless and pre-procreative days as a child, and then moved naturally into adulthood."[135] One may detect such discontent in Steinbeck's own demonstration of extremes, in the absent middle ground between hate and adoration, in the promise that, in earlier days, the movement from childhood to adulthood was "natural"—as was the movement from adulthood to death. Instead of being "revered and admired," the nation now has "a great burden of unhappy, unused, unfulfilled people."[136]

These problems prove to Steinbeck that "we are living in two different periods. Part of our existence has leaped ahead, and a part has lagged behind, because the problems have not been faced as problems, and the mores have not kept up with methods and techniques."[137] In such a portrayal he reveals his own discontent with his country, bemoaning a loss of moral moorings. If one "part of our existence has leaped ahead" and another "has lagged behind," then there is no whole. The final essay in *Americans*, "Americans and the Future," attempts to weld the past and present together, to reconcile the "paradoxes" that he has exposed throughout the book into a single, whole issue. Returning to the rhetoric of its introduction, for Steinbeck, this whole issue must be dealt with, because "many, not able to face the universal spread and danger of the cancerous growth, split off a fragment of the whole to worry about or to try to cure. But it seems to me that we must inspect the disease as a whole because if we cannot root it out we have little chance of survival."[138] The trope revealed privately in Steinbeck's letter to Covici years before *Americans* was written has been deployed: the nation is a wasting, ill body. What was once paradoxical now has a dangerous, "universal" reach, a "disease as a whole" that must be rooted out of the national body to "survive," a life-or-death matter. In its tone, the final essay of *Americans* is Steinbeck's own "Eve of Destruction." And as if the stakes are not high enough, Steinbeck amplifies the problem further:

> It is a creeping, evil thing that is invading every cranny of our political, our economic, our spiritual, and our psychic life. I begin to think that the evil is one thing, not many, that racial unrest, the emotional crazy quilt that drives our people in panic . . . the awful and universal sense of apprehension and even terror, and this in a time of plenty such as has never been known—I think all of these are manifestations of one single cause.[139]

Here, Steinbeck tries to describe the nervous system of the national body he has invented. Epic in scale and melodramatic in form, it is a body being destroyed by strong affect: creeping, awful, and terrifying. Further, it is penetrating every element of American life, "manifestations of one single cause." The synecdochical construction of this problem raises the specter of hot nationalism, for the rhetoric of hot nationalism reduces an inventory of discontents to a single cause, suggesting, as if by magical thinking, that if that cause could be corrected, resolved, or expelled, these discontents would disappear. Steinbeck may have inventoried the problems of the sixties accurately, but none of these problems he examines stem from one single cause. And it is telling that Steinbeck cannot ultimately decide on what the problem, much less its single cause is; rather, he seems overwhelmed by the discontented nation he has imagined. His conclusion is dramatic, but it is also the epitome of the merely interesting; in its omission of the answer to the dilemma he has constructed, it demonstrates how the "exact concept may itself be missing" from the merely interesting, despite its affective intensity, remaining "yet-to-be-conceptualized."[140] Steinbeck offers some possibilities, but those are plural, not the "single cause" he has asserted will remedy the nation. On the one hand, what seems to be eroding is the American's "reputation for gallantry, which, to my mind, is a sweet and priceless quality."[141] But this appeal to "gallantry" masks a more profound issue, an admission that Americans have "reached the end of a road and have no new path to take, no duty to carry out, and no purpose to fulfill."[142] There was a time, Steinbeck insists, when "those codes of conduct we call morals were evolved for this thinly inhabited continent when a man's life was important because he was rare and he was needed. Women were protected to the point of worship because they could bear children to continue the race. A cry for help brought out Americans buzzing like bees."[143] This time seems no more, for now "life is indeed cheap, and moreover it is becoming hateful. We act as though we truly hated one another, and silently approved the killing and removal of one among us."[144] "*E Pluribus Unum*" has not only reversed; it has imploded, creating a nation in which its citizens encourage the destruction of each other.

If, in *Travels*, Steinbeck outlines an epistemophilic fantasy-work to produce his portrait of the nation, in *Americans*, that fantasy-work seems nightmarish, paranoid, and apocalyptic. Here, Steinbeck sounds much like a president with whose ideology he disagreed. As Dwight Eisenhower wrote to a friend in 1965: "Lack of respect for law, laxness in dress, appearance and thinking, in conduct and in manner, as well as student and other riots with civil disobedience all spring from a common source: a lack of concern for the ancient virtues of decency, respect for law and elders, and old-fashioned patriotism."[145] Yet his closeness to Eisenhower's rhetoric shows how the gravitas with which Steinbeck has assumed that the problems of America have a single cause generates its own affective melodrama: in bringing together a whole, that whole becomes frenzied with meaning, full of gallant quests for survival, a world where everyone is needed and has an essential function, where people harmoniously come together when they hear cries for help. The nation becomes a moral epic. As Mimi Gladstein writes, the beginning of *Americans* allows Steinbeck to write "his own 'Genesis' narrative for the United States."[146] The final essay allows Steinbeck to write his own version of Revelation. Perhaps his doing so is the most extreme form of Roof's claim that "the whole story takes pleasure in the fact of an end, in the possibility of an end toward which the story goes, its specter there as a promise, a reaffirmation of the mastery we think we have from the beginning."[147] As the final essay of *Americans* demonstrates, Steinbeck brings his America to a point of self-destruction to save it, to write an ending to the nation in a way that reframes its discontents as its virtues: a new end to the story.

Steinbeck's vision of America—his desire to contain the nation—creates a nation that is on the verge of implosion, in which its citizens are antithetical to the nation in which they live. His realization of this is phrased in the form of a question: "Could it be that below the level of thought our people sense the danger of the swarming, crowding invasion of America by Americans?"[148] Here, Americans themselves have become the problem, a perspective that can only be reached when one sees a dynamic nation through a static lens. The "invasion" of America by Americans: the parts threaten to destroy the whole. "The roads of the past have come to an end and we have not yet discovered a path to the future. . . . We have succeeded in what our fathers prayed for and it is our success that is destroying us."[149] This conclusion is unbearable to Steinbeck, who has asserted throughout his book that parts represent wholes. If synecdoche allows for the part to speak for the whole, it also allows for the personal to speak for the national. Just as Steinbeck reveals his sadness about the scene he constructed in Chicago in *Travels*, Steinbeck makes a similar personal revelation after this moment of implosion, through which "the new end to the story" can be fashioned, a story of redemption.[150] In the final pages of *Americans*, Steinbeck is at his most personal. The successes now framed as discontents, Steinbeck finds himself more connected to the nation than he was before. Seeing the destruction in its successes, the author and the nation he has constructed are most intertwined: the nation continues to be a "macrocosm of microcosm me."[151] As Steinbeck writes, "if I inspect my people and study them and criticize them, I must love them if I have any self-love, since I can never be separate from them and can be no more objective about them than I am about myself."[152] His own discontent mirrors the nation he sees: his discontent becomes the nation's discontent. And once the discontent is both personal and national, once it seems shared by author and subject, as an imagined community, Steinbeck shifts from pessimism to idealism. This transition propels Steinbeck to see that his "questioning is compounded of some fear, more hope, and great confidence."[153] In this way Steinbeck is able to conclude *Americans* by resolutely pointing toward a future in which the "success that is destroying us" can be redeemed with more successes, fusing past and future. "Our restlessness," for example, "perhaps inherited from the hungry immigrants of our ancestry, is still with us. Young Americans are rebellious . . . the energy pours out in rumbles, in strikes and causes, even in crime; but it is energy. Wasted energy is only a little problem, compared to its lack."[154] The "running in all directions" that Steinbeck previously disapproved shows that, regardless, "we are running."[155] Of the future, he is assured that "our history . . . has endowed us for the change that is coming."[156] Of the present, he can only say as he concludes the book, "We have failed sometimes, taken wrong paths, paused for renewal, filled our bellies and licked our wounds; but we have never slipped back—never."[157] The optimism of Steinbeck's conclusion seems reachable only through the pessimism that precedes it: phrased in the negative, "never" shows how optimism seems to come from containing of the negative synecdochically, turning the nation's plural problems into a single story replete with a promising future, a happy ending. As much as seeing the whole through its parts presents a static portrait of the nation, for Steinbeck, there may be promise in doing so. But this is a promise that Steinbeck, as Barbara A. Heavilin suggests, ultimately leaves the reader to figure out on his own.[158] Perhaps this is because the nation in both *Travels* and *Americans* is ultimately a personal one, composed of the parts and wholes that Steinbeck saw in America, as much as in himself.

Conclusion

It is the way in which Steinbeck's shifting curiosity leads to the delights and narrative difficulties of epistemophilia in *Travels* and leads him to a discontented apocalypse in *Americans* that has interested me in this chapter. In both, through the amplification and reduction that takes place in synecdochical thinking, we can see how Steinbeck's search for the whole through its parts leads to a problematic, static portrait of the nation at a time in which the nation was undergoing drastic change. We can also see more clearly how Steinbeck's "struggle to contain the present," as Shillinglaw and Benson describe, is in part due to the synecdochical nature of Steinbeck's discontent.[159] *Travels* and *Americans* illustrate the narrative limits of synecdoche, of how the substitution of the part for the whole can be illusory, misleading even those who employ it. It is clear that Steinbeck lost his sense of novelty toward the nation, coming to see it as a discontented land, and a land that he himself was discontented with. Yet narrating his discontent through synecdoche seems to avert a reading of the tumults of the sixties that generated the discontent he sought to examine. While it was prescient, his discontent was not coterminous with the period in which he was writing.[160] In his reliance on synecdoche, Steinbeck participated in a way of containing the world, a fantasy-work which, as Alan Brinkley writes, constructed and maintained a confident world that "was not the era [its practitioners] thought it was, and did not produce the history they had expected."[161] It would take the tumults of the late sixties to show how the contained, strong readings of America composed in the fifties perpetuated fictions of their own.

At the same time, Steinbeck's attempt to understand the nation is reflective of a broader dissensus in the genre of nonfiction. As Daniel Worden has explored, by the midsixties, nonfiction had achieved split ends. On the one hand, in works like *The Autobiography of Malcolm X*, radical politics was converted into more digestible life narratives, "making any substantive political change seem unrelated to the more pressing issue of self-actualization."[162] Such narratives universalized their subjects and narratives and, in doing so, lost any radical efficacy. On the other hand, the rise of "gonzo journalism" and its fascination with countercultures is a political dead end as well, as countercultures do not disrupt the status quo as much as they are eventually incorporated by it. The supposedly individualistic and eccentric world of counterculture becomes "the place that has been created to contain and neutralize what once counted as political alternatives."[163] Thus "the hustler, the activist, the radical and the drug fiend . . . become not ways of contesting capitalism but ways of possessing rebellious individuality within it."[164] *Travels* and *Americans* thus not only reflect the limits of synecdochical thinking; they also reflect the limits of a type of nonfiction, and nonfiction more generally, to represent individuals without relegating them to being static types, even as the possibility of a national narrative was under increasing contestation. If Steinbeck reduced the complexity of the nation in search of its "one single cause," other nonfiction writers of the period inadvertently found themselves draining the complexity of their subjects in other modes of nonfiction as well.

If we examine, however, Steinbeck's nonfiction without the lens of affect, without the dynamic relationship between curiosity and discontent, we will inevitably conclude, as the critics did, that they are merely interesting, if they interest us at all. Perhaps it is the case, as Warren French observed of *Americans*, that "the better tone for a book such as this is one that shares unique experiences rather than universalizing one's own."[165] But what else do we do when we write about America? Such universalizing may be symptomatic of synecdochical rhetoric of the nation and the narrative that emerges from such rhetoric, of the desire to contain, under the guise of the nation, "the possibility of other narratives of the people and their difference."[166] It is in the relationship of the part to the whole that the narrative work of the nation takes place. Near-sighted or far-seeing, what his last works show is the sightedness, the affective intensity of Steinbeck's vision, one individual's way of fashioning his own private, albeit discontented, America. What Steinbeck captures in *Travels* and *Americans* are as much reports of the nation as they are his inventions of that nation which reveal his relation to it, inventions that are as national as they are personal. If we consider these texts in this way, the nation depicted in these books are, for our benefit, "unashamed and individual."[167] For in being so, Steinbeck is not alone.

3 HOPEFULNESS

On the Road with Charles Kuralt

The first *On the Road* segment aired on October 26, 1967, at the conclusion of the CBS *Evening News with Walter Cronkite*. After a leading story on the Vietnam War and a report on escalating racial tensions at home and unrest abroad, the segment, as the final five minutes of the broadcast, seemed both a summary of—and a remedy to—the national unsteadiness reported in the evening news. The title of the segment was "Leaves," and its subject was the changing autumn foliage of New England. With a montage of varicolored trees, the segment begins: "It is death that causes this blinding show of color, but it is a fierce and flaming death. To drive along a Vermont country road in this season is to be dazzled by the shower of lemon and scarlet and gold that washes across your windshield."[1]

The scene shifts to CBS News correspondent Charles Kuralt standing next to a phone kiosk alongside a New Hampshire highway. "They are just dead leaves," he says, "but inevitably Yankee ingenuity has turned them into a major New England industry."[2] The phone, we are told, is a line to a state-sponsored service that provides a daily prerecorded message describing where in the state the trees are at their fullest color. Next, Kuralt interviews a state forest ranger, who says that the autumn leaves can bring as many as thirty-three thousand cars on a single October day. The forest ranger admits that "it's becoming something of an industry up here. . . . We say 'keep New Hampshire green,' and the people that come up here for the foliage show leave a substantial number of dollars."[3] But at the segment's conclusion, Kuralt points out that the leaves of New England are much more than an industry. The scene shifts to four children and a dog, a leaf pile next to a tree in their backyard. As the children play, Kuralt narrates:

> But the best sight we've seen was beside the road at Madison, New Hampshire. It had nothing to do with the foliage industry or the tourist dollar. It had to do with youth and joy: Billy, Mary, and Jeannie Barclay and their friend Elaine Merritt, and their dog Thor, know the proper uses of dead leaves. They're not just to look at; they're to roll in and to laugh about and to cushion your leap from an oak limb. This is how the New England fall makes everybody feel; Billy, Mary, Jeannie and Elaine have sense enough to do something about it.[4]

"Leaves" ends with a rhetorical question, as Kuralt asks Cronkite, "Wouldn't you like to join them, Walter? All you have to be is nine years old, in New England, in late October."[5]

Though it was the first segment broadcast, "Leaves" performs nearly every rhetorical tactic of a typical *Road* segment: by juxtaposing a small part of the country with a larger ethos, the segments point toward an optimistic, hopeful future. In "Leaves," Americans are not only ingenious, but such ingenuity can make both financially and personally rewarding what would otherwise be mere dead leaves. The children's joyful play, Kuralt alludes, is a synecdoche for "how the New England fall makes everybody feel" about the leaves, thus ending the segment on a positive note that, as "the best sight we've seen," sets aside any problems the tourist industry, with its prerecorded messages and thirty-three thousand cars in one day might cause to the environment. The environment of autumn foliage and childhood enjoyment stands in sharp relief to the environment depicted in the evening news broadcast, what would become, by late 1967, a landscape of "helicopters landing, tall grasses blowing in the helicopter wind, American soldiers fanning out across a hillside on foot . . . a column of dark, billowing smoke, invariably described as a burning Vietcong ammo dump."[6] Whereas the images of burning ammo dumps and the nightly updates of the casualty count reminded viewers of mounting wartime deaths, "Leaves" evokes the language of death to describe the beauty and liveliness of the American landscape. The leaves burn metaphorically, "fierce" and "flaming." Their death brings not only a colorful landscape but a business through which Americans profit. It brings positive affects as well, the youth and joy of children playing in the leaves. All the while, Kuralt's invitation at the segment's conclusion—the first-person address that asks viewers to participate in the children's enjoyment of the leaves (and the audacity it provokes in asking the perpetually sober CBS anchorman to join them as well)— creates a heartened response that makes Cronkite's trademark closing utterance, "And that's the way it is," sound routine, detached, resigned.

From its inception, *Road* was a success. The segments would become a mainstay for the *Evening News*. From 1967 to 1980, and continuing intermittently until 1989, 395 segments were broadcast. Even though they were typically broadcast as the last five minutes of the Friday evening news—when most audiences would have "turned off" in anticipation of the weekend—CBS News was receiving, by 1972, almost fifty letters about the segments per week. By 1975 they garnered two hundred to three hundred letters per week, making *Road* the second-highest recipient of mail at CBS News, trailing only the hard-hitting news magazine *60 Minutes*.[7] Unlike *60 Minutes*, the letters the segment received were uniformly positive, often including suggestions of people or places for Kuralt to profile. *On the Road* also met with critical praise: the segment received a Peabody Award in 1968 and again in 1975; an Emmy for Outstanding Achievement in Television Journalism was awarded in 1978. CBS frequently collected segments to run as specials, and ultimately it was a series of its own in 1983. But with such popularity came detractors. A few complaints came from within CBS News itself, from hard-news-loving reporters who suggested "not altogether facetiously, that a kind of 'truth squad' should tail Kuralt around to do follow-up stories on his quaint and rustic subjects" that would expose their "less attractive qualities."[8] Most criticism came from media critics, who dismissed Kuralt's work as trite sentimentalism. Gaye Tuchman characterized *Road* as a benign "kicker," the closing story "designed to keep the audience smiling" in the midst of difficult news.[9] Herbert Gans chastised Kuralt as the finder of "harmless eccentrics" who "offered testimony to the continued resilience of individualism" without truly challenging the status quo.[10] Edward Jay Epstein wrote that *Road* championed "the nostalgia format . . . a way to reach rural audiences . . . through 'pretty pictures.'"[11] Hal Himmelstein described the segments as "human interest" stories that deliberately evoked a "myth of the rural middle landscape" strategically deployed by the network "when things get hot in the urban frontier . . . to deflect attention from the chaos" of everyday life during the period.[12] And though he found them to be "eloquent profiles," Himmelstein saw little more to *Road* than portraits of "strong-willed, commonsensical country folks" that "lent credibility to this myth."[13]

Such critical concerns sidestepped a more complex reading of the trends that developed throughout the seventies and which the *Road* segments reported on: the Bicentennial of the American Revolution, in particular, was deliberately planned as a celebration of the local in the national, coinciding with a renewed national interest in craft making and other supposedly rural practices. At the same time, Kuralt's subjects were not exclusively rural, white, or male: a notable *Road* segment is a profile of Pauli Murray, the first African American woman to be ordained a priest in the Episcopal Church. And Kuralt did not hide from exploring American history and its dilemmas: in a segment titled "Place of Sorrows," the subject was Little Big Horn, which Kuralt intoned "is the saddest place I know. . . . There is a melancholy in the wind and sorrow in the grass, and the river weeps."[14] Yet the critic's insistence that the segments were just human-interest was an accusation that the segments were not serious news. What "serious" meant to critics was a lack of emotion. Their warm affects made them unworthy of critical attention.

The skeptical tone of such criticism is pointed at *Road* as much as it is at the hopeful nation the segments portray. After all, what would a "truth squad" do—what truths would they find? The implication is that truthful reporting would render Kuralt's subjects—and the nation the segments portrayed—less appealing. And as if labeling something mythic or nostalgic makes it go away, the critical response to *Road* may be media criticism's equivalent of literary criticism's need to claim that narratives of the nation are mere banalities. As Matthew Ehrlich writes, Kuralt's "vision was one of order alongside the disorder of the rest of the news."[15] But it is not necessary to conclude, as Ehrlich does, that "one can say Kuralt's journey was designed to avoid conflict in an era full of it."[16] Kuralt's subjects, even those in the most rural or remote parts of the country, revealed their connection and engagement in the entire nation and its dilemmas. It is not so much that Kuralt's vision was one of order as much as it was his vision to present unified, emotional narratives in a medium—the evening news—which in its very construction avoided narrative complexity and whose legitimacy was based on an eschewing of emotion in the name of journalistic sobriety. That *Road* was described by critics as a "a two-minute cease-fire" can be read in at least two ways: as a cease-fire from the war and as a reminder of the war it is a cease-fire from.[17] The conflicts of the day did not disappear in *Road* but were presented from an alternate perspective, depicting how individuals responded to national issues in local, unique ways. Above all, to dismiss Kuralt's work as myth or nostalgia is to disregard the fundamental role of affect in his construction of *Road*. That Howard Rosenberg, television critic for the *Los Angeles Times*, described Kuralt as "America's official lump in the throat" points to the affective power of the segments, their ability to tap into affects of American life that were obscured in or absent from the evening news.[18] The segments captured a different side of the nation as much as they captured what the evening news did not, that "although the day's headlines bring news that the world could go up in a puff of smoke, there are people who still carry out day-to-day activities, giving a sense of endurance and vitality to the country."[19]

Road presented a hopeful nation during a period in American history that seemed rife with diminishments: Vietnam, Watergate, stagflation, retrenchment. As Natasha Zaretsky writes, "the sheer number of crises that beset the nation simultaneously" from 1968 to 1980 "challenged the exceptionalism at the center of American identity—the idea that the United States did not lose wars, its natural resources were boundless, its leaders wise and secure, and its economy capable of infinite expansion."[20] Through its synecdochical construction of hopefulness, *Road* offered an affective alternative to the sober discourse of evening news through which Americans understood themselves in the late sixties and seventies, an alternative to the way in which the news "described their world and their future in a language of loss, limits, and failure."[21] In a decade that is sometimes described as one in which "nothing happened"—or, at best, as Edward Berkowitz describes it in the title of his book, *Something Happened*—it can be difficult to remember that while the seventies "lacked the kind of emotional fire" of the sixties, it also "offered a different kind of drama," one in which "the results of the major social movements of the previous two decades became concrete in American communities and in Americans' daily lives."[22] The hopefulness the segments evoke might be thought of as a different kind of drama, especially in the context of the increasingly tenuous understanding of the nation its citizens had during this period. As the impossibility of implementing the conflicting ideals of the sixties became apparent in the seventies, the consensus of a common direction, of a national narrative, evaporated. As such, *Road* provided hopeful stories during a decade of "wholesale transformation without a narrative."[23] The seventies lacked a narrative primarily because of "a struggle over interpretation" about the meanings—and affects—assigned to the events that took place during the decade.[24] In this light, hopefulness should be understood not as a mythic panacea but as a narrative practice that demonstrates how Kuralt could script hopefulness from the local circumstances of his subjects, and of the power of such narratives to synecdochically evoke the nation during a period in which no predominant narrative was apparent. *Road* offered profiles of citizens enduring, if not succeeding, in a nation of diminished expectations at home, and offered a narrative that, despite its dramas and fractures, people still found purpose and meaning in national life. By doing so, *Road* constructed an affective portrait of the nation that was rewarding to multiple audiences but never explicitly defined: it offered hopefulness, a feeling of hope for the nation.

Such hopefulness need not be confused, as it was by the truth squad of media critics—or those who see narratives of the nation as a true fiction—with the satiation or evasion of the problems of contemporary life. In the three segments that I examine in this chapter—a small-town drugstore whose patrons have their names painted on their coffee cups; a family's anticipation of their son returning home from Vietnam; a sharecropping family whose nine children have gone to college—the hopeful reading that comes from these subjects suggests not that national problems are nonexistent but rather that the segment's subjects—and perhaps the nation—thrive in light of them. Its synecdochical way of "making room for the small pleasures" inside a broader national narrative shows how *Road* offers a strategy for reading America that scholars of hope like Sean Austin Grattan might characterize as utopic, even as it "resembles the complexities and difficulties" of living in America during the seventies.[25] In my reading of these representative segments, *Road* is shown to be hopeful because its construction of synecdoche incites feelings of hope in its subjects without expressing the full, radical nature of hope itself. Hopefulness, I argue, performs the emotional work of hope without explicitly pointing toward the cause or agent of hope. While hopefulness is an affect more dynamic than mere optimism, it is not quite hope, because, as Alphonso Lingis describes it, "hope is always hope against the evidence."[26] Hopefulness, in other words, gives the evidence, supplies the narrative to have hope. Each of the three segments points toward evidence for hope—that small-town life endures; that soldiers return home from war; that with hard work, a family can overcome racial inequalities—without explicitly announcing the path through which those hopes can be achieved. In this way, hopefulness has a dynamic role in how narratives come to be national narratives through its incitement to read the nation as more than what it presently is, while avoiding the articulation of the politics that are necessary for that potential to be realized.

Between Hope and Optimism

Hopefulness is an incitement to read an object with an appreciation for its positive qualities, for what that object promises for the future, a "promise that is always 'ahead' of itself."[27] In the weak nationalism of *Road*, hopefulness is a reading of the nation that incites a national promise: not only an assurance of the soundness of the nation but also an assurance that the nation will fulfill whatever promises have been made in its name. The affected viewers who wrote to Kuralt certainly sensed this promise, that the nation is better than the one watched on the evening news and that there is a better nation to be had, one that in the future will overcome its diminishments.

To describe the segments as hopeful is not to insist that the segments evoked this affect in every viewer. Rather, my use of the word is intended to describe hopefulness as a midpoint between two other incitements to read: hope and optimism. Both hope and optimism are strong affects: each monopolizes the object it reads in ways that neglect the complexity of the object itself. As a midpoint between two strong affects, hopefulness has an affective moderateness—a promisingness—that is neither intense nor definitive. It appreciates the complexity of an object in a synecdochical way, suggesting an interest not only in the object itself but in the broader whole that object is a part of. It is an incitement to read that does not confirm the object, as optimism does, as proof that things are fine as they are. At the same time, it is an incitement to read that does not confirm the object, as hope does, as needing a leap of faith to bring about the future it promises. Hopefulness promises us interest of a complex kind, but it does not provide a politics of what it promises. The very suggestiveness of hopefulness is what makes it distinct from both hope and optimism.

Hope is an affect of expectancy. As Ben Anderson notes, hope is often a response to a "set of diminishments within the present."[28] Hope arises out of diminishments with the incredible suggestion that in the future what has been diminished will be not only restored to its previous state but further strengthened such that those diminishments will never recur. Ahmed describes hope as an "affective disobedience" in which those who have been maligned use hope as a form of protest against current politics: in imagining a future in which the "wretched of the earth . . . will no longer be wretched," hope binds people together in anticipating a much different world than the one before them.[29] Hope goes beyond the short-term, envisioning a perhaps distant future in which what has been diminished is restored. Ernst Bloch characterizes hope as one of the "expectant emotions" whose "intention is long-term," whose "drive does not yet lie ready" before the subject.[30] The source of restoration may not be apparent, and such restoration may seem indefinite, but hope provides passion during its delay, a "dynamic imperative to action" that helps people strive onward with "a renewed sense of possibility."[31] Hope is a reminder of the potential for change, that life can take multiple, unpredictable directions.

As an affective disobedience, hope is strongly attached to its antithesis, hopelessness. Terry Eagleton insists that "it is hard to pronounce the word 'hope' without evoking the prospect of it being dashed, as adjectives such as 'faint' or 'forlorn' leap spontaneously to mind."[32] And Vincent Crapanzano argues, "Hope can never be fully divorced from hopelessness any more than hopelessness can be divorced from hope."[33] In its expectancy of a better future, hope evokes a politics that is a counterpolitics of the present, an imperative to act to make the future hoped for possible. Yet the crux of hope is that such politics are not presently possible. At its most radical, hope is "always hope against the evidence."[34] Hope goes against the evidence only because the evidence suggests that hope is impossible. In not knowing where the future will go, those in the thralls of hope take a leap, sometimes considered a leap of faith, into a fundamentally unstable and uncertain world, one which there is no evidence to have hope for. Hope is not only a leap of faith but a leap of reading, one in which other affects are overpowered by the affective charge of hope: consider the pathos of our cultural discourse in which tropes like "moments of hope" or "glimmers of hope" through which national crises are read. Hope takes monopoly over the object that has incited it, not only generating the imperative to change the present but also reframing the politics required to overcome what it perceives as diminishments.

Hopefulness should also be distinguished from optimism. If hope is the anticipation of a distant future in which present diminishments may be restored, it is markedly different from optimism, which sees its politics as innately and expectedly successful. As Massumi writes, "a concept like hope can be made useful when it is not connected to an expected success—when it starts to be something different from optimism."[35] Optimists expect success: indeed, for an optimist, the present is a success. As Eagleton notes, "optimists are conservatives because their faith in a benign future is rooted in their trust in the essential soundness of the present."[36] The optimist, even in the most ludicrous of moments, keeps a positive face in the midst of a disaster, certain that things are as they should be, and that all is well. Optimists thus practice a "blind optimism" that barely, if ever, reads its object with complexity. Indeed, optimism can be considered an underreading of its object with varying degrees of scale, perhaps the most insidious being the "cruel optimism" characterized by Berlant as "when something you desire is actually an obstacle to your flourishing."[37] Such underreading of an object is driven, for Berlant, by the latent fear that "the loss of the promising object/scene itself will defeat the capacity to have any hope about anything."[38] From the optimist's perspective, to read an object would be performing a cruelty to that object which could lead to the disappearance of the object and, ultimately, themselves. Whereas hope may require a leap of faith to effect its future, optimism requires absolute faith in its object to effect its present. In any of their varieties, optimism and hope are strong affects that regard, like hot nationalism, any inquiry into its object as a threat to itself.

By contrast, as an expression of hope, hopefulness gives evidence that the object is something more than itself: hopefulness "promises" that an object is more than the object itself. Indeed, hopefulness is the "state of feeling or expressing hope; the quality of inspiring hope" upon an object by articulating its "promisingness."[39] Its technique for bestowing promisingness on an object is synecdochical, one that relies "largely on the play between its concrete and abstract objects."[40] In making the concrete represent not only itself but also something more abstract, the construction of hopefulness is rhetorical: hopefulness takes a concrete part and enmeshes it with a broader, abstract whole. In other words, hopefulness expands its subject beyond itself. To recall Certeau's description of synecdoche, hopefulness amplifies its subject to stand for something greater than the part represented, thus connecting the part to the whole. If synecdoche miniaturizes the whole for the part, then hopefulness is a way in which those miniatures speak promisingly of the whole. The weak nationalism of such broadening may well be the horizontal work of imagined communities. Hopefulness incites a reading of an object that "goes out of itself, makes people broad instead of confining them" by bestowing promise on them; thus "the work of this emotion requires people who throw themselves actively into what is becoming, to which they themselves belong."[41] The rhetoric of hopefulness encourages people to feel broadly connected to each other, makes them feel that they share the promising object. In this way, the nation can be seen as an object of hopefulness. Instead of confining or isolating its citizens, the broadness of hopefulness provides an expansive, positive affect through which members of a community can imagine "in the minds of each . . . the image of their communion" by seeing the promisingness of their nation.[42] By doing so, hopefulness incites a reading that turns the concrete into evidence of one's abstract national hopes.

While hopefulness borrows from hope's techniques, it is also a markedly different affective valence. Hopefulness feels like hope, but more important, hopefulness is not hope. While hope offers a radical imperative that brings people together in a contingent future, hopefulness, by contrast, is not so imperative, as the hopeful present gives evidence that a better future will come. Hopefulness may, like hope, be expectant, but it is not in a hurry: it is accretive and gradual, as its synecdochical logic makes evidence for the future in the parts of the present. Hopefulness is different from hope because it assures us that there is evidence for hope, that which, by definition, there can be no evidence for. Further, hopefulness suggests that hope is there if only we looked for its evidence. Thus hopefulness authorizes a projection of the feelings of hope without acknowledging that there must be no evidence for hope in the first place. Yet in doing so, hopefulness becomes distinct from optimism. For an optimist, there is nothing to expect because there is no reason to anticipate a future different from the present. There may indeed be no rationale for synecdochical rhetoric, as there is no incitement to read the world for anything other than it already is. Hopefulness can be disproven, whereas optimism, at least for an optimist, is never subject to question. For an optimist, the labor of hopeful reading is unnecessary, as underreading the object suffices to prove what the optimist desires to read for: evidence that the present is the best possible world.

Hopefulness is suggestive, perhaps endlessly so. It promises more than the staidness of optimism without articulating a politics of hope that delivers on what it promises.[43] It may not be surprising that much like the media critics who lambasted *Road*, literary critics have similar difficulties with hopefulness as anything more than banal, wishful thinking. That literary critics, who typically love to parse distinctions, fail to see the subtle differences between hopefulness, hope, and optimism, indicates that there is something about such incitements to read that arouses critical suspicion. As Taussig writes, "There does seem to be . . . within intellectual culture, this strong temptation to bind lack of hope to being profound."[44] Hope seems to lack the profundity of criticism, perhaps because hope is easily dismissed by the practitioners of the hermeneutics of suspicion as being uncritical, as lacking in evidence, as mere optimism. And perhaps, as Taussig suggests, critics define profound thoughts by their very lack of hope, displaying their critical mastery of a subject by interpreting that which is hopeful about it as a symptom of some other thing that is unhopeful. The driving force behind—and perhaps the major reason why critics avoid—hope seems to be that the act of criticism involves a substitution of hopefulness with hopelessness. Or perhaps critics may feel more inclined to study the "set of diminishments within the present" in which hope is often a response, connecting the critical act with a social or political issue. Yet to disregard the hopeful is to miss the affective richness of the affects that articulate imagined communities. Indeed, hopefulness may be little more than wishful feeling, yet its very weakness is its effectiveness, one that, as I suggest in the conclusion to this chapter, gives it an endurance that proves superior to the intensity—and dissipation—of strong affect.

There is much about hopefulness that encourages distrust. As Christopher Castiglia writes, "That 'hope' lies at the core of so much bland political rhetoric—from Ronald Reagan's 'New Day in America' through Bill Clinton's self-promotion as the 'Man from Hope,' to Barack Obama's 'Audacity of Hope'—contributes to the embarrassment attendant on offering it as a serious critical disposition."[45] And Massumi has suggested "we want hope to be more than the wishful projection of success."[46] At the same time, "our mistrust of hope is rooted . . . in the inaction, the resignation, and the passivity that hope can promote."[47] Because hopefulness is synecdochical, the abstractions derived from the concrete can feel like wishful projections onto an object. A mistrust of hopefulness may be even more intense than a mistrust of hope, because hopefulness suggests a more imminent future, as the hopeful part of the present represents a whole future. And hopefulness may be mistrusted as mere optimism, because hopefulness, in suggesting a part to represent the whole, considers its work at least half-done and may encourage a passive, resigned reading of its object, an interpretive inaction.

Hopefulness may be the gentlest form of weak nationalism. It keeps the embers of nationalism burning without necessarily pointing toward a national solution on which hope can be pinned. But as hopefulness gives the evidence to hope, it risks evoking the nation as the exclusive agent that might fulfill those hopes. This risk is particularly worrisome for narratives of weak nationalism, because their hopefulness can slide "from a reading of what is possible to a disposition" that affirms present politics at the expense of motivating radical change to make a better future.[48] Hopefulness, because of its synecdochical construction, may construct narratives of the nation that universalize it, erasing the differences of parts to present the whole, one in which the nation itself is the site of hope, not the individuals that live in it. Kuralt's *Road* segments, with their reassuring hopeful themes, at times subsume national dilemmas under the guise of universalizing narratives that can hide the radical nature of the subject's hope. While they offer an "alternative disposition," one that Castiglia calls an "imaginative idealism" that provides a way of reading that in turn "shows that critique does not require suspicion," the hopeful whole Kuralt constructs can obscure the dynamism of its parts.[49] The segments reveal how hopefulness amplifies detail at the risk of miniaturizing the whole, potentially obscuring the realities of that whole. Yet hopefulness protects against the strong nationalisms of conservatives and liberals alike, which, in the fracturing politics of the seventies, should not be underestimated. If *Road* evoked hopefulness, it was a hopefulness embedded in synecdochical narrative, an incitement to read the nation in a hopeful way, not only as an alternative to the staccato readings of the nation that constituted the evening news but also as a reading that provided a narrative during a decade in which "there were simply no economic"—or other—"miracles waiting to be performed."[50] It reminded viewers that, even in a decade of fractured consensus and diminished expectations, there remained some form of a promising national narrative to be told.

An Alternative to the News: Hopeful Synecdoches

The appeal of the *Road* segments and the hopeful feelings they engendered were due, in part, to Kuralt's selection of material and, just as important, the synecdochical technique he applied to the material in the segments. In selecting the subject of a *Road* segment, Kuralt told Jane Tolbert, a communications graduate student who wrote her dissertation on the segments, "the first thing it must be is an alternative—not a news story, not a story you would expect to find on the news."[51] Thus the hopefulness of the segments may only seem so because they are constructed as an alternative to the subject—and rhetoric—that dominated the evening news, the rhetoric of sobriety. Such a rhetoric is "sober" because it regards "the real as direct, immediate, transparent."[52] In other words, the rhetoric of sobriety, much like realism as a literary form, is a technique that emphasizes the plainness of a situation or event by resisting the inclusion of subjective experience, including affect. Its subject may be emotional, but its reporting is not: the rhetoric of sobriety limits affect for fear of editorializing. The evening news seeks to explain itself through an almost transparent form, limiting the story it tells to staccato repetition, following the maxim to "Tell them what you're going to tell them, tell them, and then tell them what you've told them."[53] In this way, the rhetoric of the evening news "favors a kind of oracular understatement" in which narrative brevity is a sign of authoritative, neutral journalistic expertise.[54] As a defense against bias, for example, CBS executive Richard Salant would insist, "Our reporters do not cover stories from their point of view. They are presenting them from nobody's point of view."[55] Salant's defense may seem like caricature, but the evening news gained its authority by saying as little as possible in as highly an impersonal way as possible.

But the real is more than the sober will allow. The clarity of sober reporting came at the expense of a story's richness. While sobriety avoided editorializing, it also avoided interpretation—the means to incite interest in its subject—altogether. Its use of oracular understatement did not capture narrative complexity—or affective richness—in the events it depicted. It could not tell a story in a medium in which storytelling was essential for audiences to understand events. The limits of sobriety became apparent as the networks struggled with the Vietnam War. As Chester Pach Jr. writes, until the Tet Offensive of 1968, the bulk of television news about Vietnam was a "confused, fragmented, and questionable endeavor of brief reports, usually no more than three minutes long."[56] Focused on the skirmishes of the day, such abbreviated reportage "offered no interpretation in more than half the stories read. Less than one-fifth of the stories exceeded seventy-five words."[57] Fewer words may have ensured against editorializing, but at the same time, such brevity ensured that the broader narrative of the conflict and its relevance to viewers—the story of a nation—would be incomplete. The insistence on sobriety meant that while parts may be reported fairly, the whole of the story, the way in which viewers could connect themselves to the story, was seldom addressed. In its lack of storytelling, the rhetoric of the evening news created a need for other modes of narrative explanation for the events that could define the nation.

The effect of sober rhetoric on viewers is evident even in its lengthier forms. As the responses to the television news documentaries of the period demonstrate, citizens could not find their place in the news that was produced about them. In her study of audience response to television news documentaries of the period, Victoria E. Johnson noted the "disjuncture between featured citizens' sense of themselves as in accord with cultural affiliations and investments that mark the production crew's 'elite' journalistic expertise and worldly awareness."[58] If media critics accused Kuralt of appealing to a myth of middle America, it was only because they, like the producers of news documentaries, suffered from a myopia in which they could not see middle America. The sobriety of the news was, like an oracle, riddled with a pedagogic function that produced stories which did not conform to how the subjects of those stories saw themselves: neither its discourse nor the narrative produced from such discourse produced a nation others could see themselves in. As a resident of Webster Groves, Missouri, responded to a *CBS Reports* special, *Sixteen in Webster Groves*, broadcast in 1966: "I thought it was an interesting program, but I didn't particularly recognize it as the place I live."[59] The news' avoidance of "human interest" detached pressing issues from the people affected by it, as its discourse relied on trained experts and sober assessments, without supplying a narrative through which citizens could see themselves as parts of a national whole. Such reporting, often tethered in the sixties to a patriotic sense of free speech that "included invigorating democracy by offering citizens greater analysis of social issues and problems," had exactly the opposite effect in the seventies as television documentaries of the period exposed government inefficiency or corporate influence in politics.[60] In its lack of affects, such news could mute a personal interest in the national. As Nichols has argued, "News reportage urges us to look but not care, see but not act, know but not change."[61] It is little wonder that the absence of narratives in the evening news, combined with accusations of bias, either toward liberals or the "establishment," could only accelerate a national shift from the "progressive policies and activism" of the sixties that "challenged communities to extend themselves into the broader world"—a discourse of hopefulness—to a silent majority in the seventies, a "virtuous middle" valued for its resistance, if not hostility, to those who did not practice "patriarchal, white conservatism" rooted in a discourse of hopelessness.[62] Informative the evening news with its rhetoric of sobriety may be, but it comes with a cost. In such sober narratives, the affects, the incitement to interpret, the energy that propels stories forward and keeps people interested in them—their hopefulness—vanish.

By contrast, *Road* presented stories—complete narratives—that evoked hopeful parts of the nation. The popularity of the segments is due not only to the affect they engendered but also to the discourse through which such affects were presented, which attracted an audience that was previously invisible to the news establishment. Even Kuralt thought at first that "our stories would be considered terribly reactionary by my liberal friends—harkening back to sort of a simpler life. It hasn't worked that way. Much of the mail I get is from students, from college students, who are obviously not conservative in the political sense but think of these stories as illustrating an America that is better than the military-industrial-technological-scientific one they know."[63] The sober rhetoric of the evening news could not capture such an audience, much less such an audience's complex politics, hopes, and narrative needs. *Road* tapped into a national interest in a certain type of narrative, one that was neither sober nor detached but promoted identification and interest, one that assured disparate audiences that there was an imagined community worth being hopeful about.

Some of the appeal came from the segment's subjects: those who were not often reported on in the evening news. Many segments focus on an element of nature, as "Leaves" indicates, especially one common across the country, such as the migration of birds, and people's engagement out of doors, such as flying kites or making sand or snow castles. More prominently featured were people living in small towns who performed an admirable service, such as a woman in Buffalo, South Carolina, who at eighty single-handedly ran a restaurant out of her small home, allowing patrons to pay whatever they could afford, out of her desire to be "a friend to man."[64] A subset of these segments focuses on local eccentrics, such as a retired dairy farmer who took upon himself the building of a direct highway between Duluth and Fargo, and had completed nine of its two hundred miles when Kuralt interviewed him in 1978; or the owner, at the time, of the world's largest ball of twine. (Such segments almost always included an admission by the subject that they were, indeed, eccentric: as the twine owner told him, "You don't have to be crazy, but it helps").[65] In their way, such individuals Kuralt profiled reflect the seventies as "an era not of narcissism but of activism."[66] (These "eccentrics" appealed to contemporary audiences, as Kuralt often portrayed them as the epitome of the sixties counterculture's discourse of self-fulfillment, which would carry into the seventies as a more mainstream fascination with "self-realization.")[67] Whereas the national news captured the more politicized activism in school busing, minority rights, and the like, it could be said that Kuralt captured local activism, the individuals who were active in the civic life of their communities in generous, yet apolitical, ways.

Many *Road* segments focused on "archaic practices and institutions": brickmakers, teachers of one-room schoolhouses, gold prospectors, and gandy dancers, whose occupations were being replaced by urbanization or mechanization.[68] Several segments focused on communities affected by national demographic changes: the atrophying of Fort Motte, South Carolina, or the impact of the Interstate Highway System, which bypassed towns like Bosler, Wyoming, decimating the local economy. But for the most part, *Road* painted a celebratory portrait of the arcane by connecting it to the perseverance of broader American values. By connecting the arcane with the national, *Road* showed how the past survived in the present, creating a narrative of a coherent nation. The eccentrics did not seem eccentric as much as they seemed like "precursors . . . of our seemingly progressive and technological society," contemporary representatives of earlier forms of enduring American values.[69] Kuralt's focus on homey (local agriculture festivals; quilting and lacemaking), even kitschy (state fairs; the streetcars of San Francisco; the whitewashed fences of Hannibal, Missouri; covered bridges) subjects paralleled a national resurgence in the seventies of the celebration of the local. As Christopher Capozzola notes, the national bicentennial led to an explosion of interest in genealogy, community history, folk art, and Americana, which "could help Americans negotiate the tensions they felt between their local and national identities."[70] And as Suleiman Osman has noted, the seventies was the "decade of the neighborhood," which valorized the "smallness, intimacy, voluntarism, subjectivity, and privacy" of communities from national pressures.[71] That Kuralt was dispatched to cover each of the fifty states in segments temporarily rebranded *On the Road to '76* reflects not only the national interest in celebrating the bicentennial but also how it was, in a decade of diminished national identity, best to approach America state by state, through the local, to evoke the national.

The discourse of *Road* heightened hopefulness through its intimacy with viewers. Typically, a *Road* segment would begin with a brief description of the person or place being profiled, then through Kuralt's narration, directly point out the "high degree of contrast, either induced as understatement or denial, or a juxtaposition between the well-known and the unknown" of the segment's subject.[72] As Tolbert noted, "by centering around a particular individual, place or event . . . inclusion of specifics instead of generalities also gives the reports a personal angle. Thus, it is possible for the audience to identify with the series."[73] The effect of these techniques on the viewer, as a correspondent for CBS in Minneapolis told Virginia Bailey, a journalism graduate student who wrote her master's thesis on the segments, was that Kuralt approached the viewer not as an oracle with worldly awareness but "like a good friend" who "has discovered something he wants you to see and know about."[74] Kuralt's technique remained indebted to the "tell them what you're going to tell them, tell them, and then tell them what you've told them" school of sober news journalism, yet with a crucial difference: in announcing the theme of the segment at its beginning, Kuralt invited viewers to participate in the synecdoche-making process that unfolds throughout the segments. Thus Kuralt told viewers directly, like a good friend, what to see and why it is worth seeing, and in the directness of his address, Kuralt encouraged viewers to see his subject as he did, not as sober and transparent but as a synecdoche, as a promising example of the nation. Tolbert noted that the segments relied heavily on direct address—the "you" and "I" that suggests, in the space between them, a "we." In other words, while *Road* sounded much like a news segment of its time, with ample reference to individual names and specific places, as an "alternative" to the typical news subject, Kuralt's high degree of direct address, along with his direct statement of the segment's theme, created a connection between the subject of the segment and the viewer—a broader index of actors and narratives—framed in a larger, national whole. Telling the viewer what to see rather than showing them may at first seem like the epitome of literary inelegance, yet by doing so, Kuralt promulgated a unified, coherent narrative—a beginning, a middle, and an end—in *Road* that was sorely lacking in the discourse of evening news.

As an alternative to the news, the hopeful affects of the *Road* segments also stand in stark contrast to Kuralt's other work for CBS. In addition to adopting the broadcasting company's sober rhetoric when he substituted for evening news anchors, Kuralt applied synecdochical rhetoric to produce a moralistic, if not cynical, tone in other venues of reporting. Johanna Cleary has noted that Kuralt's early radio scripts focused on "what he saw as America failing to live up to its promises, a concern over damage to the environment, and a sense of cynicism about American institutions."[75] For example, a June 1964 radio essay on the realities of life in Harlem is scripted to highlight racial divides: "Harlem is the blind despair of the black man and the supreme unconcern of the white man, who daily roars through Harlem on the New Haven's 5:20 to Westport, doing the crossword puzzle in the *New York Times* as the train picks up to speed."[76] Here, "Harlem" is a synecdoche for the nation's "supreme unconcern" for black urban America through the white man's speedy escape by train to the suburbs: the *New York Times* is reduced from a report of the metropolis to its crossword section. There emerges in this radio essay a sense of a nation sharply divided, not only a racial divide between black and white but an affective divide as well, between those who suffer "blind despair" and those who live with "supreme unconcern" for national problems.

Kuralt also saved hopeful stories for *Road* as he captured, at the same time, less than hopeful ones for other CBS media. Kuralt's *Dateline America* series for CBS Radio, produced at the same time as *Road*, also reveals how he synecdochically constructed national issues through local portraits without the distinctive hopeful tone that characterizes *Road*. The *Dateline* segments, in particular, tried to capture what Kuralt told his listeners "you're trying to ignore. . . . An antic quality has crept into American public life, a kind of lunacy that makes *Catch-22* look like the book of Elijah, a book of prophecy" in which the nation "isn't the way things are supposed to work."[77] The *Dateline* segments frequently capture the frustrations of a period in which "the conventional wisdom of the postwar decades became discredited, but no prevailing philosophy or idea arose to take its place."[78] They also capture how Kuralt was able to illustrate the less than hopeful affects of his subjects with equal narrative effectiveness.

The *Dateline* segments often focused on how individuals negotiated competing and contradictory federal regulations. In a segment focused on the town of Arcola, Illinois, Kuralt noted, "The corn is so high that it blocks the view of Washington from here," yet the impress of the federal capital was felt on Arcola's farmers caught between foreign and domestic policy decisions.[79] Kuralt describes this tension synecdochically, between those in the State Department (who think "all this September bounty is good. Corn is our wealth and can be used as an instrument of foreign policy") and those in the Agriculture Department (who think "corn is our poverty: farmers are growing too much of it for their own good and next year we'll have to cut back").[80] Stuck between two disagreeing bureaucracies, Kuralt notes, "A corn farmer who came to Arcola yesterday to buy a sack of cornmeal at an inflated price told me the whole thing has him confused."[81] The farmer's confusion is also a confusion of synecdoche: if corn is made to stand for "our wealth," then whose wealth is it? Why is the farmer who grows and sells corn forced to buy a sack of cornmeal at an inflated price? Corn, as a synecdoche for divergent national policy—foreign and domestic—weighs on the minds of the farmers who grow it. But in his *Dateline* segment, Kuralt offers no hopefulness. Indeed, he amplifies the farmer's lack of hope and confusion, transforming it into a synecdoche of dysfunctional government, concluding the segment by saying, "I would just like to warn all those people in Washington that around Arcola, Illinois, the suspicion is growing that a government that cannot make up its mind about corn . . . may not be able to make up its mind about anything."[82] The contradictory politics of corn becomes representative of a government without purpose, an inert bureaucracy that its citizens find to be suspicious. The *Dateline* segment captures Arcola's—and by synecdochical extension, the nation's—lack of confidence in public leaders, spurred by the news discourse and television documentaries of the sixties, that fostered in the seventies a "skepticism about corporate leaders, the omnipresent distrust of politicians—all produced a spreading disillusionment about the competence of the dominant institutions of society."[83]

What Kuralt heard the people of Arcola say—and what he reported about them on *Dateline*—is in marked contrast to the same people who appeared in the *Road* segment titled "Coffee Cups," broadcast on November 25, 1977. The conversations about corn and politics, of contradictory bureaucracies and suspicion toward the federal government, that Kuralt heard at Arrol's Drug Store in Arcola are absent from the *Road* segment, which focuses instead on the drugstore's unique coffee cups, which have the names of their patrons painted on them. With an establishing shot of the *Road* bus pulling up to the drugstore, Kuralt begins the segment by saying, "We stopped into Arrol's Drug Store, looking only for a cup of coffee. What we found was the heart of an American small town."[84] That the drugstore is the "heart" of an "American small town" is a synecdoche that bespeaks another synecdoche: the heart suggests the body as the small town suggests the nation. Kuralt next focuses on the citizens at the drugstore coffee counter, the manager of the lumberyard talking to the town clerk about the local high school football game the day before, to note that "Bill and Ray and one hundred and sixty other regulars at Arrol's coffee counter have their names painted on their cups. . . . A hundred and sixty-two cups on the wall and everybody up there knows everybody else."[85] In a way, the cups are a test of endurance: a regular at the drugstore gets his name on a cup only after he consumes a hundred cups of coffee, after which he is put on a waiting list. But Kuralt sees community and familiarity where others may see competition and exclusivity. For him, the cups are a symbol of the persistence of small-town American traditions, and thus the vitality of small-town America itself.

The camera pans over the shelves of cups. Some cups are individualized with a symbol below the name: the first Arcola volunteer for the Korean War has a star painted on his, the town banker a dollar sign, the town mechanic "won a crossed wrench and screwdriver" on his cup after helping Charles Lindbergh repair his airplane engine decades ago: the drugstore proprietor explains that a man named John has a black key painted beneath his because his grade school nickname was "Blackie."[86] The symbols, in effect, become synecdoches that stand in for the town's citizens, binding their occupations to their names, indexing a person's place in the community, and occasionally, as with "Blackie," evoking a language that only those who live in town could understand. Kuralt sees the cups as a symbol not only of small-town pride but of a national pride as well, in its patrons' service to national icons such as Lindbergh and to the nation through military service such as the Korean War. Kuralt's affection for the cups also raises their hopeful appeal. The cups—and their hopeful connotations—make him "wish—just for this morning—that we didn't have to travel on interminably. We wished we could stay and drink our five gallons and get a cup up there with our name on it."[87] By expressing his desire to stay, he suggests to viewers that they would want to stay, too, in their hometowns with their prideful traditions. "Coffee Cups" concludes with shots of men and women consuming coffee in the cups with their names on them. Kuralt reflects, "To have a cup with your name on it—it is such a small thing."[88] But the smallness of the cup makes it a part that Kuralt, in his conclusion, embeds in a larger whole. "But when you die, or leave town, they take your cup down from the rack. . . . The cups may not be such a small thing after all. They are a town register, and a history, and a confirmation that life goes on in a small American town."[89]

"Coffee Cups" shows the hopeful work of synecdoche that is prevalent throughout the *Road* segments. The smallness of the cups is juxtaposed with the smallness of the town, such that the cups become a "town register" of the endurance of American community. The coffee cup, "such a small thing," becomes a big thing, a "confirmation" of one's life, a symbol that "life goes on in an American small town," and therefore that life goes on in all towns across America. The part, the coffee cup, becomes a whole, just as the town's denizens become a conformation of the life of small-town America, and, subsequently, a confirmation that the nation is alive. The presence of the cups confirms—synecdochically is made to confirm—the life of the country. Through Kuralt's scripting, each patron of the drugstore is something more than the one hundred cups of coffee they have consumed. Through their cups, and through Kuralt's scripting, they become a representation of an even larger imagined community.

Yet Kuralt has been selective in scripting this *Road* segment, as his *Dateline* segment on Arcola indicates. The drugstore patrons are not talking in the *Road* segment about their dismay at domestic or foreign policy. They are not talking about contradictory politics in tones of frustration; their talk is more moderate, about yesterday's football game, pheasant hunting, the big town dance: the rituals and minutiae of local everyday life that Kuralt suggests keep a community together and make it a place he—and we—should stay. The cups themselves represent the everydayness of the community—the drinking of coffee at the drugstore—as much as they represent each of the people that are part of the community. The presence of the cups, Kuralt says, is a "confirmation," a ceremony that admits people to the community but also a testament to the life and liveliness of the town, a more abstract, imagined community. Such synecdoches are hopeful because they have been selectively scripted to be so: by focusing on the liveliness of the town, Kuralt evokes a hopeful whole where other concerns, like the contradictions of corn policy and its effects on farming and the local economy, might not evoke such hopefulness. Such selectiveness has its effects: the Arcola of *Road* risks reducing its citizens to their coffee cups, making them seem eccentric as a result, disconnected from the nation as a whole. That the segment is titled "Coffee Cups" is telling: the story about the cups is meant to stand for something larger than Arcola itself, that is, all small-town Americas.

Rather than deploying synecdoche to show divide between the local and the national as he does in the *Dateline* segment, the deployment of synecdoche unites them in "Coffee Cups." The construction of hopefulness is a matter of the selection of parts to suggest a promising whole.

If, as Burke suggests, synecdoches are reductions that allow for representation to take place, Kuralt's techniques are synecdochical. As Kuralt told Bailey, his strategy was to craft a narrative of one subject, because "by focusing on a single thing, you can evoke the whole thing. . . . If you focus on a barker, you can evoke the carnival."[90] And as he told Tolbert: "I know that there's no point to do a story about Arizona. It's just too big a subject. What you have to do is a story about one man who lives in one small house or one corner of Arizona. You may say a lot about Arizona that way. More than if you tried to cover the whole state."[91]

More than if you tried to cover the whole state: this is the promise of synecdoche, a rhetorical technique that takes a small subject and makes it, like Bloch's description of hope, something broader than itself. And in Kuralt's synecdoches, the result is quite broad, even broader than what covering the whole would allow. At the same time, the risks of synecdoche are also apparent in Kuralt's miniaturization of a state to "one man who lives in one small house" or one corner of the state. As Kuralt admitted to Bailey, "You always have to narrow it down," which raises the question of what is lost in the narrowing that produces synecdoches.[92] Such a narrowing may produce a rich narrative but does so in miniature. At the same time, it may universalize the part in ways that obscure its distinctiveness and risks turning that part into something it is not. This is where hopefulness is in marked contrast to hope: to build a hopeful portrait of the nation from one citizen does not evoke hope as much as it evokes hopeful feeling. How hopeful feelings were scripted in the *Road* segments may also show how distant actual hope was at the time, such as in the nation's ongoing war in Vietnam.

Waiting for Roger

Filmed in October and broadcast on November 11, 1970, "Waiting for Roger" was a favorite *Road* segment of Leslie Midgley, an executive producer of the *Evening News*, as it epitomized Kuralt's discovery of hopeful narratives by traveling the nation without a fixed destination: the crew, as Midgley described it to Bailey, "literally came across the story by the side of the road, the sight of a family waiting for their son and brother to come home from Vietnam. Just standing out there."[93] Saved for Veterans Day, thus connecting the segment to the national holiday and subsequently a national narrative of celebrating veterans, the evening news was relatively undramatic: Vietnam and Cambodia were secondary to a tentative contract reached between General Motors and the United Auto Workers. The broadcast devoted lengthy coverage to the mourning of Charles de Gaulle in France, as well as an Energy Department proposal to sell environmental bonds to help fight pollution.

The segment begins with Kuralt standing in front of the Soldier's and Sailor's Monument in the Public Square of Cleveland, Ohio. As the camera pans across the monument's reliefs, Kuralt's narration begins: "Time was in America when veterans were heroes. They came home to waving flags and marching bands, and we raised great gaudy monuments to them, like this one."[94] The camera, which has zoomed in on the tip of the monument, moves downward to Kuralt, who continues, "But times have changed, wars have changed, monuments and heroes are out of fashion. Nobody much thinks about veterans anymore—except, of course, the people they left behind."[95] Kuralt's introduction at the Public Square frames the story with a past (heroes for whom gaudy monuments were raised) and a present (war itself has changed, as has society's responses to war) as well as a hopeful feeling: that even though monuments and heroism are "out of fashion" and war no longer brings national solidarity, veterans are still loved by the families awaiting their return home.

The scene shifts to a two-story white house perched close to the side of the road in a country hamlet. With typical understatement, Kuralt says, "We weren't thinking about veterans when we passed Sam Lambert's house in Carrothers, Ohio. We were on our way somewhere else."[96] Yet the reason for their stopping is quickly evident. The front of the white house is festooned with flowing streamers and handwritten signs. "But seeing the signs and the people in the yard, we stopped, and spent an hour or two with the Lamberts, waiting for Roger to come home."[97] In the narrow space—perhaps ten feet—between the state highway and the house, a dozen people stand, leaning on trees or automobiles, chatting with each other as they look down the road, scanning the horizon. They are watching for a red car with a white top owned by Roger Lambert, who is returning home from Vietnam.

Kuralt admits that Roger "didn't come home while we were there. But there was something timeless and affecting about the waiting that made us want to tell you about it on Veterans Day."[98] What is "timeless" and "affecting" about the waiting is the family's hope for Roger's return. No one is sure when Roger will arrive because, Kuralt says, "The thing about Roger is, he never calls. He just drives up. The Lamberts weren't sure what day that would be. Maybe today."[99] The family mills about the front of the house, as the camera cuts from one family member to another, standing outside, waiting not only for Roger, it seems, but for time to move on with him there beside them. Their waiting is affecting because their hope is as much about Roger's arrival as it is the image they want him to see when he drives up. Kuralt notes, "His wife, Jane, had the idea that she wanted to be standing in the yard holding Harold Lee when he arrived, so she kept the baby outside until it began to get too chilly."[100] The waiting, then, is not only for Roger's return but for the hopeful tableau they wish to present him when he arrives home, the wife holding the four-month-old baby he has never seen in front of the family home, a symbol of the return to the normalcy of civilian life. Thus what is "affecting" is not only a hopefulness for Roger's return but a hopefulness for a certain sort of life after his return. Perhaps this is why "the Lamberts stood beside the road, waiting, nobody wanting to be inside and miss everything if he really did drive up."[101] What is "affecting" about the timelessness is their waiting: the Lamberts are caught in the expectancy of Roger's return, suspended in time as the hours pass.

After introducing Roger's wife and child, and a distant uncle who stops by with a jug of cider for him, Kuralt notes, "There were cousins and nephews and sisters and a brother and a father, all waiting, but nobody waiting more eagerly than Roger's mother."[102] While Kuralt interviews

Mrs. Lambert, the camera focuses on her. As she talks, she looks at other members of the family, who have formed a semicircle around the camera against the front of the house, as if to confirm she is speaking synecdochically for them. His birthday will be in mid-November, and she plans to "have a lot of company in" and bake him his favorite cake. As the camera pans across the family, the elders holding the children, she says:

> Even if he was working in a finance office you don't never know what's gonna happen. But I turned him over to the Lord, and I asked him to watch over him like he did David when he was . . . when David was in those places lots of times, he watched over him, and so has Roger been in those places, and he's watched over him. And I'm still trustin' in the Lord.[103]

As Mrs. Lambert talks to Kuralt, we hear that her hope is anchored in a faith that has given her a way to hope. It comes from a story, the biblical story of David, fighter of Philistines and Goliath. In her prayers, she asked God to watch over her son as he did for David: she asked that God not only watch over her son but that her son's life be plotted like David's life. In effect, her hope is anchored in a story. The story sustains her hope: it is as much a discourse as it is a narrative. A higher power watches over her son, as he has others' sons before. She is still "trustin' in the Lord."[104] Kuralt asks Mrs. Lambert when she is expecting Roger to come home. "About this day and time, she responds. "We don't care how soon it is, just so it ain't too long."[105] Mrs. Lambert is aware that she is not in control of time, that she is caught in the arrest of hope, that while it may be a long time, she hopes that it won't be too long before Roger arrives home. How soon does not matter; what does is that soon be, indeed, soon, that "it ain't too long" before her son arrives home. Mrs. Lambert is caught in the waiting that so characterizes hope: her expectancy, expressed in double negatives, is evident for viewers to see.

From its tableau of his wife waiting for his return to his mother's vision of his life as one like the biblical narrative, "Roger" constructs a cohesive narrative—complete with plots and subplots—that was the opposite of the staccato reporting offered by the evening news. In the reporting on his family as they wait for him, Roger takes on a narrative complexity as soldier but also as father, son, and cousin. Viewers see how others relate to Roger, identify with him, and are thus themselves spurred to identify with Roger. (Indeed, "Roger" was such a popular segment that in response to overwhelming viewer mail, Cronkite announced at the end of a broadcast the following week that Roger had indeed returned home safely.) Such is the power of synecdochical rhetoric to connect members of an imagined community with each other through hopeful narratives in which one can identify as part of a hopeful whole. The rhetoric of synecdoche can, as Bloch writes of hope, make people feel broader by going outside themselves and identifying with another member of the imagined community.

After the interview with Roger's mother, the camera shifts to the cars going up and down the road as the Lamberts watch them. "Nothing exactly happened this afternoon, except what was happening inside people," Kuralt notes.[106] The shift from the family's hope—what is happening inside them—to their hopefulness, their evidence as a synecdoche for a larger national dilemma, takes place in the segment's conclusion. What is going on inside the Lamberts, Kuralt suggests, is also going on inside most Americans. As the camera pans back to the house and the streamers and the signs, Kuralt says, "No parade is planned in Carrothers. And that is a measure of how times, and wars, have changed."[107] As the segment ends, the camera, attached to the *On the Road* bus, departs the Lambert home. As the house recedes in the distance, Kuralt says, "Nobody in the yard beside Ohio Route 4 was waiting for news of victory in Roger's war. They were just waiting for Roger."[108]

Though no one in the Lambert family ever says it, Kuralt's narration asserts that "what has been happening inside people" is hope. And by focusing on the hope inside the Lambert family as they wait, Kuralt aspires to evoke hopefulness in viewers, too. That Roger does not arrive in the segment is made indicative of a larger waiting, a national waiting. In the numerous shots of the family milling about the thin strip of yard between the house and highway, in the lengthy interview with Mrs. Lambert, what has become apparent is that the Lambert family is waiting, hoping for Roger's return. As Crapanzano writes, "hope is the field of desire in waiting."[109] It is an affect that leads a family to put streamers and signs on a house, to stand by the side of that house, and wait, expectantly, for their loved one to return.

But at the conclusion of the segment, the juxtaposition of the Lambert family with the national war serves as a reminder of how times have changed, just as the segment offers evidence of hopefulness rather than hope itself. The most glaring difference between hopefulness and hope in "Roger" is that unlike many viewers who did not know the status or whereabouts of the soldiers close to them, the Lamberts know that Roger is alive and returning home. Less obvious is the lack of talk about the war itself. The Lamberts never reveal their own political views about the war, nor does Kuralt, in his interview with Mrs. Lambert, attempt to solicit them. Viewers do not know if Roger was drafted or enlisted, or if he supports the war or has become a critic of it. Roger himself is never pictured on screen: his anonymity was a deliberate choice. Kuralt's cameraman noted that while he filmed footage of family pictures for broadcast, including pictures of Roger, Kuralt did not include them in the shooting script, telling him, "We don't need to see Roger . . . it's better that we don't."[110] In being unseen, Roger becomes an everyman, a synecdoche who stands in for all the soldiers whose families are waiting. Thus Kuralt urges viewers to interpret Roger's story as an index, as a "measure of how times, and wars, have changed."[111] That change—the anxiousness and anonymity in comparison to the gaudy monuments and town parades—is not necessarily a positive one that viewers might associate with the family's hope. The focus, Kuralt suggests, is no longer on building monuments to war heroes but on assuring their safe return. That Mrs. Lambert thinks of the story of David may show that she is not thinking of a story of American patriotism: such narratives of patriotism are no longer convincing but are rather, as Kuralt describes the statue in Cleveland's Public Square, gaudy. The segment suggests, as an index of how times have changed, that the nation does not have much hope for the outcome of the war. At the same time, it comes close to perpetuating an optimistic disposition that the war will eventually end if families just wait it out. By focusing on the family's waiting for Roger, the anticipation of his arrival substitutes for a larger anxiety, one without solution, about the hopeless situation in Vietnam.

It could be said that Americans, after the Tet Offensive and the widening of the war into Cambodia, and far beyond that, through the energy crisis and Watergate and stagflation, were throughout the seventies "caught in the structure of waiting. What they hoped for was a solution—something they could not envisage. They had a hope so indefinite as not to have an identifiable object. As such, they could not turn it into effective desire."[112] In "Waiting for Roger," this indefiniteness is most telling in the handwritten signs on the Lambert home, such as "We Love You," "Waiting for Daddy," and, the most evocative, "Leave Viet Nam Far Behind." If the Lamberts are waiting for Roger to come home, they are also waiting out the war that sent him away. The sign asks him—and viewers—not to have hope for the war but to have hope that it can be left far behind. In miniaturizing the narrative around Roger, Kuralt evokes the broader, national waiting for the war to end, without directly addressing the unlikeliness of a national victory in it. The nation's desperation to rid itself of the war is subsumed beneath the family's hopeful waiting for Roger to return. In this way, "Roger" is not a story about Vietnam: it is a story about Roger. The microcosm hides the macrocosm: the intense contentiousness of the war is hidden by the hopefulness of Roger's return. And even that is not national nor public but private and internal. A family that is caught up in national turmoil only reflects on it inwardly: nothing happens in "Roger" "except what was happening inside people."[113] There is no heroism on display in parades throughout town, only families waiting expectantly beside the road.[114] There is no outpouring of communal (or national) patriotism planned in Carrothers, no marching bands or waving flags: the soldiers drive home separately in their individual cars, each returning to the isolated, private lives awaiting them.

"Roger" may be hopeful, but at the same time, the segment reflects a turn toward what Capozzola describes as "the localization of American patriotism" during the seventies, when "there was an uneasiness about outspoken patriotism," when "it became increasingly clear that one historical narrative could not tell the whole nation's story."[115] Scripting the segment as one in which the family waits for Roger, Kuralt sets aside larger narratives of the nation and instead individualizes and miniaturizes the narrative to one of a single family waiting for a single soldier to come home. In doing so, the segment captures the affective complexity of the family's hope, all the while synecdochically suggesting that viewers identify the Lamberts' hope as a moment of national hopefulness. The segment thus constructs a narrative that viewers can identify with, all the while evoking the nation without directly engaging in its unease. Only by pointing to "what is going on inside people" does the segment speaks to larger national issues. It also shows Kuralt's synecdochical technique for capturing the national: by scripting a part to represent the whole, Kuralt was able to produce segments that intrigued both the television news establishment and viewers alike. Yet the way in which Kuralt substitutes part for whole to evoke hopefulness also risks subsuming national problems in need of resolution. The conflict between the radicalism of hope and Kuralt's scripting of hopefulness in the *Road* segments is apparent in one of its most popular—and problematic—segments.

Chandler Reunion

"Chandler Reunion," alternately known as "Coming Home," may be one of the most enduring *Road* segments: Kuralt thought it "the most moving" segment of the series.[116] Originally broadcast on November 27, 1978, the Monday after Thanksgiving weekend, the evening news began with developments in the November 18 mass suicides at Jonestown in Guyana. The lead story included an update on the number of bodies found at Jonestown and detailed the ongoing search for cult members presumed alive. Also prominently featured was the murder of San Francisco mayor George Moscone and city councilman Harvey Milk by a former city supervisor. The evening's news broadcast also ran segments on the possible reinstating of price controls on home heating oil, and of skirmishes with truckers who were not being compensated at the rate of inflation, which was at 8.89 percent and rising.

The segment begins as Kuralt walks down the road to the Chandler house near Prairie, Mississippi. Walking toward the camera, Kuralt reflects, "This is a long road. It took nine children out of the cotton fields, out of poverty, out of Mississippi. But roads go both ways, and this Thanksgiving weekend, they all returned."[117] Leaning on the family's mailbox outside their house, Kuralt intones, "This is about Thanksgiving, and coming home."[118] As with "Coffee Cups" and "Roger," by telling the viewer what the story is about, Kuralt performs the synecdoche that is the subject of the story: it is a story not about cotton fields nor poverty nor Mississippi individually, nor is it a story about cotton and poverty and Mississippi combined, but each are subsumed as parts of a hopeful narrative about holidays and coming home.

There is an immediate shift to the Chandler family, cheering in the yard as another carload of family members arrives at the reunion. (One cannot help but think of this as the anticipated conclusion to "Roger.") Thanksgiving, Kuralt informs us, is the elder Chandlers' wedding anniversary: this year is their fiftieth. The camera pans over each of the Chandler children, who arrive, "one after the other, and from every corner of America."[119] Kuralt provides each of the Chandler children's names, occupations, and professions, including their degrees and the names of the colleges from which they were earned. Why is this important? Because "all nine children had memories of a sharecropper's cabin and nothing to wear and nothing to eat. All nine are college graduates."[120]

In fact, many of the Chandler children have earned more than their bachelor's degrees: three of the daughters have earned their master's degrees; one son has earned a doctorate. All have gone on to well-regarded, middle-class occupations: preacher, technical manager, schoolteacher, university professor, and hospital dietitian. The camera pans through the Chandlers' home: the daughters, donned in aprons, are preparing the Thanksgiving dinner. Then Kuralt interjects, "I thought you ought to meet their parents," as the segment shifts from the abundance of food being prepared in the kitchen to the backyard, where the elder Chandlers are framed by an old, rusted tractor in a barren autumnal cotton field. The listening shot is established, and the camera focuses on Alex Chandler, the head of the family. The camera is so closely focused on Mr. Chandler that the deep wrinkles of his face are evident. As he talks of his first son's desire to go to college, his eyes look away from the camera. "We didn't have any money," he says slowly.[121] "We went to town and borrowed two dollars and a half . . . and when he got there, that's all he had."[122] Alex Chandler's furrowed face is juxtaposed with a shot of the smiling face of his eldest son, Cleveland, snapping pictures of his family as Kuralt says, "From that beginning, he became Dr. Cleveland Chandler. He is chairman of the economics department at Howard University."[123]

This hopeful reading suggests that, in America, even those who start on borrowed money can become masters of it, such as professors of economics. Continuing to juxtapose the abundance of the Chandler children with their family's poor surroundings—the camera quickly returns to chickens roaming the backyard near a decrepit coop—Kuralt rhetorically asks, "How did they do it, starting on one of the poorest farms in the poorest part of the poorest state in America?"[124] The question may be rhetorical, but it recalls the synecdochical process he explained to Tolbert: much like telling a story about Arizona by focusing on one person or one house or one part of the state, Kuralt here reveals his thinking about telling an American story by focusing on one family in one house in one part of Mississippi. Much like the segment's opening description of the road that took the children away from home and into the nation, Kuralt telescopes outward. The rhetorical question thus reveals the synecdochical process of *Road*, in which local, miniature parts are dramatically amplified—"one of the poorest farms in the poorest part of the poorest state," which makes the Chandlers' successes all the more astounding and all the more hopeful—to speak for the whole nation.

The answer to Kuralt's rhetorical question is provided by Princess Chandler Norman, who is framed standing in front of the decrepit chicken coop:

PRINCESS: We worked.
KURALT: You picked cotton?
PRINCESS: Yes, picked cotton, and pulled corn, stripped millet, dug potatoes.[125]

The dialogue, as it is presented in a book of Kuralt's favorite *Road* segments, does not capture the visual drama of this interview. Princess says "We worked" simply and with pride: labor is a way of life that is obvious to her. Uncertain how to draw her out—perhaps uncertain of how to get Princess to project hopefulness—Kuralt pauses, then asks anxiously, "You . . . uh . . . picked cotton?" As soon as he finishes the question, Princess's eyes, like Alex's before, look down and to the side: the look of shame. Her answer, "Yes," is said with a great sigh, her face seeming to recall the hard labor she and her family have undertaken in their lives. The question, of course, is the most insensitive one an interviewer could ask of an African American growing up in Mississippi in the middle of the twentieth century, for it recalls not only the structural but also the racial inequalities of the period. Kuralt's question sets aside Princess's successful present to compel her to dwell on the struggles of her past. (At no point in the interview does Kuralt ask Princess about her master's degree or her occupation as a schoolteacher.) It also frames Princess as being evidence to hope, all the while tacitly presuming that where that she has succeeded, others can too, even in the poorest part of the country, if they work hard enough. Kuralt has asked the question strategically, then, to draw out that tension, to show how hard the Chandlers have not only worked but also hoped through their toil for a better life. Their struggle is telescoped through Kuralt's question into a hopeful feeling for the nation. It is a hopefulness that is both deserved by the Chandlers as much as it is appropriated by Kuralt.

The segment shifts back to the abundance of the Thanksgiving dinner, as if suggesting that the fruits of the family's labors are on display at the table filled with "ham and turkey and sweet potatoes and cornbread and collard greens and two kinds of pie and three kinds of cake."[126] The plenitude of food on camera is paralleled with the plenitude of family: the youngest of the Chandler children arrives just as the family is sitting down to eat. The camera once again zooms in on Alex Chandler's face as he says grace, giving thanks to God for "all that you have provided us through all these years."[127] The furrows of his face obscure his tears; he covers his pursed lips with a napkin as if trying to prevent himself from sobbing. As he is overcome with emotion, the camera pans back to show that the Chandler children are crying too, some openly, some with cloths close to their eyes to absorb their tears. As he finishes the prayer, Kuralt supplies in voice-over narration what he presumes Alex Chandler is recalling: "Remembering all those years of sharecropping and going hungry and working for a white man for fifty cents a day and worrying about his children's future, Alex Chandler almost didn't get through this blessing. And neither did the others."[128] In his narration of Alex Chandler's remembrance, Kuralt keeps the Chandler story to one of family: economics and race are subsumed to his worry for his children's future. Kuralt's shooting script indicates that the elder Chandler's prayer be synced with his narration, so that when Kuralt says, "And neither did the others," Chandler concludes the prayer with an "Amen," affirming the message Kuralt has scripted. The entire family says "Amen," there is a pause, a bolt of nervous laughter, sighs of relief, and then Thanksgiving dinner begins.

Over a montage of food being passed about and family members eating, Kuralt says, "The Chandler family started with as near nothing as any family in America ever did. And so their Thanksgiving weekend might have been more thankful than most."[129] As the extremity of their former poverty has been juxtaposed with their current plenty throughout the segment, Kuralt connects the Chandler family to the nation, noting that they "started with as near nothing" as any American family but are "more thankful than most" Americans who have not endured such extremes. The Chandler family, Kuralt insists, is an American family, one that reflects a nation that has become ever more prosperous because of hard work and merit. They are "more thankful than most" families because they started "with as near nothing as any family in America ever did."[130] By shifting the focus to the Chandlers as representative of American families, they synecdochically come to stand as exemplary Americans: they come to embody a hopeful American story.

The segment concludes with the family sitting around a piano, as Alex Chandler plays "I'll Fly Away," his favorite spiritual. "His nine children flew away," Kuralt says, "and made places for themselves in this country, and this weekend, came home again."[131] As the family sings along, the camera establishes midrange shots of several of his children and grandchildren. "There are probably no lessons in this," Kuralt says as the segment concludes, "but I know that in the future, whenever I hear that the family is a dying institution, I'll think of them. Whenever I hear that anything in America is impossible, I'll think of them."[132] The camera lingers as the family finishes the spiritual, then fades out.

"Reunion" may be one of the most enduring segments because of Kuralt's ability to script hopefulness through synecdoche. Not only in the themes—family, work, faith—that dominate the segment but in the synecdochical way that Kuralt attaches the Chandlers' successes to the nation, "Reunion" provides a lesson, even if Kuralt understatedly dismissed it, that family and nation are thriving. The segment is, to use Kuralt's word, "moving" because it produces so many hopeful feelings about the nation. Such hopefulness, moving as it is, is also carefully scripted, as Kuralt's notes indicate. While the crew began taping with the arrival of the family, all the interviews used in the segment were shot after the emotional Thanksgiving dinner. Kuralt's notes also indicate that Alex Chandler was crying intermittently throughout the taping—his tears of joy in seeing his family together on both a holiday and his fiftieth wedding anniversary is understandable—but Kuralt saves Chandler's tears only for when he says grace, thus using his tears as a sort of catharsis that fits the synecdoche being scripted. Of greater concern is Kuralt's interview with Princess Chandler Norman. While the entirety of the interview was not transcribed, Kuralt's notes demonstrate how he pressed her to talk of her youth as a struggle, despite her certainty, even at a young age, that she would have a better life than her parents:

KURALT: You picked cotton?
PRINCESS: Yes, picked cotton. And pulled corn, stripped millet, dug potatoes.
KURALT: When you were doing all that hard work in the fields, did you know you were going to leave all that someday?

PRINCESS: Oh yes, we knew we would do something, be somebody else than farmers.

KURALT: How did you know that?

PRINCESS: You decide you're going to do something. And the details may need to be worked out a little later, but you're just going to do what you want to do, and if it's important enough to do, it's possible to do it.[133]

Princess Chandler Norman has given, in her way, the very definition of hope, the radical expectancy that one way of life is coming to an end and that another will eventually emerge in its place. The details "may need to be worked out a little later" because the experience of hope is that in which "the 'not yet' impresses upon the present, such that we must act, politically, to make it our future."[134] That Kuralt found this, according to his notes on the shooting script, to be "no good" indicates that he was not as much interested in her radical hope as he was in presenting a hopeful family, one that might be scripted to stand in for the American family. Kuralt's notes indicate a lack of interest in the details of individual family member's stories: he has also written "no good" next to Princess's description of how segregation made her unable to ride the school bus to town, as well as Fortson Chandler's description of the segregated commodity lines of the Great Depression, in which Alex Chandler often came home with nothing for the family to eat.[135] In Kuralt's scripting of hopefulness then, the challenges of the elder Chandlers' lives are subsumed by the successes of their children, as are the children's challenges subsumed by their educational and vocational successes. And the structural inequalities that Kuralt highlights, that Alex Chandler worked in an economy in which "he had a horse and a cow and tried to buy a mule, and couldn't make the payments, and lost the mule, the horse and the cow," are made to seem minor in light of the middle-class occupations his children have, and made to seem past tense in comparison with his children's successful present.[136] In the case of the Chandlers, the radicalism of their hope is subsumed by hopefulness as Kuralt attempts to fit them into a wider national narrative.

Their hope becomes a hopeful story. As such, the segment comes to sound more optimistic than the Chandlers' story actually is, the Chandlers' hopes more certain than they ever were in reality. In becoming representatives of the endurance of the American family, in turning the Chandlers' hopes into a narrative of hopefulness, the segment sidesteps the radical determination of the Chandlers to overcome the economics of sharecropping and the inequalities of race in the nation.

As narrative is affected by its discourse, Kuralt's selection and arrangement of affects in "Reunion" rearrange affects to interject a hopeful narrative trajectory. In the continuous juxtaposition of poverty and bounty, Kuralt provides viewers with evidence of a story in which the American family is thriving, and as a synecdoche, the nation, despite its diminishments, is thriving as well. We are encouraged to think of the Chandlers as representations of the nation, to recall them in times of diminishment. Kuralt, glossing Steinbeck's *The Grapes of Wrath* while bypassing its political radicalism, intones, "Whenever I hear that anything in America is impossible, I'll think of them."[137] Thus the Chandlers serve as an example—a synecdoche for the promises of American life and a cause to have hope for the nation. Through Kuralt's synecdochical rhetoric, the Chandlers affirm the nation's potential, a reminder that nothing is impossible in America. The hopeful sentiment of Kuralt's claim affirms the Chandlers as exceptional Americans as much as it affirms a narrative of American exceptionalism. Yet the segment is curious for the nation it does not evoke, what it does not ask us to think about when we think about the Chandlers.

Just as "Roger" captures an unease surrounding Vietnam, "Reunion" captures an unease surrounding the roles of family and race in national life. The scripting of family in the segment, particularly in its conclusion, alludes to a discourse of family decline that became predominant in the seventies. This vocabulary was innately connected to a broader narrative of national decline as the family served "as the site where the origin of national decline could be discovered and where the damages wrought by it could be assessed."[138] The family, in short, came to serve as a synecdoche for the nation, particularly as concerns about changes in family structure, it was feared, "undermined the family's ability to transmit the traits that had been essential to its survival under industrial capitalism: discipline, abstinence, and character."[139] Kuralt's assurances point toward each of these concerns: it is the Chandlers' discipline to work and their ability to endure hardship that generate their positive character. That such abstinence was imposed on them by the racial inequalities of the period also evokes the specter of race in American life, one that Kuralt subsumes under a broader, pluralist narrative: the Chandlers' struggle is a family struggle, an American struggle; that it is an African American struggle is not in the foreground but in the background of "Reunion."[140] The segment thus participates in a dominant rhetorical strategy of the seventies, perhaps best seen in narratives of the Bicentennial that evoke a weak "pluralist nationalism" to "create a sense of national unity precisely through a carefully controlled showcasing of difference."[141] Such pluralism was rhetorically enacted by subsuming difference through synecdochical approaches to practices all had in common: school, work, leisure, and individual family practices. In such narratives, much like "Reunion," "discrimination and prejudice would not be ignored . . . but the emphasis would be on the affirmative ways that ethnic and racial groups had adapted."[142] In this way, the Chandlers are seen as representative not of American race relations but of American family life, as the starkness of their differences from "most Americans" celebrating Thanksgiving are subsumed under the ways their family has succeeded.

Kuralt's attempts to script hopefulness also demonstrate the challenges of maintaining hopefulness's moderateness. The motif of coming home strains: it is clearly not that roads go both ways, but only one way, out of the poverty of Mississippi, as Kuralt reminds the viewer that the Chandler children left, that "they all flew away."[143] Such going away is paralleled in the spiritual that concludes the segment, as the family sings "I'll Fly Away." That the Chandler children "made places for themselves in this country" makes them sound like pioneers, when in fact, they are escaping a part of the nation that actively refused to sustain them. Their struggle is relegated to subplot: the segment is not about their leaving but about their "coming home." As such, the segment skirts how radical the Chandlers' perseverance and resilience are. It avoids any intonation of competing nationalisms of the period, including Black Nationalism, itself predicated on the synecdoche of the nation as a family, a family that could thrive only in a home of a "separate black nation."[144] Instead, the segment demonstrates how the Chandlers sought to assimilate into mainstream American culture, which keeps their story within the domain of the American pioneer tradition rather than the self-determination espoused by Black Nationalists during the period. Race is relegated to the background in narratives of weak nationalism, as a more thorough exploration would hinder weak nationalism's hopeful pluralism. And in its attempts to obscure the role of race, the segment's substitution of race for family comes with its own dangers. By concluding the segment with the Chandlers singing the spiritual, Kuralt risks connecting their achievement and prosperity not to the national holiday, nor the nation in general, but to a strong affect, the potentially messianic hope of the spiritual. That very evening's news offered a reminder of the affective power of the family in American culture and the strong nationalisms it could solicit: the mass suicides at Jonestown proved all the more chilling because they were performed under the aegis of a "family" of believers who fled the nation out of a paranoid sense of persecution as much as a sense of radical hope in their religious community and, when told that they had reached the "place where hope runs out," were willing to follow their leader, who they called their "father," to oblivion.[145]

"Reunion," like many *Road* segments, thus walks a fine line between competing strong nationalisms. To do so, it transmutes the radicalism of the Chandlers' hopes into a hopefulness for the nation, a reminder that the "affective disobedience" of hope can be synecdochically rearticulated to "work as a form of assimilation: hoping for freedom is converted into hoping to have a place in the nation, in a way that keeps the nation in place as the distributor of hope."[146] The success of the Chandlers makes for hopeful feelings, then, at a cost. It optimistically affirms a disposition that through hard work, racial divides remedy themselves. By no means did Kuralt misrepresent the Chandler family's successes. Rather, he adapted their hope to craft a hopeful story for a mass audience, and in doing so, synecdochically turned their story from one of an African American family's struggle against racial and economic inequality into one of the endurance of the American family, hard work, and faith. Such a synecdochical shift is subtle but potent in a decade of transformation without narrative. At a time in which an emerging conservative movement would find new freight in the catchphrase "family values," the segment offers reassurance that family values persist in American life. And at a time in which equal rights continued to be a vexed political issue, the segment reassures viewers that with hard work and merit, a better life can be had. It is in this way that *Road* constructed an affective portrait of the nation that was rewarding to multiple audiences but never explicitly defined: it offered hopefulness, a feeling of hope for the nation, where perhaps hope—and the radicalism of hope—was needed more.

Conclusion

As the midpoint between optimism and hope, the hopeful affects of the *Road* segments had special currency, providing promising narratives in a period that lacked a clear national narrative. The segments provided hopefulness through a narrative by which viewers could see a part of themselves seldom represented in the evening news. As such, *Road* offered a "cease-fire," an alternative to the sober rhetoric of the evening news, through synecdochical narratives that constructed a hopeful narrative of the nation. Through his use of synecdoche, Kuralt crafted stories that suggested evidence of a better nation than the one the evening news presented without suggesting a politics by which that better nation could come into existence. His scripting of a hopeful national story occasionally bypassed pressing political, social, and economic issues to construct a hopefulness in the successes of the present.

But as the seventies progressed and the politics of consensus collapsed, the moderateness that characterizes hopefulness would be subsumed under the hope elicited by the rise of a new, strong nationalism promulgated by the political right. The rhetoric of hopefulness that the segments relied on seemed hackneyed, almost antique by the late seventies, in part because the politics that perpetuated such hopefulness had become fractured. What was once a predominant national rhetoric that "clustered together freedom with responsibility and discipline; peril with wisdom, leadership, firmness and resolve," already under strain in the late sixties, would eventually become totally decoupled by the early eighties.[147] And the hopefulness that attended such rhetoric, that with freedom came responsibility to others, and that through individual efforts the common good could be fulfilled, no longer had appeal as the diminishments of the seventies became evident. "Freedom, once so tightly tied to its contexts of challenge and destiny, had become disembodied, unmoored, imagined" by the time Reagan was elected to the presidency, at which point "the nation disaggregated into a constellation of private acts."[148] The shift in politics also affected the power of synecdoche as a trope: that an individual could represent the nation, and perhaps represent the nation better than the nation itself, a core assumption of Kuralt's writing, could not be sustained once individuals retreated inward and no longer found synecdoches to be inspiring or convincing. By the late seventies it was apparent to a consensus of journalists, political scientists, and commentators that "the crisis of leadership lies not merely in Washington but in the nation as a whole."[149] As the individual was decoupled from the national, the nation was no longer something to participate in but something to be kept at bay. No wonder that the rhetoric of Reagan, with its dour assessment of the role of government in an individual's life, with its promise of fulfillment without federal intrusion, gained traction during this decade. The diminishments of the seventies exposed an exhausted, weakened nationalism and, in the rhetoric of conservatives, a weak nation.

Yet in its moderateness, hopefulness has an endurance that the strong affects of national hope and optimism do not. Hope may be intense but, like any form of strong affect, ultimately proves monopolizing, prone to political extremes, impossible to implement without creating reactionaries and potentially evoking even hotter forms of nationalism. Hopefulness, as a weak affect, may not be as intense but, as an incitement to read, has a persistence that survives well beyond the hopes of the political season. As the gentlest form of weak nationalism, neither radical nor conservative, hopefulness has a persistence that is as eccentric as it is enduring.

The promise that the nation can be incited from reading an object chanced upon the side of the road is central to the premise of the segments. For example, the segment broadcast on September 8, 1978, titled "Blackie," focused on what Kuralt saw as the *Road* bus traveled Illinois Route 16. The evening news that night began with coverage of protests against the shah of Iran, an update on the negotiations that would soon lead to the Camp David Accords, and comprehensive coverage of ongoing teacher strikes in fourteen states. Like "Roger," the segment begins with Kuralt's typical understatement "We were going somewhere else, like all the other traffic, when we noticed what looked like a grave beside the highway. Funny place for a grave, so we stopped and asked around."[150] The site, "just a crossing of country roads," Kuralt says, again with understatement, "has a special meaning for the people around here, because of something that happened here once."[151]

The segment shifts to Kuralt interviewing Bill Stiff, whose family owns the land on which the grave stands. In the summer of 1965, a small black dog appeared at the intersection. "Nobody can fully explain why he was here," Stiff states: the dog may have become lost, or been abandoned, but as Stiff sees it, "he just stayed here and was waiting for his master to return."[152] The scene shifts to a close-up of a "cross traffic does not stop" sign underneath a stop sign. And the scene shifts again to a car speeding down the country road, as if to suggest that the car could contain Blackie's owner, as Kuralt explains, "The summer went by and the fall came, and Blackie kept his place here at the crossing."[153] Shifting again, the camera, now behind the grave marker, looks out at the highway, capturing traffic as it passes, as if Blackie himself were still waiting for his owner. Kuralt describes how the dog's persistence aroused the worry of the people who live nearby, who repeatedly tried to adopt him. But Blackie refused to leave the intersection.

"I think that unless some motorist hadn't killed him, I don't think he would ever have left," Stiff says.[154] As the camera scans the intersection, Kuralt finally confirms what we have known since the segment began and what Stiff has just said: Blackie was struck by a car on an icy February morning and died. As this fact is revealed, the camera is at ground level, such that individual blades of grass obscure the lower half of view. As Kuralt says that Blackie was "killed," a car speedily passes through the frame: still at ground level, we are given the perspective, from the dog's point of view, of the event itself.[155]

Blackie's death, much like his refusal to leave the intersection, cast an impression on the people who lived nearby, even twelve years afterward, an impression that Kuralt finds "hard to explain."[156] The segment shifts to a young girl mowing the grass at Blackie's grave marker, which is surrounded by a chain-link fence and covered in yellow flowers. A large white cross stands next to the grave marker. "He was just a lost dog, and it all happened a long time ago," Kuralt says, yet even today "kids still take turns mowing the grass and keeping the place cleaned up."[157] Why the locals are so affected might be explained, Kuralt says in the segment's conclusion, by "what they wrote on Blackie's grave marker," which Kuralt reads aloud as the camera, which has focused on it, pans back. The marker reads: "Blackie, Feb. 6, 1966: Know Ye Now True Loyalty & Love."[158]

As hopefulness gives evidence to hope, Kuralt has given evidence for many hopes, each replete with the trite sentimentalism his critics accused him of, yet with the different kind of drama that characterizes the seventies, a drama seldom seen on the evening news. Blackie, though a dog, the segment suggests, was in a state of expectancy that characterizes hope, waiting—and hoping—for his master to return. Throughout the segment, the camera—when not focused on the interview between Kuralt and Stiff, or on Jenny Whitmore, who mows the grass around the grave marker—focuses primarily on the road: the speeding traffic, the warnings at the intersection that traffic on Illinois Route 16 does not stop. All evoke the dangers of the intersection that Blackie loyally refused to leave. The transitoriness of the road, as much as Kuralt saw it as a synecdoche for the promise of the nation, becomes a synecdoche for the transitoriness of life. Miles away from the nearest village, the intersection of roads is in the middle of nowhere, surrounded by cornfields.

The nowhere that Blackie was abandoned, the grave marker suggests, led him somewhere, much like the cars on the road, to a destination, first to the care of those who live nearby, and through accident, ultimately to an afterlife where he will know loyalty and love in perpetuity. In this way, Blackie becomes not only an index of small-town America but also an index of the values and faith shown in their care for him. Their care for his grave marker, even twelve years after his untimely demise, indicates an endurance of their values and, by association, the endurance of American values, even if on a microcosmic and eccentric scale. Rural America watches over all those who come to live in it, the segment suggests, and watches over them long after they have died.

One of the easiest ways to dismiss a positive affect is to complicate it. By problematizing the positive, critics attempt to wield power over it; in being professionally suspect of warm feelings, critics drain the positive affects of their profundity through the demonstration of critical prowess. "Blackie" could be complicated and problematized, parsed in ways that encourage the critical dismissal of *Road* as banal by critics. But the positive affects require, much like weak nationalism, something more than what criticism can provide. It requires seeing strength in that which is not perceived as strong, seeing complexity in that which is not perceived as critical. It requires a type of reading that is aware of the dynamism of the affects—and their synecdochical construction—the emotional work that critical reading would protest or dismiss. The persistence of hopefulness does not reveal the panaceas of nationalism: its evidence for hope may be contrary to the radical project of hope itself, but in keeping the embers of nationalism warmly glowing, it has an endurance in its very weakness that envisages new audiences where the sobriety of the evening news could not, encourages an interpretation that the suspicions of critical hermeneutics would bypass, and creates an incitement to read that can span generations, uniting them in the imagined community of the nation. If the community is crafted by Kuralt as a synecdoche of the national, then the community—the part—can endure even when the whole—the nation—wanes.

At the southwestern edge of the intersection of Illinois Routes 16 and 49 between Ashmore and Kansas there is a grave. The road has since been widened and new electric poles and gas lines installed, and the chain-link fence and white cross are no more, but fifty-two years after Blackie's death and forty years after Kuralt reported it in an *On the Road* segment, the grass is trim and the grave marker is clean and flowers still adorn the stone.

4 INCREDULITY

Reading Sarah Vowell

As she protested outside the 2001 presidential inauguration of George W. Bush, Sarah Vowell revealed that before the contested election which led to his presidency, "there was a part of me—the part of myself I don't like—that harbored a secret, perverse desire that Bush would defeat Gore."[1] Vowell described how her "pre-election daydream" of a Bush II presidency would offer her "four illustrious years of taking the high road" in comparison with the Clinton era, during which "being a civics nerd of any political stripe was like having the school bully paste a 'Kick Me' sign on your back every day year after year."[2] By contrast, in her daydream of this administration, Vowell's knowledge of politics, her role as a "civics nerd," would be sorely needed, even appreciated. "I imagined that I would criticize his policies and lambaste his statements with a civic-minded nobility. All my venom, spite, and, as long as we're dreaming, impeccable logic, would be directed at *our* president. As in 'Look how *our* president is wrecking *our* country.'"[3]

In the daydream, the Bush II presidency offers Vowell a way to focus her "venom" and "spite" on an object that enables her to define herself—and the nation—through her opposition to it. In what may be the most fantastic component of the daydream, Vowell sees her criticizing and lambasting as a way of inducing others to agree with her: the daydream constructs—it literally imagines—a community of supporters who agree with her that the president is "wrecking *our* country."[4] The community defines "our" country, an "our" that becomes clear, in Vowell's daydream, only when it is being wrecked by "our" president. Thus her criticism of him is both civic-minded and noble because it enables her to put the whole before the part, the nation before the president. In her daydream, Vowell is the nation's true representative.

Yet the daydream reveals a problem. The nation is constructed from Vowell's "secret, perverse desire" of being opposed to the president: that "our" president is wrecking "our" country makes one wonder if Vowell's imagined community would only exist if there were an antagonist to wreck it. The nation is constructed out of an opposition. And in its revealing of a part of Vowell that she does not like, the "secret, perverse desire" shows how the nation is as national as it is personal, as the nation she daydreams of exposes inner desires. The daydream reveals how from such opposition comes self-fashioning: in being opposed, Vowell finds her purpose in the nation. With such opposition also comes a fount of affects, not only in her daydream but in the discourse through which she describes it, apparent in Vowell's hyperbolic word choice, which simultaneously exposes the genuineness of her feelings as it sarcastically dismisses their intensities. The "perversity" of her desire, the "impeccability" of her logic—these modifiers describe in an amplified way her wish for a role in the nation in which her civic nerdiness will not come with a "Kick Me" sign but is instead considered an asset. The hyperbole that describes her opposition never fully conceals an attachment, a desire to be seen as part of, and to be of value to, America and its imagined community.

Her experience at the inaugural—and the daydream that preceded it—may explain why Vowell describes her engagement with the nation as a "relationship" in which "I feel like a battered wife. Yeah, he knocks me around a lot, but boy, he sure can dance."[5] Such rueful sarcasm seems to belie another affect: her feelings toward the nation are maudlin if not sentimental, such as her refusal to cancel a subscription to the

Chicago Tribune because Abraham Lincoln was once a subscriber.[6] Or her identification with Anne Hutchinson, whose testimony during her 1637 trial reminds her of "the sort of smart-alecky diatribe for which I've gotten paid for the last twenty years."[7] Or, even though he evoked a part of herself she does not like, her insistence that George W. Bush not be called "W" because, as she told *Vanity Fair* in a 2011 interview, "I still have enough respect for the presidency that the idea of referring to the president by his middle initial in a derisive manner just seems childish and mean-spirited."[8] Her solution to this conundrum, of how to have respect for the presidency but not for the president, may strike one as passive-aggressive: "I handle that by never mentioning his name at all."[9] Vowell would rather not mention Bush II's name than reduce him to the synecdoche of his middle initial because she still respects the office, for the office is not just the executive function of the government but a synecdoche for the nation.

The blend of rue and awe, of hyperbole and sincerity, in Vowell's work has proven difficult for critics to grasp. Her prose has often struck critics as overdone; simply put, many critics do not like its intensity, nor the tone through which that intensity emerges. Her contributions to the radio series *This American Life* have been panned. As Marc Fisher wrote, "For every couple of breathtaking tales of some cluttered alley of the nation's life, brought to life in captivating voices, there is a whining, pointless memoir by the likes of the show's resident cloying artiste, Sarah Vowell."[10] Virginia Heffernan's review of *The Wordy Shipmates*, Vowell's 2008 study of the Puritans, is no less intense: "Sarah Vowell is a problem. . . . She's double-annoying, because she styles herself as annoying—provocatively annoying—and if you become annoyed by her you seem to be conceding the point."[11] Such strong reactions speak to Vowell's synecdochical reading of the nation as much as her insertion of her persona—a combination of "sarcasm, flat indie-girl affect and kitsch worship"—into the narratives she composes.[12] What provokes critical annoyance is the moody, affective sway of the persona in her prose, a voice that sways between extremes of adoration and sarcasm in tones of belief and disbelief. What provokes critical annoyance is

Sarah Vowell's incredulity, which chastises and exhorts the nation, often simultaneously. If critics feel annoyed by her swaying tone, it is because her annoyance is a rhetorical effect of her incredulous approach to America and its synecdoches.

Incredulity, as I explore it through Vowell's work, is a mode of weak nationalism predominant between the Reagan and Obama administrations. Incredulity is a response to the strong nationalism birthed out of a reaction to the rise of Reagan, a response whose intensity waxed and waned during the end of the Cold War, the Clinton and Bush II administrations, and the emergence of the War on Terror. Through Vowell's work, incredulity can be traced throughout an entire generation: a generation developing their sense of nationalism in opposition to the strong nationalism of Reagan, coming to terms with post-Reagan administrations that lack such strong nationalism, and reacting to the evocation of those Reagan-era tropes in the Bush II administration and beyond. In this way, incredulity is an affect that others have characterized as a Generation X response to the contemporary world. Writing of Reagan, Alex Woloch notes that "for our generation, he'll always be *the* President," indicating that for such a generation, Reagan's presidency, and the incredulous response to it, is the one from which all other presidents—and responses to the president—follow.[13] As this chapter explores incredulity over time, it tracks Vowell encountering changes in American politics and its metanarratives with Reagan not only in mind but at the forefront: her perception of the nation, and herself, reflect attempts to construct an identity from eighties discourse, even decades after it has passed. The result of this ongoing construction is that the political is reduced to the personal: the nation becomes a resource for coping with one's eccentricities, and its history becomes a way of coping with the personal incommensurabilities of the post-Reagan era, including the contested 2000 election, the events of 9/11, and, ultimately, the election of Donald Trump to the presidency.

How does America become "our" nation? For the practitioners of what I describe as incredulous nationalism, America becomes "our nation" by being opposed to it. In effect, an incredulous nationalist would answer the question "What is America?" by describing what the nation, at present, is not. But as Vowell's preinaugural daydream demonstrates, incredulity's reliance on opposition to generate its contrarian ethos creates a problem of self-definition. Incredulity never generates its own politics: it never goes beyond criticism of the politics of others. It relies on others to define itself: it needs strong nationalism to define its weak nationalism. Such dependency is a problem. Vowell herself writes of it as a kind of love as much as it is a kind of abuse: as she describes herself, she becomes the nation's battered wife. Such a metaphor is symptomatic of incredulity's weak reaction to prevailing strong affects of the nation. Incredulity feels like abuse because incredulity focuses on disbelieving the nation rather than constructing a nation that it can believe in. The incredulous still believes in synecdoche's ability to construct the imagined community of the nation and its metanarratives, and even in their disenchantment with the nation, still believes in the ability of synecdoche to fashion themselves as participants in it. Despite her daydreams and her critiques, despite her feeling abused by the nation, in Vowell's work, the nation is still worthy of a credulous reverence. Incredulity reveals a disenchantment with the nation, a disbelief waiting to believe again and be enchanted again by the nation: thus the incredulous is always reacting to its own credulity as if doing so will hide it from view. As such, its own moments of genuine credulous belief come off as emotional moments in an otherwise flatly affected narrative. For all its cool, what incredulity ultimately reveals is the intense, sincere desire to believe.

The inauguration reveals the living nightmare when one's daydream comes true. Vowell is reduced to tears as she watches the inauguration proceedings. "Alas," she writes, "my tears are my picket sign."[14] There is neither venom nor spite, no impeccable logic: her tears synecdochically evoke her protest. Why does Vowell cry at the inaugural? Perhaps because George W. Bush, whose politics she disagrees with, has become president. Her tears may be read as the physical demonstration of her incredulity: the inauguration will require her to take on a role daydreamed by that part of herself she does not like. But it is equally likely that Vowell cries because her credulous idea of the nation, that which she sincerely believes, has been torn asunder by Bush II's inauguration. Thus her tears may also be read as the physical demonstration of her credulity: the nation she loves has been handed over to a president she does not trust. And even though her perverse desire is now a reality, listening to his inaugural speech, Vowell wishes that Bush would acknowledge his tenuous election to the office so that "the rest of us suckers might cut the new president some slack for a day or two."[15] That Vowell describes herself as a "sucker" hyperbolically characterizes the degree of her credulity: even she, who has daydreamed her noble civic engagement against Bush II, would give the new president a chance if he asked for it.

In defining the nation by being opposed to it, incredulity's contrarian ethos can be easily misread as negative affect. That Vowell's critics, who may be sympathetic to her politics, find her narrative style so "cloying" and "annoying" suggests that incredulity risks becoming its own cause for attention. Its affective flatness—its dependence on demonstrations of quirkiness and smartness—can be mistaken for no affect at all. Yet the incredulity of Vowell's nonfiction reveals a complex, if not vexed, relation to the synecdochical rhetoric of nationalism. Incredulity's contrarianism flares up in moments of intense affect, surprising us because it deviates from its typical flatness: we are put off by the incredulous's change in tone. But in this way, incredulity's contrarianism sufficed, even during Democratic administrations, to sustain a weak nationalism, as it offered a way of coping with the seeming lack of strong nationalism in those administrations. But in its perpetual return to Reagan as an index for their identities, the practitioners of incredulity were unable to foresee the rise of a nationalism that became more virulent during the Obama administration, a nationalism so hot its boiling over would dominate—and ultimately win—the 2016 election. The election of Trump revealed the weakness of incredulity's contrarian ethos, the way in which it credulously remained subscribed to a metanarrative—the very idea of a nation—that was unable to mount an effective political challenge to Trump's hot nationalism. Perhaps, if we think of incredulity as a fount of affects that make the incommensurable tolerable, there may be a place for incredulity as Americans attempt to cope with the politics of the Trump administration. At the same time, the rise of Trump may itself be a sign of a necessity for a different politics altogether, not one that sees itself as a contrarian alternative to the political mainstream, but one that envisions synecdoches of the nation which actively depart from hot nationalism's strong affects.

Incredulity and Its Valences

To use the word "incredulity" to describe Vowell's writing is to evoke Jean-François Lyotard's definition of the postmodern as the "incredulity toward metanarratives," in which the "narrative function is losing its functors, its great hero, its great dangers, its great voyages, its great goal."[16] Incredulity is a reaction, a response to the erosion of metanarrative, the loss of "narrations with a legitimating function."[17] Vowell's personal essays and her book-length retellings of American history display their incredulity as the very purpose of their composition: the loss of the nation as a legitimate metanarrative on which the affects of nationalism can be entrusted. In particular, Vowell's interest in retelling narratives of colonialism (early Puritan life in *The Wordy Shipmates* or the life of Hawaiian missionaries in *Unfamiliar Fishes*, for example) seems inspired by current events, to point out that the metanarrative of the nation is inconsistent with contemporary politics. Vowell's incredulity, like incredulity in general, is as much a reaction to the erosion of metanarrative as it is a disenchantment with the legitimacy of that metanarrative as it is used in the present. Yet the disenchantment of the incredulous is contingent on an affective attachment to what was once enchanting and legitimating. The word "incredulity" has its roots in the word "credulity," the willingness to believe. Incredulity is the opposite of credulity, yet in the affect's deployment, much like the very construction of the word, incredulity evokes credulity. If the credulous is too eager to believe, the incredulous is too eager to disbelieve. If the credulous is enchanted by metanarrative, the incredulous is disenchanted by metanarrative. Incredulity is thus bound together with credulity: they travel as a pair of extremes that the subject—and her affects—sway between.

From the perspective of affect theory, incredulity is a response to the disenchantment with metanarrative. Tomkins writes that disenchantment is the result of a contamination of the mode of communion.[18] Disenchantment with "primary identification figures is perhaps the most serious threat to communion to which the human being is vulnerable" because "contamination of the idealized identification figure jeopardizes the very possibility of identification, evokes shame and threatens radically the sense of identity."[19] Much like the inability to commune with a figure with whom we identify robs us of the opportunity to fashion ourselves like the identification figure, the inability to commune with a national metanarrative with whom we identify robs us of the opportunity to fashion ourselves as a member of it, requiring an oppositional, contrarian stance from which we fashion ourselves and our participation in the nation. The contamination of a national metanarrative that is perceived by the incredulous inhibits the very feelings of communion on which an imagined community is constructed. The nation is, after all, a prime site of incredulity because disenchantment is a response to "the inevitable gap between the most satisfying and least satisfying . . . the discrepancy between the latter and the idealized constructs based on the former."[20] The gap between most and least satisfying not only is a gap through which one can posit one's incredulity but a gap that gives incredulity a heated emotional tone. It is also a prime site for ironical comparisons between what the nation is and what it should be. Underneath Vowell's incredulity is the credulous demand that the nation be better, as she sees better to be, and thus the heated emotional tone of incredulity also has a connotation of moral judgment that reveals the contamination which led to disenchantment.

And just as incredulity is locked into the terms of credulity, disenchantment is locked into the terms of enchantment. Tomkins asserted, "The outcome of disenchantment is ultimately a renewed quest for the lost love object," as the "relationship provided enough past enjoyment to have generated an uncompromising demand that it never be adulterated or attenuated."[21] The incredulous pursues an object because of their faith that the object can still be credulously enjoyed: the incredulous never abandons the metanarrative. Vowell's own love of country never vanishes, though it takes on an overcast of disappointment, as the title of her book, *The Partly Cloudy Patriot*, indicates. Even if their critique of it is intense, the incredulous is still in search of the metanarrative's great goal. The incredulity toward metanarratives, Lyotard insisted, "refines our sensitivity . . . and reinforces our ability to tolerate the incommensurable."[22] For Vowell the nation does not match the credulous feelings she has for its metanarrative; thus her descriptions of contemporary policy, such as the inauguration of George W. Bush that she sees as "wrecking" the country, threatens to spoil the metanarrative itself. The same threat of spoilage is evident in Vowell's vexed writing of Reagan: her incredulity is reflective of the appropriation of the nation by strong nationalists in the rise of Reagan as much as the inability of his opponents and successors to reclaim the metanarrative that Reagan fundamentally altered. Incredulity offers a way to tolerate this incommensurability, a way that preserves metanarrative as a source of credulity while rebuffing its appropriation.

Incredulity negotiates incommensurability through incomplete concealments of its affective intensity. The intensity of affect itself is at issue in most of the affects attributed to Generation X, which takes the form of numerous valences of incredulity. Peter Stearns has described the practices and affects known as "cool" as an "anti-intensity emotionology" in which emotional maturity is judged through the repression of intense emotions in most instances of daily life.[23] Just as in the fifties, "it was safer to be 'tired' than to be emotionally upset," in the eighties, it was safer to be "quirky" or "smart" than to be publicly opposed to Reagan.[24] And such avoidance of affective intensity typifies a style of writing predominant in the nineties that has been alternately described as "quirky" or "smart." As Michael Hirschorn writes, "quirk is an embrace of the odd against the blandly mainstream" through "unexplainable but nonetheless charming character traits" that make quirkiness more mild and appealing than eccentricity.[25] To describe a person or a text as quirky is to describe them as unusual, yet with an assurance that their unusualness will not generate embarrassment or trouble. Quirkiness avoids strong affects, which might bully it in response. "Quirk is odd, but not *too* odd. That would take us all the way to *weird*, and there someone might get hurt."[26] The mildness of the quirk is a reaction against the mainstream but never one that challenges its primacy. Quirks are unusual in an entertaining, "merely interesting" way whose affective "minimalism is somehow understood to secure its link to ratiocinative cognition and to lubricate the formation of social ties."[27] People and texts become known for their quirks; perhaps they are actively sought out for them, in part because their quirks evoke incredulous responses within us as "interesting" judgments which divert "attention away from itself so as to throw the spotlight entirely on the question of its own legitimation."[28] Legitimation is a core concern of incredulity, as the disbelief of the incredulous challenges the legitimacy of its object. Yet incredulity still legitimates its object by trying to indicate how interestingly contrarian it is, thus legitimating the metanarrative it claims to resist. All the while, the incredulous writer, seen as "interesting," struggles for legitimation: in labeling her as "double-annoying" or "pointless," Vowell's critics show how this struggle for legitimacy resonates not only at a textual level but at the level of the persona: there is an emotional intensity to her work that transcends the mildness of the "interesting" and provokes in critics not only a critique of her writing but of its "annoying" persona. And much of this struggle for legitimation is interpreted as a personal struggle: perhaps this explains why Vowell feels, when she is attending the 137th anniversary of the Gettysburg Address, that her attendance indicates that "something's missing in your life."[29] Though incredulously framed through Vowell's persona as a quirky personal deficiency, what is missing is the legitimacy she thinks her attendance should bring: a legitimacy of being seen as a credulous caretaker for the nation and its history. As she admits in *Assassination*, her "fantasy is to one day become a docent," a legitimated caretaker of the objects that constitute the American metanarrative.[30]

As Lee Konstantinou has noted, "Quirkiness might well be the stylistic and institutional form the avant-garde takes when it reconciles itself to the reality of the market, no longer seeing its mission as social revolution but as the cultivation of the smartness, the dumbness, or the smart dumbness of the individual person."[31] "Smart" in this sense means, as Jeffrey Sconce describes it, "an aura of 'intelligence'" that distinguishes the smart person as different from "the perceived 'dross' of the mainstream."[32] In the nineties, such an aura was transmitted through "a predilection for irony, black humour, fatalism, relativism, and nihilism," all of which are consumable, middlebrow diminutions of postmodernism's aesthetic interest in irony, plurality, contingency, indeterminacy, and entropy.[33] As much as "smart" texts may cultivate an air of wry detachment from their subjects, Sconce notes, particularly through a heavy reliance on irony, that "behind their veneer of studied detachment, cultivated disaffection and ironic posturing . . . many are extremely politicized and even rather moralistic."[34] Irony seeks to dampen the intense affects behind its potent moral charge. If quirkiness is a mild way of expressing an interest or an identity, the use of "smart" irony attempts to build a community of fellow ironists in ways not recognizable to the mainstream. "The entire point of ironic address is to ally oneself with sympathetic peers"—fellow smart people aware that irony is being used—"and to distance oneself from the vast 'other' audience, however defined, which is often the target of derision. If I think you are an idiot, I can use irony to insult you without getting punched in the face. If I think you are like-minded, we can use irony to laugh at, or express our disengagement from, those around us."[35] The concern with "someone getting hurt" because of their quirks or "getting punched in the face" because they are being ironic reflects Generation X's concern with being attacked, physically as much as affectively, by those who subscribe to the triumphalist mainstream of the Reagan era. It is a concern for avoiding affectively intense moments with others as much as within themselves.

The "question of Generation X," Kevin L. Ferguson notes, "is whether the slackening of social engagement is a continuation of or a response to the culture of the eighties."[36] Ferguson's use of the word "slackening" seems deliberate, to describe a cultural label that would become mainstream in the nineties, the "slacker." From the perspective of incredulity, such slackening is both a way of engaging with as much as it is a response to the eighties and its incommensurable legacies. Incredulity perpetually returns to its credulous roots to find itself, to define itself in opposition by slackening against its credulities. In doing so, incredulity demonstrates its reliance on quirks, smarts, and ironies to mark itself as contrary to the strong affects of the Reagan era and beyond. Vowell is very much a Generation X writer, as her writing, regardless of the decade of its production, displays "its uneasy situation between precision and elision, specificity and negation. . . . X crosses out *and* marks the spot."[37] It is the very resistance to credulity—an attempt to cross it out—that generates the incredulity—that marks the spot—that Vowell's prose displays. The nation may be a source of disbelief, but for incredulous nationalists like Vowell, such disbelief only returns to a further, even more emotionally avid belief in its exceptionalism.

Reacting to Reagan

Incredulity, as I examine in this chapter, is a reaction to the rise and dominance of Reagan and Reaganite politics, which brought with it a wave of strong affects. Ellen Schrecker describes such affects as "Cold War triumphalism," which was marshaled to support Reagan's revival of the Cold War and the increase of military expenditures (and the gutting of social programs as well as the running of high deficits to support those expenditures) as a "moral parable" between the forces of democracy and communism, capitalism and socialism, good and evil.[38] Such triumphalism perpetuated a portrait of the nation in which individuals could be morally righteous only if they subscribed to Reagan's political and economic policies. As such, triumphalism posited a world of winners—free-market capitalists in particular—and losers—those typically caught in the abuses of the free market—within its moral parable. Such triumphalism was mapped onto the Reagan administration itself: the president became synonymous with victory, whereas those who did not subscribe to his political vision proved to be fodder for it. This moral parable made it impossible to truly oppose Reagan: weak nationalism's affective dynamism was dismissed as a losing attitude. Woloch has noted that "Reagan's ascendancy opens a period that makes hope difficult and can work, with ruthless alchemical dexterity, to transform pragmatism into insufficient compromise (co-optation, selling out) and principle into sectarian isolation."[39] Those who critiqued triumphalism were encoded as losers and, as such, were locked into triumph's terms. They became the losers pointed at by the victors as the very evidence of their triumph.

Reagan's ability to act like a victorious president was an essential display of triumphalism. His credulity—whether he was acting a part or was aware he was acting at all—was compelling not only to conservatives who took him seriously but also to a broader public who participated in the decade's importance of acting out of labels, regardless of political orientation. Grossberg noted, "Many of those who voted for Reagan did not vote for a set of meanings or values that they subscribed to; they voted for the 'acting president.' They voted, paradoxically, for the more real of the candidates, the less boring, the one entirely defined as a media object and who could negotiate that identity successfully—a real measure of success" in the eighties.[40] All the while, the credulousness of Reagan's rhetoric brought to the surface the role of affect in the political. "Reagan uses the media affectively to recharge the political clichés which have lost their power, but, in the process, he articulates them into larger ideological structures. He uses the very strategies of the autonomous affect, reducing questions of politics, values, and meanings to individualized images of morality, self-sacrifice, and community."[41] In other words, the Reagan administration's ability to reduce the nation to the synecdoches they deployed gave neoconservatives power over the tropes that defined the nation. Their appropriation of three generations of rhetoric framed neoconservatism as the culmination of the American project. As Rodgers notes, "into the network of associations with the term 'freedom,' Reagan and his speechwriters drew the language of the self-actualization psychology handbooks of the 1970s, the *Jonathan Livingston Seagull* phrases, the Esalen notion of freedom, the slogans of the 1960s cultural radicals."[42] Reagan-era "freedom" was thus a mélange of the popular and the academic: the self-help manual and the supply-side economics treatise; the quest for individual fulfillment and theories of cultural autonomy. And much like their disdain toward what they perceived as big government, neoconservatives displayed a disdain toward synecdoche: their tropes miniaturized the nation into such small parts that they were representative no longer of a whole public but of parts of the private. The only viable national synecdoche remaining was the president. Reagan himself came to serve as a synecdoche not only for the political agenda of his administration but for the nation itself.

Thus the eighties gave way to "the struggle for self-definition" within the decade's "stark polarity of optimism or pessimism" facilitated by triumphalism.[43] The saturation of Cold War triumphalism can be seen in the decade's overt fascination with optimistic displays of "power" and the infusion of such displays into virtually every facet of everyday life: Ferguson notes the attachment of the modifier "power" to virtually all facets of everyday life, as if eating a "power breakfast" before putting on a "power tie" and going "power shopping" defined one's identity.[44] The eighties' fascination with cultural labeling points to the formation of a new language of cultural taxonomies that sifted people into new classifications within the economic and affective polarities of the decade. "Such cultural labels were crucial alternatives to the peril of sameness."[45] At the same time, the eclecticism afforded by the increasingly globalized and deregulated economy made "identities increasingly easy to own and discard," making it "more challenging to act ethically in the absence of a sense of self-consistency or a feeling of belongingness to something larger."[46] In this way, being contrary at least gave one an identity: one that rejected the perils of sameness by building an identity that was opposed to it, a sense of belonging by not belonging to the mainstream.

At the same time as triumphalism became embedded in the affective fabric of the nation, the struggle for self-definition in the eighties would become another struggle, for economic self-definition (if not survival), as the children of the eighties faced the consequences of Reagan-era economics in the nineties. As Sherry B. Ortner outlines, "Starting in the 1970s . . . and accelerated by Reagan-Bush policies in the 1980s, the middle class started pulling apart at the middle. The economy suffered a series of setbacks, and the overall level of prosperity began to slip. But Reagan-Bush policies favored and protected the top of the structure. The top and the bottom of the middle class began pulling away from one another."⁴⁷ The result is that Generation X found that "there are not enough jobs, there are certainly not enough well-paying jobs, and there are particularly not enough quality jobs available for the level of education and qualification many members in the cohort have achieved. People are basically overeducated (or anyway overcertified) and underemployed."⁴⁸ Such circumstances could only foster incredulity in the incommensurability between the metanarratives on which they were raised and the actual world in which they came of age. When "smart" people who have been raised on triumphalist moral parables—metanarratives—of meritocratic and economic achievement find that the economy has no room for them, the result is incredulity. Similarly, when "smart" people who have been raised on a metanarrative of American exceptionalism and triumphalism find that politics has no room for them, the result is incredulity. Generation X makes a cultural style out of such difficult straits, one that defends one's privilege even as one knows such privilege is being taken away by larger economic forces, one that defends one's upbringing in such metanarratives even as one is discomforted by the politics such metanarratives support.⁴⁹

Generation X responds to the incommensurabilities of Cold War triumphalism by negating their affective intensity. To do so, they take on a persona of weakness that contrasts and runs contrary to strong nationalism: they aestheticize their position as losers to avoid the victors of triumphalism's moral parable. Generation X aesthetics embrace the "loser" as a cultural category and perform this social position through displays of irony, self-defeat, laxity, and cluelessness. In other words, the "flat indie-girl affects" that Heffernan takes issue with in Vowell's work is as much aesthetic and affective as it is a political practice.⁵⁰ As Woloch noted, "thought . . . is torn, in the 1980s, in an elaborate intertwining of rejection and engagement."⁵¹ Much like crossing the X marks the spot, incredulity combines rejection with engagement: its rejection of strong nationalism marks its engagement with it. The result is an aestheticized disenchantment, in which "the very dynamics of discovery or immersion are strangely intertwined with rejection and withdrawal."⁵²

Yet underneath such withdrawal is a reservoir of credulity toward strong nationalism. Vowell's work demonstrates Woloch's claim that, for a generation, "waking up to the world, we discovered Reaganism, and Reagan will always limn the contours of discovery itself. Like first love—or heartbreak—the first government you learn to know stays with you."[53] While Woloch feels heartbreak and Vowell feels abuse, for both, Reagan is a source of enchantment and disenchantment. His administration becomes the primary identification figure for a generation despite his administration's contamination of the national metanarrative. He becomes the way to measure "the inevitable gap between the most satisfying and least satisfying . . . the discrepancy between the latter and the idealized constructs based on the former."[54] And as Vowell's writing makes clear, Reagan is as much the discrepancy as he is the norm that limns; he is both the most satisfying object of their attack and the least satisfying object of their credulous love of the nation.

Vowell's essays for *This American Life*, collected in anthologies including *Take the Cannoli* and *The Partly Cloudy Patriot*, explore her coming of age in the era of Reagan. The essays are a reminder that, as Jon Fox writes, "we are not born into our nations, we have to acquire them, and that process of acquiring a national identity is an arduous one."[55] Indeed, as Vowell does, one can fashion one's identity by being contrarian to the national identity that is foisted on them. The essays in *Take the Cannoli* provide a biographical sense of how she grew up credulous, as they explore her early upbringing as a Pentecostal and her subsequent teenage rebellion. In "The End Is Near, Nearer, Nearest," Vowell writes that "I was a believer. . . . But there was something stronger than my belief in God. The thing the preacher said that I believed more than anything else I heard at church was that I was a sinner. . . . Even as a six-year-old I knew I'd never be good enough to get into heaven."[56] A family move at age eleven from Oklahoma to Montana led to a change in churches, yet neither Vowell's strong beliefs nor their affects waned. Instead, "I merely replaced one apocalypse for another," from the end of the Bible to the end of the Cold War, as "President Reagan made so many mortifying announcements . . . that I was utterly convinced I was not going to grow up."⁵⁷ What Vowell dismisses as "merely" a "replacement" is in fact a more profound incitement to read the nation: from one figure of identification in the Bible to another figure of identification in the nation. And with that substitution of identification comes a substitution of disenchantments: if Vowell is disenchanted by religion because she feels she will never be able to get into heaven, she comes to feel equally disenchanted by the nation because she feels that those in charge of the nation do not adore the nation in the same way she does. The credulity of her faith, and her incredulity that despite her faith, she will not get into heaven, transfer onto a credulity of the nation, and her incredulity that despite her adoration of its metanarratives, it will not accept her in the same way that her faith will not accept her in the afterlife. Thus the synecdoches of the "evil empire" of the Soviet Union or the "Star Wars" of the Strategic Defense Initiative were not political rhetoric for her; rather, they were realities to be believed in. Indeed, Vowell finds that "I owe my life to Ronald Reagan," because being able to oppose Reagan gave her a way to express the zealotry she learned as a child in a different form, something she could be opposed to.⁵⁸ By her junior year of high school, she joined the local "Youth for Global Peace" club, who she sees as "the most glamorous people I'd ever met.... They played in rock 'n' roll bands and wrote poetry and didn't eat meat... and debated whether or not William Burroughs's *Junky* was better than his *Naked Lunch*."⁵⁹

The nation—and the synecdoches that evoke the nation—come to substitute for the credulities of her earlier Pentecostal upbringing. By sixteen, the mysteries and paradoxes of evangelical faith are replaced with an ardent, if not literary, patriotism. Quoting from his poem "America," Vowell asserts, "Later in the poem Ginsberg writes, 'It occurs to me that I am America.' I loved that line because it solved a problem, because it shook its queer fist at the rest of the words, words about being a stranger in a strange land."⁶⁰ The "problem" that it solves is Ginsberg's—and by appropriation—Vowell's synecdochical relationship to the nation: one becomes an "American" by becoming an outcast within it, by being outside the nation all the while proclaiming "I am America." Vowell's incorporation of the phrase from Exodus 2:22 forms a seamless bond between her religious and her national credulity: the Bible, Ginsberg, and Vowell are all now exiles in a nation—and a metanarrative—to be incredulous about, which defines them as the nation's true representatives. A few pages, though many years later, a friend asks Vowell what her favorite book is:

> ... and I said "*On the Road.*" He smiled, said, "That was my favorite book when I was sixteen." At the time, I thought he was patronizing me, that it was going to be my favorite book forever and ever, amen. But he was right. As an adult, I'm more of a *Gatsby* girl—more tragic, more sad, just as interested in what America costs as what it has to offer.[61]

Vowell seeks to identify herself through synecdoches: the American canon in this case, texts that are considered to embody quintessential national metanarratives. Rebuffed by her friend, Vowell changes the title of her favorite book to another that she perceives as more "adult," a state she attaches to affects like "tragic" and "sad." She switches parts—books—but remains credulously attached, "just as interested" in the whole of the nation. It is not that Vowell has lost her credulity as much as she has moved from one canonical text to another, only to look back on her first choice, as her friend does, credulously, even evoking the religious language of "forever and ever, amen" to point out the innocence of her reverence.

The nation provides Vowell, even when she is incredulous about it, with a source of belonging, an imagined community that she may critique but never abandons. "We all grew up, those of us who took *On the Road* to heart. But . . . we got what we needed, namely a passion for unlikely words, the willingness to improvise, a distrust of authority, and a sentimental attachment to a certain America, still so lovely, as Kerouac wrote, 'at lilac evening.'"[62] What Vowell describes are the ingredients for an incredulous nationalism: a vocabulary that makes one sound smart, improvisation that generates displays of quirkiness, distrust that perpetuates skepticism, and a sentimentality that provides a source of attachment and affective investment. All of these provide incitements, sources of enjoyment that come with them "an uncompromising demand that it never be adulterated or attenuated."[63] At the same time, such incitements demand the sort of bipolar identification that Berlant has described, as the incredulous citizen demonstrates their competence by reading "conveniently and flexibly between the lines [of nationalist rhetoric], thus preserving both utopian national identification and cynical practical citizenship."[64] The incredulous nationalist reveals both the utopian and the cynical: the credulous, utopian faith in the national metanarrative, and the incredulous, cynical criticism of that nation as it is presented in historical events and everyday life. Thus Vowell's attachment is to "a certain America," of Kerouac and Ginsberg, a subcultural, metaphorical, and literary nation more than it is the actual one. It is an attachment to a national metanarrative, a canon, though of a nontriumphalist kind.

Armed with these metanarratives and their affects, Vowell attempts to interpret objects as synecdoches but often finds that the parts she has selected do not make wholes. Vowell herself is an avid consumer of stories. Reflecting on that staple of the 1990s, the Starbucks Mocha, she finds,

> The more history I learn, the more the world fills up with stories. Just the other day, I was in my neighborhood Starbucks, waiting for the post office to open. I was enjoying a chocolatey caffé mocha when it occurred to me that to drink a mocha is to gulp down the entire history of the New World. . . . The modern mocha is a bittersweet concoction of imperialism, genocide, invention, and consumerism served with whipped cream on top.[65]

History fills up the world—like coffee filling a cup—with stories for Vowell to tell. As such, history is consumed by Vowell as the fuel for the retelling of it from her quirky perspective; the "bittersweet," emotionally jarring leap from imperialism to genocide to whipped cream. The affective magnitude of history does not seem to matter, as much as the way in which it can be consumed to further the telling of her incredulous version of it. The mocha may be a synecdoche for imperialism, genocide, invention, and globalization, but what the example of the mocha serves for Vowell is to demonstrate that she can make a story out of it; in this case, a story of the "entire history of the New World." Her knowledge of history and her means to convert it into a narrative offer a respite from the economic pressures of everyday life: "When you know such trivia, an act as mundane as having an overpriced breakfast drink becomes imbued with meaning, even poetry."[66] History and its narratives defamiliarize and make bearable the incommensurabilities of the present—the globalized economy in which third-world farmers are exploited and first-world bourgeoisie are overcharged—that makes the mocha a "mundane" object. Incredulity, Vowell asserts, turns the trivial into the meaningful.

If the "entire history of the New World" is too vast a subject to evoke from the Starbucks Mocha, Vowell's focus on smaller objects seems to evoke a similar grandness that synecdoche cannot contain. Her essay "Michigan and Wacker" begins: "I had this theory, a Chicago theory. After four years of walking back and forth across the Michigan Avenue Bridge, I had accumulated a few random facts about the bridge that coalesced into an actual hypothesis. Namely, that I could tell the whole history of America standing on that bridge. I thought I might be able to swivel around and point at the whole dark, inspiring tale."[67] Vowell searches for an object—a bridge—on which to build a "dark, inspiring tale," the affects which to her make for a compelling national metanarrative. At the same time, she admits the affects must be stronger than the facts on which they are based. "As any journalist knows, three instances are enough to establish a story, if not an actual trend, so I thought that's enough American history, and I could just make up the rest."[68] But as she works through the facts within sight of the bridge—the Chicago Tribune building, a commemorative plaque on the bridge, knowledge of an Indian massacre that occurred near it in 1812—Vowell's "Chicago Theory" warps and wanes as she tries to handle the thicket of facts that form her metanarrative, her personal "whole history of America." The sheer weight of history proves to her that "my theory was only too right. The intersection of Michigan and Wacker, I found out, isn't just a corner, it's a vortex."[69] The bridge, and its inability to tell the whole story, forces her to concede in Generation X terms: "Up, down, north, south—whatever. The point is that the bridge was."[70] Vowell finds that the synecdochical relationship she has sought offers too many parts for a whole to cohere. The result is an incredulous response: the corner, and with it, her "Chicago theory," turns into a vortex: the bridge cannot bear the load of the metanarrative Vowell places on it. Her response to this is not defeat as much as it is the response that so characterized the slacker of the eighties, the incredulous cool of the nineties: a literal "whatever."

Vowell's incredulity extends to a disenchantment with post-Reagan administrations. Their very lack of a triumphalist, strong nationalism gives fodder for her incredulity. The essays in *Patriot* reflect this disenchantment. In "Ike Was a Handsome Man," presented in the form of a memo to "Former President William Jefferson Clinton" from "Citizen Sarah Jane Vowell" makes a variety of suggestions about how Clinton should organize his presidential library. Noting that Eisenhower's library mostly focuses on his military career, Vowell intones, "What about a similar stage set, only in your library, instead of being a soldier leaving the boat for Omaha Beach, the visitor could walk in the shoes of Fed chairman Alan Greenspan, as he steps out of a Lincoln Town Car and into the Dirksen Senate Office Building to endorse the Clinton deficit reduction strategy before the Senate Banking Committee!"[71] Vowell is being ironic, but she is also exasperated by the lack of a triumphalist metanarrative—events replete with winners and losers—in the Clinton administration. That the policies of the Clinton administration, such as the reappointment of Greenspan indicates, are moderate variants of Reagan era policies suggests that Clinton lacked a political metanarrative of his own aside from a vague oppositional sense of not being a Reagan Republican.[72] "Eisenhower's greatest achievement," Vowell writes, "was liberating Europe. Your greatest achievement? Balancing the budget."[73] Searching for the president's "greatest achievement," Vowell searches for a contribution to a triumphalist metanarrative, one that frames the presidency, and synecdochically the nation, through one pinnacle act. Balancing the budget does not suffice, as it lacks the affective intensity of a triumph. The very lack of drama evokes Vowell's sarcasm, if only because it is difficult for her to fashion a contrarian stance to something as affectively sober as deficit reduction. National drama, it seems, is a key component of the presidential metanarrative, which allows not only for feelings of enchantment but for disenchantment as well. What Vowell suggests makes for the best presidential library—the Johnson and Nixon libraries are her favorites—is that "they deal with quarrelsome subjects."[74] But more important, it is through their "quarrelsome subjects" that they, for Vowell, represent America. At the LBJ, in the brief walk from a display on the Voting Rights Act of 1965 to a photograph of a serviceman who had been killed in Vietnam, "I felt like all of America was in that ten seconds: the grandeur of civil rights, the consequences of war."[75] In other words, what Vowell likes most about the LBJ is how it evokes the incommensurable affects of the period through synecdoche, how the museum represents the whole nation through the dilemmas of its parts. Yet beneath the quarrelsome subjects, Vowell clearly subscribes to a credulous vision of the president, one "first advanced by Progressive reformers" who "not only in his actions or policies, but in his presence and voice was imagined as the suture that could bind together public opinion and political institutions."[76]

Quarrelsome subjects, and the synecdoches they can evoke, are prime fodder for an incredulous nationalism. They allow for the incredulous to fashion themselves as a smart citizen, to demonstrate their knowingness of the nation: they also allow a quirky, special language through which the nation provides a way to understand the self. In "God Will Give You Blood to Drink in a Souvenir Shot Glass," Vowell admits that she is "a *history buff.* I am one 1–800 number away from ordering the Time-Life World War II series off the TV. I have set my alarm so I wouldn't miss a C-Span morning live remote from the house of the Revolutionary War pamphleteer Thomas Paine. I celebrated my thirtieth birthday at Grant's Tomb."[77] It is intriguing that Vowell's interest in history seems more about an interest in metanarrative than history itself: the Michigan Avenue bridge, the trips to presidential libraries and national monuments, the Time-Life series, and C-Span remotes all suggest that she is interested in the stories that can be told through the appropriation and affectation of historical narratives. The appropriation is as historical as it is personal: one of the essays in *Patriot,* titled "Rosa Parks, *C'est Moi,*" Vowell, punning on the apocryphal statement by Gustave Flaubert of himself as Emma Bovary, notes that "analogies give order to the world—and solidarity. Pointing out how one person is like another is reassuring, less lonely. . . . Who wouldn't want to be in the company of Rosa Parks?"[78] Her interest in history is a coping skill for Generation X anxieties. In American history, Vowell finds friends who make her feel less lonely, events that help her negotiate contemporary everyday life. "In my self-help universe, when things go wrong I whisper mantras to myself like 'Andersonville' or 'Texas Book Depository.' . . . 'Texas Book Depository' means that having the delivery guy forget the guacamole isn't nearly as bad as being assassinated by Lee Harvey Oswald as the blood from your head stains your wife's pink suit."[79] In such moments, Vowell becomes history: she becomes the president, if only at the moment of his assassination. Such historical events, reduced to "mantras," spoken in response to banalities, become a private language in which history functions as a synecdoche of her affects. As an incitement to read, the nation provides her with personal meaning, a figurative language through which she can mitigate anxiety and regulate her affects. The nation, almost literally, becomes an ontological safety net.

And because the nation provides an ontological safety net, because it proves enchanting even in its worst moments, incredulous nationalists remain perpetually credulous toward the nation and its metanarratives. In "Dear Dead Congressman," a mock letter to a deceased representative, Vowell recalls an experience as an eight-year-old:

> At the Braggs rodeo, you shook my hand and gave me the "Synar for Congress" button off your own lapel—which I still have—and told me it was the last one off the printing presses. You'd think Elvis was handing me a scarf or something. I was so excited. I realize now how young you were. You were twenty-seven then, younger than I am now.[80]

The younger Vowell equates congressmen to superstars. Like an adoring fan, she "pull[s] out of the envelope and reread[s] a thousand times" a thank-you letter Synar wrote to his supporters, reflecting that she would, as the letter states, "get involved in government and our government will be better."[81] The older Vowell's enchantment takes on intonations of romance. To the dead congressman, and to the reader, she confides: "I think of you every time I draw the voting booth curtain behind me, every time I pull the lever. . . . I love it in there. I drag it out, leisurely punching the names I want as if sipping whiskey in front of a fire. I mean, how many times in a life does an average person get to make history?"[82] Voting intoxicates her: she does not consume it like a mocha but savors it like fine liquor. Yet such sentimentality toward the congressman, her unrestrained reverence for voting, and her idealism in believing that average people make history when they vote, transcend her incredulous persona.

At the same time, such enjoyment informs her struggle to avoid the perils of sameness that characterized coming of age in the eighties. In the middle of her mock letter to Synar, Vowell informs the deceased congressman that she "pined to vote" after seeing *The Breakfast Club*, finding that "I identified with Anthony Michael Hall's nerd, Brian. (Though I was only about nine months away from turning into black-clad, antisocial Ally Sheedy.)"[83] Vowell seems to have taken Brian's defense for having a fake driver's license—so he can vote—not absurdly, but seriously; not ironically, but literally. Her version of *The Breakfast Club* is one that gives her an identity from which she can demonstrate her uniqueness from eighties types yet—one part nerd, one part goth—remain grouped within them. She accepts her identity credulously, seemingly unaware that the film mocks the adolescent pretense behind these supposedly "distinct" identities in the first place. As Ferguson notes, the film itself is not so much about the uniqueness of the character's identity as it is their struggle to see what they all have in common. "Instead of completing the assignment, however, they realize that they each embody some of the traits of their peers and that they have only been brainwashed to think of themselves as representative of rigidly defined, stereotypical roles."[84] In the film, the parts these roles represent are ultimately exposed as fictional: the group becomes a cohesive whole who realize they are trapped in the perils of sameness. But Vowell's resistance to being part of any one group, intended to mark her as the most individual, is surreptitiously an American cliché, the iconoclast who considers themselves as outside or beyond categories. Yet her incredulous nationalism reveals, for all its quirkiness, smartness, and irony, how the cynical is intertwined with the utopian, how her disenchantment is intertwined with her enchantment. Incredulity hides—at times barely—the affective pull of credulity and the metanarratives that perpetuate it.[85] The affective spectrum of such incredulity, despite its cool veneer of weak affect, is prone to moments of intense credulous reaction because the incredulous continues to identify with that credulous part of themselves: the person who found herself through Ginsberg and Kerouac, the writer of mock essays to dead congressmen and living presidents. As such, Vowell's incredulity is bound to her credulity: they travel together to incite her interpretation of the nation.

Reagan is never far away. If anything, for Vowell, events perpetually evoke him. As she tries to make sense of the War on Terror after 9/11, how America could have strayed so far from its ideals to encourage torture and to doctor evidence to support the invasion of Iraq during the Bush II administration, Vowell comes face to face with Reagan when she writes, "In the U.S.A., we want to sing along with the chorus and ignore the verses, ignore the blues. . . . And that's why the citizens of the United States not only elected and reelected Ronald Reagan; that's why we *are* Ronald Reagan."[86] Reagan is the apex of Vowell's synecdochical thinking. The synecdoche—that Americans have become Ronald Reagan—shows how Generation X continues to live, twenty years after he left office, in his shadow. For Vowell, the synecdoche is totally personal: as she wrote in *Cannoli*, she owes her life to Reagan for giving her a way of escaping the credulity of her Pentecostal upbringing and a way to express her incredulity, to fashion herself in reaction to his triumphalist affects. At the same time, this synecdoche wobbles: it is a credulous sense of synecdochical representation to argue that because Reagan won office that he somehow became the nation, or that the entire nation became him. And to write that "we are Ronald Reagan" is to do literally what neoconservatives did figuratively in their placing

Reagan at the epicenter of triumphalist metanarrative. In this potent synecdoche, Vowell still finds herself, decades after his administration and his death, tethered to Reagan. For her, he has become the nation: his triumphalism continues to triumph. Yet if America has become Reagan, and he is her opponent, it is only through a contrarian stance toward the nation that she continues to fashion herself. Thus perniciously, Vowell affirms the synecdoche she so ardently opposes. By turning Reagan into a synecdoche of America, Vowell has turned Reagan into a synecdoche of herself. In the intersection of her incredulity toward Reagan and her credulity toward national metanarrative, Vowell's prose marks the X of her personal identity.

The political economist Francis Fukuyama concluded his seminal 1989 essay "The End of History" by writing, "The end of history will be a very sad time. . . . The worldwide ideological struggle that called forth daring, courage, imagination, and idealism, will be replaced by economic calculation, the endless solving of technical problems, environmental concerns . . . the satisfaction of sophisticated consumer demands . . . the perpetual caretaking of the museum of human history."[87] Given what Fukuyama spells out as "the end of history," to call it a "very sad time" is an understatement to say the least. The end of history reads more like the end of humanity, the end of pathos. Even the "powerful nostalgia" for Cold War triumphalism that Fukuyama holds on to as the last, tenuous string of community—he feels it in himself and sees it in others—is nowhere near as evocative as Cold War "daring," "courage," and "idealism."[88] Fukuyama sounds much like the right-wing equivalent of Jameson's thesis of the "waning of affect." For both Fukuyama and Jameson, there are fewer things to feel because of late capitalism: unlike the modernist adage, less is not more. Substituted for imagination is the careful maintenance of the past, the "perpetual caretaking" of relics for the temporary satisfaction of "sophisticated consumer demands."[89]

"The end of history" never came, of course. And neither did its promised—from both the left and the right—affective flatness. What authors like Vowell show us is that affect is alive and thriving in the post-Reagan era as Generation X continues to cope with the metanarratives of Cold War triumphalism, which still informs their use of synecdoche in the contemporary. This is not the "powerful nostalgia" for a triumphalist time Fukuyama writes of: it is the living nightmare that Vowell experiences at Bush II's inauguration; the feeling that Cold War triumphalism and its agents refuse to set us free into the future where they will not have such control over the national metanarrative.

Incredulity after 9/11

If the daydream that preceded his inauguration brought out a side of her that she does not like, it is during the Bush II administration that Vowell was forced to engage most directly with the part of the nation she does not like. The George W. Bush administration—not only in the way it absurdly adapted Reagan's triumphalism (think of the president proudly standing in front of the "Mission Accomplished" banner flying on the USS *Abraham Lincoln*) but also in the way such triumphalism proved a veneer for the administration's atrocities—challenged most directly the anti-intensity emotionology of Vowell's incredulity.

Though she did not explicitly use the word, Joan Didion described the appropriation of 9/11 by the Bush II administration as a revival of synecdoche, in particular the Cold War synecdoches of a moral struggle between a "them" that required attack in order to defend "us." At first expecting the event to be seen with "annihilating economy," as a synecdoche of "the complicated arrangements and misarrangements of the last century into a single irreducible image," Didion instead discovered that the event reactivated Reagan era tropes that made the actual attacks "less readable than it had seemed on the morning it happened."[90] Through the reactivation of the tropes of triumphalism, Didion found that "the irreconcilable event had been made manageable" as the synecdoches redeployed by the Bush II administration never acknowledged the complicated history of American foreign relations, but instead used the event as a rationale to justify those very policies. The events of 9/11 were "reduced to the sentimental, to protective talismans, totems, garlands of garlic, repeated pieties that would come to seem in some ways as destructive as the event itself. We now had 'the loved ones,' we had 'the families,' we had 'the heroes.'"[91] As Rodgers notes, "The most striking expression" after 9/11 "was an outpouring of nationalist signs and sentiments. Not even at the height of the Bicentennial celebrations had they been so numerous."[92] Such synecdoches unleashed a fear that was carefully contained in Cold War metanarratives, even when pushed to their apocalyptic extremes by the Reagan administration, as the Bush II administration turned "discrete, nonnuclear threats into the emotional equivalent of the Cold War nuclear crisis."[93] The logic of the Bush II administration extended the Cold War buildup of nuclear arsenals to the domain of affect, fighting a "war on terror"—an affect—with terror itself instilled domestically through a discourse of "homeland security" and internationally through torture and an ultimately preemptive war.

For writers like Vowell who were raised on—and took literally—the triumphalist rhetoric of Ronald Reagan, 9/11 reinvigorated their incredulous nationalism. Vowell's essay "The Partly Cloudy Patriot" captures the brief affective rupture between the event and the politicization of its meaning. This rupture she sees through a synecdoche, the American flag. "Immediately after the attack, seeing the flag all over the place was moving, endearing. . . . Seeing them was heartening because they indicate that we're all in this sorrow together."[94] But Vowell finds that "the meaning" of the flag soon after "changed, or let's say it changed back. . . . The flag again represented what it usually represents, the government."[95] The meaning of the flag for Vowell shifts from representing a "we" of the people to a "we" of the government: the Bush administration. Thus the flag comes to make Vowell feel "nervous" because it no longer stands as a synecdoche for national sorrow but for the legitimacy of another synecdoche: Washington.[96] In doing so, the flag comes to mean the federal government, something a citizen raised in the antigovernment rhetoric of Reagan would find innately alarming. Thus like the nerdy citizen, the true patriot is "smart" and skeptical about their government: "this deep suspicion of Washington is one of the most American emotions an American can have."[97]

Such patriotic feeling, that the "most American emotion" a citizen can have is a distrust of the government, is an assertion that national feeling transcends governments or politics. Such distrust bespeaks the continued power of Reagan-era tropes to describe the nation, even decades after his presidency.

After 9/11 the rift between the national metanarrative and contemporary politics became even more incommensurable. The Bush II administration undermined so many of its tenets that it became more difficult for the nation to suffice as an ontological safety net. Indeed, Vowell's writing about the period points toward the spoilage of that metanarrative's ability to connect past to present. *The Wordy Shipmates* begins with John Cotton's prayer before the Puritans' landing, which Vowell connects, through prolepsis, to a number of events throughout American history, as part of a broader whole:

> By the time Cotton says amen, he has fought Mexico for Texas, bought Alaska from the Russians, and dropped napalm on Vietnam. Then he lays a wreath on Custer's grave and revs past Wounded Knee. Then he claps when the Marquis de Lafayette tells Congress that "someday America will save the world." Then he smiles when Abraham Lincoln calls the United States "the last best hope on earth." Then he frees Cuba, which would be news to Cuba. Then he signs the lease on Guantanamo Bay.[98]

The Puritan preacher and politician John Cotton is transposed into the narrative of American exceptionalism: the nation that will someday save the world, "the last best hope on Earth."[99] He is also synecdochically transposed into the nation's great atrocities: the savagery of Wounded Knee, the rendition and detention of inmates at Guantanamo Bay. Thus he is turned into an American Everyman, part military general, part secretary of state, with scattered traces of soldier, president, congressman, and everyday citizen. Strangely, as a synecdoche, throughout Vowell's proleptic narrative, he does no good: he is merely in the audience of Lafayette and Lincoln, all the while fighting and buying land, bombing

Vietnam, "liberating" Cuba for American interests, signing the lease on the military base that will also serve as a prison.

Vowell's interest in American history points to her fascination with—and desire to construct—an origin narrative of the nation that verifies her incredulous relationship to it: in *Shipmates*, a desire to demonstrate the contemporary relevancy of the Puritans—and the relevancy of her writing about the Puritans. Vowell's interest in the Puritans is also due to their appropriation by contemporary politicians. *Shipmates* reveals a credulousness intensified by the events of 9/11. Vowell admits early in the book that she has lied to her friends about why she is writing about the Puritans. "I would never answer with the honest truth. Namely, that in the weeks after two planes crashed into two skyscrapers here on the worst day of our lives, I found comfort in the words of [Puritan leader John] Winthrop. When we were mourning together, when we were suffering together, I often thought of what he said and finally understood what he meant."[100] The "words" are from Winthrop's "Modell of Christian Charity": "We must delight in each other, make other's conditions our own, rejoice together, mourn together, labor and suffer together, always having before our eyes our commission and community in the work, our community as members of the same body."[101]

The former Pentecostal has found solace in a sermon, a plea to believe in a synecdoche, for a community to become a national body by being intimate with each other's affects—their rejoicing, mourning, and suffering—and working together to achieve a shared goal. For Vowell, 9/11 was a literal reincarnation of synecdoche. "We were breathing sooty air. The soot was composed of incinerated glass and steel but also, we knew, incinerated human flesh. . . . We were members of the same body, breathing the cremated lungs of the dead."[102] Yet this is a reincarnation birthed from destruction, not creation. The defensive tone of *Shipmates* strives to hide a profound sadness, a disenchantment that one must cope with the contradictions, the incommensurabilities, in the wake of 9/11, of the nation one loves. Unable to find a synecdoche that unifies the metanarrative of the national past with the actions of the nation at present, Vowell writes:

> I can't really fault Gore for saying that what happened at Abu Ghraib is sickening, not only because it's just plain sickening but because America is supposed to be better than that. No: best. I hate to admit it, but I still believe that, too. Because even though my head tells me that the idea that America was chosen by God as His righteous city on a hill is ridiculous, my heart still buys into it. And I don't even believe in God! And I have heard the screams! Why is America the last best hope of Earth?[103]

What are the screams that Vowell hears? Are they the yawps of Pentecostals, speaking in tongues? The cries of those fleeing the fleshy dust of the collapsing towers? Or the howls of those tortured by the very soldiers whose nation promises freedom from torture? Vowell does not answer: her credulity will not let her answer. Using a synecdoche perhaps most infamously attributed to Richard Nixon, she separates the head from the heart of her body, and by extension, the body of the nation. Her head remains incredulous at the Puritan synecdoche—one brought back into the public sphere by Reagan—that the nation is a city on a hill. Yet her heart buys into the metanarrative that the synecdoche has birthed: that America is the last best hope of Earth. She has bought into the exceptionalist metanarrative, the idea that America is better than others, that others look on America as an example to follow. In credulous anger she writes, "*The eyes of all the people are upon us.* And all they see is a mash-up of naked prisoners and an American girl in fatigues standing there giving a thumbs-up. As I write this, the United States of America is still a city on a hill; and it's still shining—because we never turn off the lights in our torture prisons."[104] Playing on Reagan's addition of the word "shining" to the phrase "city on a hill," an addition that, as Stephen Prothero notes, "merged the Sermon on the Mount with the New Jerusalem from Revelations," taking credulous triumphalism to its prophetic, apocalyptic extreme, Vowell evokes from that synecdoche the manipulation of the entire American metanarrative by the Bush II administration, its perverting the national story through its acts of torture.[105] The light from the "shining" city reveals the evil inside it. In the discrepancy between what the nation was in the narratives she has constructed and what it is at the present in which she writes, Vowell captures the depths of her disenchantment with the nation.

Vowell's later work still searches for a part that can stand in for the whole nation: if not a president, a state (Hawaii in *Unfamiliar Fishes*), or in her most recent work to date, a military figure. *Lafayette in the Somewhat United States* begins with Vowell attempting to parallel contemporary events with historical ones: the constitutional convention is paralleled with the 2013 federal budget debate, in which she finds "the quintessential experience of living in the United States: constantly worrying whether or not the country is about to fall apart."[106] But underneath such incredulity, Vowell finds a figure who has brought the nation together:

> The thing that drew me to Lafayette as a subject—that he was that rare object of agreement in the ironically named United States—kept me coming back to why that made him unique. Namely, that we the people have never agreed on much of anything. Other than a bipartisan consensus on barbecue and Meryl Streep, plus that time in 1942 when everyone from Bing Crosby to Oregonian schoolchildren heeded FDR's call to scrounge up rubber for the war effort, disunity is the through line in the national plot—not necessarily as a failing, but as a free people's privilege.[107]

Whereas Vowell articulates, from the perspective of history, her argument in *Patriot* that disagreement and disunity are the true measure of the nation, in *Lafayette*, her perspective becomes the metanarrative of the nation, the "through line in the national plot" of its history.[108] By doing so, Vowell performs a move similar to Steinbeck's in *Americans*—that what unites Americans is their very division, and that division is "not necessarily" a failing but a strength, a "free people's privilege." To do so, much like Steinbeck in *Americans*, Vowell takes the nation literally. Irony—that technique that Vowell frequently employs—is no longer just a literary device but is itself literal, in the very name of the nation, the "ironically named United States." Whereas Steinbeck asserted that the nation has a genetic tape that keeps it together, Vowell comes to see the tape that keeps it together as generic, the genre of irony. To effect such a move, however, is to subordinate the historical events that would show otherwise, to obscure parts in order to make a whole: Vowell affectively dismisses the national unity during the Second World War as a mere linking of arms by describing it as "that time in 1942." Vowell similarly dismisses a metanarrative of unity by evoking other synecdoches—barbecue, Meryl Streep—to stand in for the ultimately minor matters Americans seem to agree on.[109] Perhaps, as she puts it, "getting on each other's nerves is our *right*" as Americans.[110] Such a "right" justifies her contrarian stance, especially in light of the critics who find her style cloying or annoying. Her annoyance, in this sense, becomes a demonstration of her patriotism. But that Lafayette, as Vowell sees him, is a "rare object of agreement" seems to be her fascination with him. At the same time, through her interest in Lafayette, Vowell continues searching for that which the nation agreed on—what unites parts as a whole—that makes "the ironically named United States" not as ironic as she may prefer it to be. Despite her incredulity, Vowell remains incited to interpret the nation credulously.

Her later work also continues to fashion herself and the nation's history through attempts at self-definition in a distinctly eighties syntax. Vowell's work continues to blend historical metanarratives with popular culture, such as in her description of Prussian general Steuben. Considering Steuben's uncertainty as he travels—he is in fact fleeing—to America, Vowell writes:

> Who could have predicted that more than two hundred years after this washed-up Teutonic mercenary bummed a ride across the Atlantic because he had nowhere else to go, the director of *Pretty in Pink* would hire the kid from *WarGames* to play a high school student who skips school and crashes a German-American celebration in Steuben's honor, commandeering a float of buxom Bavarians to lip-synch to Wayne Newton's "Danke Shoen."[111]

In this passage, Vowell reads Steuben not through his military achievements and not through the parade that Chicago holds for him, but through the 1986 John Hughes film *Ferris Bueller's Day Off* in which the parade is depicted. She subordinates the despondency she presumes Steuben felt at the time to Hollywood hiring practices and the teen celebrity of Matthew Broderick: the rhetoric of Reagan and triumphalism reappears in the reference to the film *WarGames*. Vowell is still reading contemporary events but through the lens of eighties film, a genre that is becoming increasingly historical itself and may be alien to audiences reading *Lafayette* when it was published in 2015. Her struggle for self-definition, the struggle Ferguson characterizes as paradigmatic of those who were children during the Reagan era, continues. Regardless, there is, in this context, nothing merry about the parade: the suggestion, through Vowell's exaggeration, is that the parade floats like an empty signifier detached from a metanarrative. And if it is not an empty signifier, then Steuben is like Broderick, a smart-alecky high schooler, similar to Vowell's earlier characterization of herself. Her reading of the parade depicted in *Bueller* ultimately connects the Prussian general back to Vowell herself: her quirks; her position within eighties types. Vowell's pastiche of metanarrative with popular culture continues throughout *Lafayette*, blurring historical reality with entertainment and simulation. Later in the book, Vowell finds herself enchanted with Williamsburg, Virginia. At first concerned that it would be "too chipper, too reassuring, an infomercial for the preindustrial good olde days," she "falls in love" with a simulated angry mob giving a performance of storming the royal governor's palace: "if they are sentimental, it is only because they're nostalgic for a time the government of Great Britain respected their constitutional rights as Englishmen."[112] Perhaps she has become so enamored with disagreement and argument as signs of civic-minded nobility that the actors playing the angry mob strike a real chord in her, but Vowell has momentarily forgotten that what she is seeing is a dramatic reenactment for tourists and has credulously "fallen in love" with American actors playing a group of incredulous Englishmen.

By the conclusion of the book, Vowell is concerned that "nowadays, Lafayette is a place, not a person," that the illustrious general has been cast aside by history.[113] She finds it "eerie how one day in 1824 two-thirds of the population of New York City was lining up to wave hello at Lafayette and nineteen decades go by and all that's left of his memory is the name of a Cajun college town."[114] What Americans see as history, Vowell sees as something alive: in the book's last paragraphs, Vowell quotes at length a speech given in Lafayette Square in Washington DC by Evelyn Wotherspoon Wainwright, leader of the National Woman's Party and a force behind the passing of the Nineteenth Amendment. The conclusion of the book is not so much Vowell's, then, as it is Wainwright's, as she addresses the bronze statue of the general, urging him to "'speak, Lafayette, dead these hundred years but living in the hearts of the American people.' 'Lafayette,' she said, 'we are here!'"[115]

Vowell's presentation of Lafayette and the synecdoches she uses to evoke his place in contemporary life is much like Wainwright giving a speech to the statue of Lafayette: he becomes a prop that is addressed but remains a dead object. Wainwright talks at Lafayette but not to her audience: as if talking to the statue will announce to the nation "we are here."[116] Vowell's mode is similar to Wainwright's: Lafayette becomes a prop through which she can describe the nation, as if the motley crew she assembles, from Steuben to Wayne Newton to Matthew Broderick, will bring Lafayette to life, that the nation will become alive through the composition of these parts. But that Vowell concludes with a speech given almost one hundred years ago indicates that Lafayette is, indeed, not alive or current in people's memory. Thus the conclusion is synecdochical but also apostrophic: the dead address the dead. Vowell's evocation of Wainwright parallels Wainwright's evocation of Lafayette: as such, her engagement with contemporary politics is increasingly historical. Vowell's history of Lafayette ends on a moment of nascent triumph, as readers know that the Nineteenth Amendment was passed. And history itself has become less a living narrative than a justification for Vowell's credulity—that there could be a figure who can "live in the hearts of the American people," a synecdoche within a synecdoche, a figure of identification and enchantment—as much as a justification for her incredulity: the statue of Lafayette is a sign that "the only reason there's a statue of him staring at the White House is because as a teenager he defied his father-in-law's edict to settle into a boring job, explaining afterward, 'I did not hesitate to be disagreeable to preserve my independence.'"[117] Lafayette's life sounds suspiciously like the plot of an eighties coming-of-age movie, or a reminisce of Vowell's adolescent shift from credulity to incredulity. Much like her disenchantment with Reagan spurs her self-fashioning, through Lafayette, Vowell's own life is projected as a synecdoche, a metanarrative of American history.

Conclusion: Incredulity in the Wake of Trump

After the 2004 reelection of George W. Bush, Vowell told *Vanity Fair* that "I kind of lost my rosy colored glasses about the electorate. . . . I just fear them. . . . This country is really schizophrenic and insane."[118] While the contested 2000 election was a source of disenchantment, Bush II's reelection in 2004 was for Vowell a source of disappointment, a confirmation that the nation and its metanarrative had tilted permanently to the right. In a way, Vowell's turn to book-length histories can be seen as a sign of this disenchantment: the nation's past gives her a way of articulating a metanarrative that runs counter to the one articulated after 9/11. At the same time, such a turn can be seen as a sign of retreat from the contemporary, an infatuation with a past of one's own construction that only engages in a contrarian way with predominant metanarratives.

This is not to say that Vowell has gone unaffected by changes in the political landscape. In two separate articles for the *New York Times*, written in 2008 and 2016, Vowell describes how each of the Democratic candidates for president left her in tears. In 2008 she wrote, "I have spent the last eight years so disgusted with the incompetent yahoos of the executive branch that I had forgotten . . . that government can be a useful, meaningful and worthwhile force for good in this republic instead of just an embarrassing, torturing, Book of Revelation starter kit."[119] The nation Obama promises is appealing to her—"the ideal America just about any registered Democrat would dream up"—which Vowell embraces with hyperbolic praise: a "wind-powered public school classroom of 19 multiracial 8-year-olds reading above grade level" whose parents "work only eight hours a day in a country at war solely with the people who make war on us."[120] In 2016 Clinton's candidacy evoked in Vowell the challenges women face in politics. Watching Clinton's acceptance speech, she describes how she "cried like a 14-year-old girl for the 14-year-old girl [she] once was and because [U.S. vice president candidate] Geraldine Ferraro and [Montana U.S. representative] Jeannette Rankin did not live to see it," connecting her tears to the joy she experienced in watching Ferraro's acceptance speech at the 1984 Democratic National Convention. In a way, Clinton's acceptance speech serves as a confirmation of Ferraro's role in Vowell's youth and thus Vowell's contrarian self-fashioning: her tears are as much for Clinton's success as they are for Ferraro's defeat as much as they are for the adolescent Vowell's credulity toward the nation.

Watching Clinton's acceptance speech, Vowell concludes, "Feeling represented does matter in a representative democracy."[121] In parentheses, she adds, "(It matters more to elect the candidate who is not bonkers)."[122] Of course, feeling represented matters in a democracy: feeling that one's imagined community is represented, that one is a part of a broader whole. Yet Vowell's parenthetical addition, that feelings matter less than the candidate who is elected, is a premise that the 2016 election would contest. It makes sense, from the perspective of an incredulous nationalist raised during the rise of Reagan, to relegate one's affective intensity to the background, to slacken off in the face of strong nationalism. Such a tactic enabled the contrarian perspective that generation became known for, a fount of ways for them to fashion themselves against the appropriation of the national metanarrative by neoconservatives. In a way, Vowell's parenthetical addition is a reading of Trump along eighties lines: the candidate who is "bonkers" is too intense, too hot, not cool enough. Indeed, these were the accusations of the Clinton campaign against Donald Trump: that his emotional displays were a sign of his inability to govern as much as they may be signs of a mental unfitness for office.

Yet "feeling represented," that which Vowell sets aside, is exactly what supporters of Donald Trump did not, to the incredulous surprise of Vowell and the majority of Americans. The power of Trump's strong nationalism remained inconceivable to weak nationalists during the 2016 campaign as late as August: Vowell herself, in her article "Join the Army, Love the Constitution and Pray to Whomever You Like," wrote, "The Republican old guard will spend the coming years trying to figure out how to salvage the moral foundation built by the original [party] delegates . . . while warding off barmy xenophobes."[123] Thus three months before the election, Vowell was certain enough of Trump's defeat to imagine a future Republican party without him, a certainty confirmed by most pollsters and the political establishment. Reducing hot nationalism to "barmy"—foolish, crazy—xenophobia, incredulous nationalism dismissed the affective power of Trump as much as those who sought to profit from Trump's success. Reading the 2016 election as an extension of the 1984 election, Vowell could see neither the affective intensity, nor the appeal, of Trump's hot nationalism.

We are now living in an era when the federal government has become a laboratory for hot nationalism and its strong affects. Weak nationalism seems to be undergoing an interregnum as hot nationalism flexes its muscle in reshaping federal policy, as it maintains its loudness through domestic social media as much as revelations of foreign scandal. Incredulity is difficult when there is so much to be worried about, when it seems like every day is a living nightmare, much like Vowell's witnessing the inauguration of George W. Bush. Even something as simple as the election of a congressman can prove daunting. On May 24, 2017, Greg Gianforte, a Republican seeking election in Montana's sole congressional district, grabbed the wrist of a reporter for the *Guardian* during a campaign stop. Reports vary as to why Gianforte grabbed the reporter's wrist: the reporter's question about Gianforte's support for the Republican-sponsored repeal of the Affordable Health Care Act may have spurred it. But Gianforte's grabbing of the reporter's wrist was read as a synecdoche for a change in American politics, in which political candidates have become openly disrespectful, as President Trump has been, toward the free press. Some media outlets reported Gianforte's grabbing of the reporter's wrist as a punch, others reported it as a "body slam." Regardless, Gianforte was elected to the district, and the Speaker of the House, Paul Ryan, declared that Gianforte would still be seated in the House after his encounter with the reporter. Gianforte would eventually plead guilty to a misdemeanor assault charge, his sentence was deferred, and he was ordered to perform community service, take an anger management course, and pay court costs.

Gianforte's behavior is the subject of Vowell's article in the *New York Times Sunday Review* titled "Don't Judge Montana for a Single Body Slam." Her response to Gianforte is reminiscent of Jane Smiley's essay written after the 2004 election. While the premise of the response is the same, their tones are markedly different. Both begin by evoking the red-state–blue-state dichotomy. "If there are two Americas," Vowell wrote, "there are at least that many versions of Montana."[124] There are, by her tally, at least fifteen different types of Montanan, ranging from members of the seven tribal Indian nations to constituents including miners (politically left) and farmers (politically right), artists and college faculty, and the occasional "coastal refugee" like Gianforte and a medley of "dirt bags," a term of affection for those who "look like a bunch of Hillary-voting hippies" but who, because they are also "stingy tippers," might be "secret Republicans."[125] Vowell asserts that Gianforte is not a true Montanan: jokingly referring to him as a coastal refugee who has sought sanctuary from the busy life of the American coasts, Vowell casts illegitimacy on his ability to represent the state. Yet while Smiley affirms the red and blue dichotomy as one that threatens to destroy the whole, in which the unteachable ignorance of the red states must be countered by pedagogic displays in the blue states, the sheer political diversity of Montana, Vowell writes, shows that "Montanans are not unlike the founders who came up with the Electoral College in the first place": though the state may be "one of the biggest red blotches" on the map, the state is "nevertheless too diverse and too geographically spread out to cohere."[126]

This diversity does not mean, though, that the state of Montana is like the Michigan Avenue Bridge, the "vortex" she found so frustrating in *Cannoli*. The tension of "Don't Judge," like the tension of weak nationalism, emerges in the ability of the part to represent a whole. This bespeaks an even larger tension, for it returns to Burke's claim that synecdoche is "present in all theories of political representation, where some part of the social body (either traditionally established, or elected, or coming into authority by revolution) is held to be 'representative' of the society of the whole." Vowell's disconnection of Gianforte from Montana evokes a question of legitimacy, as Burke would describe it, the issue that "any act of representation automatically implies a synecdochic relationship (insofar as the act is, or is held to be, 'truly representative')."[127] What Burke has placed in parentheses is the problem of Vowell's essay: her insistence that the state not be judged by the acts of its representative is problematic. That the part does not represent a whole is a problem when the part represents the whole, such as Gianforte's representation of the state in Congress.

When synecdoches expose dilemmas, incredulity incites a reading that turns inward, that fashions the self as the part that represents the whole. Characteristic of its slackening turn inward, Vowell offers a counterexample of the exemplary diversity of Montana: herself. Her youthful protesting of Iran-Contra or her riding her bike thirteen miles to hear Jesse Jackson speak at the 1988 state Democratic primary was not her acting like a "beatnik outlier" as much as it was her "carrying on the longstanding nonviolent tradition" of Montana representative Jeannette Rankin.[128] As the essay continues, Vowell does not seem as concerned about Gianforte himself, his politics, or those who voted for him as she is in asking, "Would the early voters who cast absentee ballots for Gianforte before his hissy fit have changed their minds?," reframing the representative-elect's physical altercation as a childish, feminized "hissy fit."[129] She is more concerned that readers of the newspaper will see Montanans only as "authoritarian hotheads" without remembering that some are "lily-livered liberals" committed to nonviolence.[130] In other words, Gianforte's violent outburst is unrepresentative of Montana, and it would be unfair for readers to judge the state based on his actions. Vowell, ever the contrarian, insists that the majority of Montanans are "nice."[131]

Nice: the word has a timid rosiness that seems intended to incite a reading of the state that counters their representative's "body slam." Yet there is something vague in the use of that word, almost aggressive in its passivity. The disposition of being "nice" promises, as Carrie Tirado Bramen has written, "to convert animosity into affection."[132] But "nice," in the distinctly American sense of the word, as Bramen suggests, is merely the other side of a binary between the "nice American" and the "ugly American" that has dominated political discourse, a tension in American politics between the nation as benevolent hegemon and as genocidal expansionist.[133] At the same time, "nice" is a word bound up in its own banality, a disposition so ambiguous that it can mean almost anything—or nothing. Indeed, "nice" shares an etymological history with the "foolish" and "trivial."[134] Vowell's claim is not that Montanans are good or virtuous or exemplary Americans: they are only, vaguely, merely, nice. Nice does not confer much in terms of national identity; indeed, there is something markedly banal about "nice"—think of the "Have a Nice Day" buttons that adorned so many wearers in the seventies—that connotes a lack of affective intensity. Not only a lack but the antithesis of the intensity that strong affects like triumphalist nationalism prizes: to evoke the cliché, nice people finish last. There is something slack in Vowell's description of her home state, a slackness that suggests the exhaustion of incredulity's contrariness. That "nice" is considered a characteristic of the majority of Montanans is reflective of a broader political disregard for weak affect altogether: that Vowell feels compelled to ask readers not to judge them because the majority of Montanans are "nice" is reflective of hot nationalism's predominance in political life. "Nice" may sound like a plea for a new sort of politics, yet it is anything but. The political tradition that Vowell yearns for in her insistence on Montanan's "niceness" recalls nineteenth-century ideas of civility and domesticity. Yet "nice" has its own conservative politics "in that it helps sustain the status quo by keeping other values, such as fairness, at bay."[135] Thus in her proclamation of their niceness, Vowell captures the incommensurability of being an American during the Trump administration—one in which the affects that promise to "make America great again" are in the hands of hot nationalists.

Vowell's incredulous nationalism suggests that the nonfiction of Generation X is perpetually reacting to the triumphalist affects of the eighties and has yet to escape either the political agenda or the strong affects of the Reagan era. Perhaps this is because of the generation's insistence on quirky ironical smartness as a contrarian response to the rise of neoconservatism in the eighties and its triumphalist rhetoric, a reactive response without a politics—or an arsenal of synecdoches—of its own to posit an alternative to the triumphalism they are locked into. Vowell's work demonstrates how a different generation of writers would better cultivate "an ironic understanding of our own countercultural inheritance" while developing "a nonironic commitment to learning how to build enduring institutions . . . to dismantle the power of those whose strength partly depends on our cynicism."[136] Vowell's latter work attests to the almost nostalgic quality the Reagan era has on Generation X, especially after 9/11. It provided them with an orderly world, one in which they were contrarian but found their aesthetic through the incommensurabilities of the period, which they fashioned and continue to fashion themselves.

Yet the nation allows Vowell to invent herself as much as she invents it in her nonfiction. As a source of self-fashioning, Vowell's incredulous affect serves as a reminder of the incitement to read the nation synecdochically, and of the affective intensity of nationalism, if only because she sees herself, at times, as more American than the nation itself. By doing so, Vowell reminds us that the affects of nationalism have not waned as much as their intensities have become obscured in response to Reagan-era triumphalism. Perhaps such obscuring is the culmination of neoconservatism, which often proudly announces itself as the only way in which patriotism can be expressed, the only affectively "strong" way to express one's participation in the nation. The challenge of writers like Vowell—and others who seek to reclaim nationalism—will be in the story they tell of the nation but also in the affects those stories enable and encourage. It will take a reassessment of weak affects to accomplish this reclamation, not from the disenchanted perspective of wry contrarians, not with reactive passiveness nor with ironic defensiveness toward the metanarrative coopted by neoconservatives, but by creating a metanarrative that opens up new stories of the nation, one that enchants through the dynamism of weak affects, one that facilitates not an alternative but a departure from contemporary American nationalism and its underlying and ultimately unquestioned credulities.

CONCLUSION

Affected Critics, the Nation, and the Limits of Critique

Throughout this book I have examined the role of synecdoche in weak nationalism. In conclusion, I examine why critics have given little attention to the issue of weak nationalism by exploring the vexed emotional engagement critics have with the nation. Criticism itself is an index of narratives, a set of stories we tell ourselves about the material we study. And if affect, as I have used the term throughout this book, is the incitement to read, it is worth examining how criticism constructs incitements to read. The incitements that make criticism possible may also make other modes of inquiry less possible: what they bring to attention may simultaneously obscure or make invisible other incitements to read, other paths toward inquiry. And so here I sketch out some preliminary answers to the following questions: How are critics, like the authors I have studied in this book, affected readers in an imagined community? And how does the monopoly of one affect—suspicion—dominate and limit criticism's ability to imagine and critique its subject? If the synecdochical affects of weak nationalism should be studied more closely to fully engage with nonfiction representations of the nation, then it follows that critics, in turn, need to be more aware of the affects of our criticism to fully engage in the critical act.

Critics are trained to be suspicious, a stance that Felski has described as "professional suspicion," a "detached, dispassionate, and skeptical demeanor" toward its object of inquiry.[1] Yet as dispassionate as it may seem, criticism also brings a certain "ludic delight . . . a form of engrossing, high-level, intellectual stimulation" that is both "addictive and gratifying."[2] At the same time, professional suspicion is dominated by a negativity that portends to "tabulate a limit, to discern a lack, to heave a sigh of disapproval or disappointment" toward its object.[3] Suspicion, it seems, flows easily between being a method that applies critique to illuminate an object and being a disposition, an affective orientation toward the object that does not illuminate but rather dismisses, one that does not explore but rather deplores its object.

Critics have been trained to be suspicious in general, but they have been trained in particular to be suspicious, if not dismissive, of nationalism. When Spivak writes that what "nationalism conjures is not a positive affect," critics can feel, through its negative and cautionary framing, a tone of critical suspicion that perceives nationalism as a site of negative affects exclusively.[4] Or when Ignatieff writes, "The repressed has returned, and its name is nationalism," critics hear the professional suspicion of the analyst toward the analysand, in which nationalism is dismissed as a symptom of something more worrisome and insidious.[5] The way in which critics approach nationalism, either as a sorcery that is conjured or as an unconscious that has resurfaced, presupposes inquiry's ability to dismiss it. Such presuppositions, as Felski and Fraiman write, "pave the way for ideas, helping to determine what will matter to us (or not)" as inquiry just as the affects of "curiosity, wonder, irritation, or optimism animate us to pursue a certain path of inquiry."[6] Yet within Americanist criticism, a suspicion toward nationalism encourages the exact opposite of interpretation. For the most part, critical curiosity ceases when the issue of nationalism appears. We are so suspicious, so dismissive of it, that nationalism does not seem worth being curious about.

This wariness speaks to the broader problem of how critics approach the nation itself. As Liam Kennedy vividly describes it, the affective modus operandi of Americanist criticism is that "America does not make

Americanists happy. As Americanists, we commonly approach 'America' with suspicion, fear, even anger; we view it as a powerful, duplicitous force to be denounced or demystified."[7] This is criticism's equivalent of strong affect, "a pathological stance" toward the nation that is "wary of sentiment . . . wary of nationalism."[8] Such a modus operandi too often serves to perpetuate a mode of critique that according to Felski, "*does not tolerate rivals.*"[9] To discuss the possibility of nationalism in a nonpejorative sense is to risk triggering a strong affect that sees any alternatives as rivals who cannot be tolerated lest the critical enterprise fall asunder. Spivak and Ignatieff dismiss nationalism so easily because they do not see its potential for inquiry: it is, to them, antithetical to inquiry. Felski's conception of "the limits of critique" is driven, at least in part, as a reaction to such intolerance. A technique that once provoked feelings of excitement and community among its practitioners, suspicion no longer offers these positive affects because it reached a limit and became an end in itself. Being suspicious has become "an efficiently running form of intellectual machinery, modeling a style of thought that is immediately recognizable, widely applicable, and easily teachable" and so strongly marks "the boundaries of what counts as serious thought, so that the only conceivable response to the limits of critique seems to be the piling up of yet more critique."[10] My work in this book suggests that a suspicion of nationalism has so monopolized the critical act in Americanist criticism that critics' suspicion of nationalism reveals "less its murderous brutality than its potential banality."[11]

Suspicion toward the nation closes the doors of inquiry. Indeed, as Russ Castronovo writes, it seems that critics "willingly cloak themselves with a hair-shirt logic that makes their own penance about nationalism a prerequisite for progressive critique."[12] When critics use the word "nationalism" they often presume it to be aggressive and violent, disregarding a site of intellectual novelty and political boldness. Our difficulty in seeing the dynamism of nationalism seems to lead critics down the same path as Jane Smiley's essay, which I explored in this book's introduction, such that we only see nationalism as the domain of the "unteachable." Yet nationalism is far richer than the rote critical performances of the nation as a "true fiction" or "the return of the repressed" or the seemingly obligatory nod toward demystifying American hegemony will allow. Being professionally suspect of nationalism makes nationalism's weaker and more fruitful valences like the ones I have examined in this book banal if not invisible. But to engage them, criticism must open itself up to an affective complexity that the hermeneutics of suspicion, in its strictest form, cannot allow. Critics must come to terms with the dynamic affects that incite their work, affects that determine not only the archives which suffice as objects of critique but also the range of affects that determine what constitutes the act of critique itself.

An Affected Critic

While Felski has contemporary criticism in mind, the limits of critique are visible whenever a critic attempts to engage with the nation. Criticism's oppositional tactics toward the nation are evident in work that preceded the rise of "theory" as well. Consider, for example, the work and career of Lionel Trilling. Early in his career, Trilling wrote, "There is only one way to accept America and that is in hate; one must be close to one's land, passionately close in some way or other, and the only way to be close to America is to hate it; it is the only way to love America."[13] Trilling's statement is at first bewildering. The intensity of his affects—acceptance, hate, love—are intertwined in such a way that they become embedded in each other: to accept the nation is to hate the nation, which is the only way to love the nation. Such intense affects, and the transitive way in which affect is linked to affect, cannot be reduced to a single affect alone. What is felt instead is an intensity of closeness to the nation as Trilling comes to ultimately love the intensity of his attachment, to love his hate, to accept his closeness to the nation.

Trilling's feeling, his "intensity of closeness" toward America, is reminiscent of the closeness toward the nation displayed by the authors I have studied in this book. Yet Trilling's attachment to the nation evolved into what Felski might call a "rhetoric of againstness" in which the critic's acceptance of the nation enables only the opportunity to critique it.[14] Trilling's tortuous semantic work demonstrates this: to convert his acceptance into hate, then into love, marks the work of a critic who feels compelled to convert one set of emotions into another more acceptable for the cause of criticism. For Trilling, at least, such againstness made his critical career. As Mark Krupnick has explored, Trilling often pivoted in his understanding of the American mainstream to establish his own position. By being suspicious of the mainstream, he found the opportunity to critique. "In the forties the liberal intellectuals were sunk in a drab and soulless materialism, and so Trilling argued for vivacity and variety, for wit and style."[15] Yet by the sixties, when "the orthodoxy of dissent had become 'the adversary culture' . . . Trilling shifted course, arguing now for reason and expressing skepticism about the literary values he had once celebrated as a corrective for an excessively rationalistic liberal culture."[16]

Yet such againstness culminated, in the latter part of his career, in ambivalence. While there is some promise in his admission to Richard Sennett that "between is the only honest place to be," being between for Trilling seemed little more than being torn between opposing forces, a double againstness. Sennett himself reflected, "In the last few years, I've come to see how anti-liberal this seemingly liberal statement is. . . . A body that can immobilize itself through the search for gratification; a nature that can, like the Stalinist reactionaries of Trilling's youth, immobilize its citizens in the name of freedom—these are the antimonies of his morality."[17] And the result of being between seems to have ultimately furthered in Trilling a detachment from the nation itself. His refusal to take a stance on national events, such as the Vietnam War, endeared him to no one. "Writers on both the left and the right had reason to feel let down by Trilling. His remoteness saved him from the polemical excess of intellectuals more deeply involved in the cultural debates of those years. But Trilling's coolness was purchased at too high a price."[18] The critic who once saw the nation as a site of affective engagement, where hate led to love and ultimately acceptance of the nation, seemed increasingly uninterested in examining the contentious issues that would reactivate such intense affects. Trilling's abstention from the politics of Vietnam was not an acceptance of the hate and love that bring one close to one's nation but ultimately an indifference toward the dynamic affects the nation evokes.

The high price that Trilling paid was not only political but affective as well. As Seigworth and Gregg write, affect "arises in the midst of in-between-ness."[19] Yet Trilling's "between" is the critic's between: one that does not delight—or display any positive affect—in the work that takes place in being between but instead finds traction in being doubly against (of both the mainstream and the avant-garde), doubly suspicious (of both style and dissent), opposing everything at the cost of feeling nothing. Instead of provoking inquiry, as it does in affect theory, Trilling's "between" effectively closed the door to inquiry because it closed the door to the dynamism of feeling.[20] The result of such unsustainable double againstness is intellectual and affective exhaustion, and for Trilling, a turn inward. By the end of his career, as Marianna Torgovnick, who briefly attended Trilling's graduate seminar at Columbia University notes, the critic "had taken to reading aloud long passages from his essays and praising them as 'elegant' or 'well-put' without—and this was the curious part—ever identifying them as his own. Looking up at the ceiling and not at his students, reading his own prose aloud, Trilling made himself into the anonymous third person" of his own criticism.[21] Such againstness, while positioning the critic as a suspicious and supposedly superior interpreter of the nation, at the same time limits critique to the point that the critic is left talking to himself, impressed by his critical prowess but speaking to no one. (I wonder what critics could learn if we looked the nation in the eye rather than staring at the ceiling in its presence.) To Torgovnick, Trilling "had disappeared into the tradition, a tradition he felt that most of the students before him no longer respected and therefore no longer deserved. His manner was both effete and distant—and, finally, both defeated and hostile. His 'we' was directed at the ceiling, not toward his students, sitting there before him. We were the barbarians inside the gates; he wanted none of us."[22] Trilling's critical trajectory may demonstrate how "the positive turns out to be a temporary way station en route to the negative, whose sovereignty is rousingly affirmed" by the hermeneutics of suspicion.[23]

Trilling's againstness toward the nation—and its affects—eventually led to critical inflexibility and, ultimately, disenchantment and resignation. Such againstness and its consequences are a reminder that to be in opposition to the nation may make for critical fodder, yet it ultimately proves to be opposition for its own sake, with the effect of affectively exhausting and blinding the critic to the nation's richness and realities. Such is the result of an oppositional stance that is "unwilling to admit the possibility of peaceful coexistence or even mutual indifference" of other modes of inquiry and "concludes that those who do not embrace its tenets must therefore be denying or disavowing them."[24] Trilling's career reveals how such an oppositional stance becomes a problem for critics not only in the way it ultimately reduces the field of inquiry to rote performance but also in the way it limits criticism's ability to reach new audiences and maintain its position in a changing world.

Beyond the Limits of Critique: An Affectively Aware Criticism

Trilling's problem is an Americanist's problem. For the most part, this problem plays out latently in criticism, reaching one of two conclusions. One dominant conclusion of this problem, as I examined in the introduction to this book, is reflected in a poststructural reading of the nation as "true fictions." Such an argument risks sounding like an intellectualized dismissal of the nation: the nation is an illusion that only the trained Americanist, reading against the mainstream, can see as such. (If only the barbarians at the gate could see the incommensurability between the sign and the signified, they would be free of their illusory nationalism.) Another dominant conclusion is the nation not as a fiction but as a real and insidious site of imperialism. "Empire *is* US history," Matthew Frye Jacobson announced in his 2013 American Studies Association presidential address.[25] As an example, he encouraged his audience to "think of the aesthetic of the common guitar, whose rich combination of rosewood, ebony, mahogany, teak, abalone, mother of pearl, and ivory originated in Spanish imperial ostentation, meant to show off at one glance the magnificent reach of empire."[26] It is worth notice that Jacobson's example is synecdochical: the individual elements of the guitar represent the global reach of colonial exploitation, the resulting product representative of imperial aspirations. Jacobson is aware that the guitar itself has been used to perform music of resignation as well as rebellion, of the "many artists who have used the guitar to *decry* power—Phil Ochs . . . Joan Baez . . . Jimi Hendrix . . . The Dixie Chicks . . . Who did not play a guitar but a banjo—an instrument that originated in Africa and made its way into [Pete] Seeger's hands by way of Caribbean slaves."[27] But the suspiciousness of empire is knotted into the interpretation of America; for Jacobson, it cannot go unnoticed. That the instruments of empire also serve as instruments of liberation are exceptions to the rule of America as empire. And while Jacobson makes clear that the tools of colonialism can also serve as the tools of criticism and dissent, he seems preoccupied in pointing out their imperial sources at a much more microcosmic level. (If only the barbarians at the gate could see their imperialism that the critic has deftly exposed, the barbarians would adopt progressive politics.) But in seeing their art only in service of liberation from American empire, Jacobson sidesteps the complexity of these artist's affects and their role in an evolving nationalism. One need only listen to Seeger's "Dear Mr. President" or Ochs's "The Power and the Glory" or the Dixie Chicks' performance at the post-9/11 *America: A Tribute to Heroes* telethon fund-raiser or Baez's performance of "We Shall Overcome" at the White House to see that each of these artists have feelings toward the nation that are evolving and complex, a more dynamic sense of nationalism than an exclusive focus on American imperialism will allow. The critic misses how the affective valences of nationalism are perpetually appropriated and rearticulated. Particularly of Hendrix's performance of "The Star-Spangled Banner" at Woodstock, it is apparent that while "he had taken one of the best-known tunes in America and made it his own . . . for Jimi, it was a musical exercise, not a manifesto."[28] That his performance was turned into a synecdoche of political radicalism does not square with what Hendrix himself said of his performance: "We're all Americans . . . it was like 'Go America!'"[29] What was the nation that Hendrix had in mind, the community he imagined, as he performed his version of this synecdoche, the national anthem? In his analysis, Jacobson perpetuates what Hendrix's biographer Charles R. Cross forewarns, that "ultimately, however, Jimi's pro-army stance or his own political beliefs hardly mattered—the song became part of the sixties zeitgeist."[30] It is not that Jacobson is incorrect in his analysis. Rather, he seems caught up in a certain type of affect—a suspicion of the nation as an empire—that emphasizes one avenue of inquiry at the expense of one which could reveal not only these artist's complex affects toward the nation but also varieties of nationalism that are complex tapestries in themselves.

Such conclusions show the limits of critique when the subject is the nation. Yet these limits are often seen as symptoms of nationalism itself rather than as the limits of critical hermeneutics. J. Gerald Kennedy has recently written, for example, in his study of literary nationalism in America that "nationalism produces a way of seeing that is also a not-seeing, and the strange, unresolved contradictions of nationhood and nationality lurk in this cultural blind spot."[31] Yet the panoply of affects studied in this book suggests that nationalism is not so much a blind spot as it is a vision of synecdochical seeing, the seeing of a connection between the part and the whole that constitutes the nation. "America" exists in the transferential, affective space of synecdoche. My exploration of the affects throughout this book that emerge from these synecdoches leads me to wonder: have critics considered what nationalism sees, before the seemingly inevitable, critical dismissal of nationalism for what it does not see? If nationalism is a blind spot, it may be not the concept but how critics approach it that leads it to being so.

Americanists construct themselves—and an imagined community of similarly affected critics—around a suspicion of nationalism. Of course, to study America, one not need be a nationalist. Yet, by proximity, nationalism is there, lurking because we have put it in a lurker's position, prowling about our discourse as if waiting to ambush us. The lurking proximity of nationalism "is felt as a negation . . . a turning away from others . . . as a turning towards" the academic self.[32] Our tacit agreement that nationalism, as Kennedy writes, "lurks" is part of what constructs an imagined community of our own; the affective admixtures—like Trilling's hate which becomes the only way to love—that lead us to study this nation, as a way of being close to America by keeping nationalism at bay. But as suspicious as we are, even the trope of the blind spot is a synecdoche, suggestive of an eye, suggestive of a national body. That nationalism lurks is a key component of our professional suspicion. To think of the nation as "lurking" suggests a different type of closeness: not the "passionate closeness" through which the young Trilling found his affective way into the nation but a closeness that we are aware of, and like the older Trilling, disturbed by if not ambivalent toward. The affects Americanists deploy to understand nationalism indicate the effects of this proximity: nationalism is suspect, insidious, and dangerous. Yet my archive has demonstrated that many writers find the nation to be a source of a moodiness that incites interpretation, of curiosity as much as discontent, of hopefulness, and of the incredulity that reveals credulity itself. Whereas critics seem trapped by synecdoches that reveal fictions, empires, and blind spots, it is possible to find an archive of affects with more dynamic incitements to read the nation.

So if nationalism lurks near criticism, criticism lurks near nationalism, with only a sense of its shadows. By paying closer attention to what we see and how we see, and how we feel about our seeing, critics may strengthen our understanding of what nationalism is and what it is not. The weak nationalism I have described in this book is an interpretive blind spot only because it has been so seldom studied. Perhaps it is easier for critics to deal with the nation as if it were a fiction, or an empire, or a blind spot, to dismiss the flow of their critical affects instead of attending in their criticism to the moodiness, curiosity, hopefulness, and incredulity that motivate their scholarship in the first place. Americanists may disavow nationalism as unworthy of inquiry, but by doing so they, much like Trilling, also disengage from national problems and disavow their stakes in them. And in doing so, we contribute to the disenchantment presumed and perpetuated by critique, one that discourages "affective connections in contexts where detachment is dangerous."[33] We limit our scope of inquiry. How we move beyond this limit requires not the abandonment of suspicion so much as a more affectively aware criticism. This is not to say that I agree with the claims that "postcriticism" can overcome the limits of critique. For to replace criticism with another mode of criticism merely perpetuates the problem: postcriticism runs the risk of merely replacing the hermeneutics of suspicion with a new set of strong affects. Eve Kosofsky Sedgwick noted, "A disturbingly large amount of theory seems explicitly to undertake the proliferation of only one affect, or maybe two, of whatever kind."[34] This is concerning, for as Tomkins wrote, strong affects are fixed, inflexible theories of the world. Tomkins gives the example of a person whose strong affects toward avoiding being hit by a car first lead him to avoid busy streets, then to avoid leaving the house in the daytime, such that "if his house were to be hit by a car, he would have to seek refuge in a deeper shelter."[35] Criticism's virtually reflexive jump to suspicion, much like Ransom's reflexive disdain of the "vulgar rhetoric" of synecdoche that I explored at the beginning of this book, is a jump to strong affects. And while strong affects make for a predictable world, they form an empire of their own, an affective monopoly, through which texts are read in ways with a "rigorous exclusiveness" that risk "being strongly tautological."[36] The strategies that yield such strong affects encourage a narrowing of what constitutes the scope and act of inquiry.

What is needed then is not a criticism that limits some affects and privileges others but a criticism that embraces the entire range of affect: one that does not monopolize one or two strong affects but acknowledges, as Tomkins wrote about affect theory, that affects must be weak for them to be effective. Suspicion should be one of many affects in play in a critical reading. Above all, it should be recognized for the affect it is—an angle into a subject but only one of many angles that affect the tonality of the interpretation it yields. Diana Fuss reminds us that the positive affects offer a fount of incitements for criticism, that "transference, love and deep attachment are not mere footnotes in psychoanalysis. They are bedrock theories—places where conflict and connection, agon and eros, are never far apart."[37] And as Sedgwick noted, even "paranoid reading" yields multiple affects; not only suspicion but the hope that in exposing the object for what it truly is, all will see the light the paranoid reader, no longer paranoid but wise all along, shines on its object of inquiry.[38] In this way, the paranoid reader is not far from the critic who takes glee in the moment, through its critical interrogations or problematizing, when "the object betrays itself."[39] And even that language is affectively encoded: betrayal is an emotion. But critics have become so accustomed to suspicion that we take such betrayal not as an affect but as a method. Objects do not betray themselves. Rather, the line of inquiry looks for betrayal: the critic looks to feel betrayed as the impetus for inquiry. Why do we indulge in the language of betrayal other than to conceal the fear that, lurking in the distance, the object will somehow betray us, and mock the love we feel compelled to convert into critical suspicion? Our affective investment in the critical act certainly must be more complex than this. Perhaps the first step toward a more affectively aware criticism is to cease converting hate into love but to acknowledge the dynamic interplay of such affects. To be aware of the manifold affects at work in the act of criticism would yield a criticism more aware of itself, more attuned to its affective registers, and more engaged with its subject. We become better critics when we engage with our affects.

And so what would the criticism I propose look like? First, it would have to engage with a range of affects. Even as she was saddened by the affects of his latter career, Torgovnick still found value in Trilling's definition of culture, one that incorporates the "hum and buzz of implication . . . the whole evanescent context in which statements are made . . . the half-uttered or unuttered, or unutterable expressions of value . . . the things that for good or bad draw the people of a culture together."[40] Notice how Trilling embeds the suspicions and implications of a culture within a "whole evanescent context" that hums and buzzes, how he attends to the evident as much as the implied, to the good along with the bad: the parts and the wholes that draw people together. Critique is limited when it cannot show the enthusiasm—its own hum and buzz—that foregrounds its endeavor; it is limited when it cannot show the hopes that motivate its writing in the first place. Criticism can show affection as much as astonishment, can show anger as much as admiration. By doing so, an affectively aware criticism can remedy what Sedgwick called the "unintentionally stultifying side effect" of the hermeneutics of suspicion, which "made it less rather than more possible to unpack the local, contingent relations between any given piece of knowledge and its narrative/epistemological entailments for the seeker, knower, or teller."[41] Consider how the hermeneutics of suspicion has affectively charged nationalism as a site of anti-intellectual nonsense. Doing so has only led to fewer venues of inquiry. And yet for the authors I have studied in this book, the nation has a rich, emotional meaning for them, which carries through in the rhetorical constructions of the nation they produce.

Thus secondly, to go beyond the limits of critique will require for Americanists, as Grossberg writes, that a new balance "be struck between the local detail and the national structures. The United States is neither New York nor Texas nor Main Street. It is, somehow, scattered among all of these."[42] Grossberg is suggesting a way of reading that is not so much like reading a novel but rather like "driving by the billboards that mark the system of interstate highways, county roads, and city streets that is the United States."[43] Reading between signs and signposts is not necessarily a way of "reading" in the way literary critics define the term. But to read between is to read the nation for the feelings that cross over between part and whole, to show how the nation gives meaning in ways that can be appreciated without resorting to the strong affects that dominate the hermeneutics of suspicion. To understand the nation, one must "travel" it affectively as much as "read" it critically. One must read for the messy experiential nature of the between, a process that the strong affects of the hermeneutics of suspicion can only miss. To answer the question I raised at the beginning of this book, theories of affect illuminate "the durability of nationalism . . . how deep is the human need for an ethnos of accessible proportions and how portentous are the affiliations people choose or are coerced into accepting. Not all nationalisms are alike."[44] That not all nationalisms are alike should open the door to studying them, but such a door is locked by the hermeneutics that declare it suspect.

Affects and the Horizon of Inquiry

Critics are too often baffled by a nationalism that their critical tools presume to be suspect. Trilling was himself of the generation of American writers who, as Susan Hegeman writes, found themselves torn between the uniqueness of the nation and its inability to develop a coherent, unifying cultural tradition. Even "though they were interested in the *possibility* of an authentic artistic tradition rooted in America . . . these writers were often insistent on the *failure* of the nation to produce a hospitable creative environment, precisely because the very idea of the American nation was itself sadly incoherent."[45] Yet the "very idea of the American nation" is not incoherent but overwhelming in its plurality and plenitude. Its affective complexity cannot be gauged through suspicion alone. As Anne Norton writes, Americans are "people of the text," a text that is by design, out of sync with the present of its participants, even as it aspires for communion with others.[46] It is not that the nation is incoherent as much as it is densely affective and synecdochical. The nation can only be seen through the relation between abstraction and particulars, parts and wholes. As I have explored throughout this book, synecdoches "stick" the nation together, primarily because of the affective valences of weak nationalism that synecdoche evokes, which cross over between expectation and reality, make the incoherent cohere, and construct an index of narratives.

Consider how openly the authors in my study express their vexations with the nation. The nation, by default, exceeds their grasp. Neither facts nor personal experience, nor any solitary critical approach, can capture a full portrait of the nation. Even early in *America*, Beauvoir concludes that America "will have to be discovered slowly; it will not let you devour it like a big piece of candy."[47] Steinbeck found in *Travels* that in his studying America, it "became huge beyond belief and impossible ever to cross."[48] Kuralt's admission that more could be said through the story of one man living in one house in one part of Arizona rather than through a story of the entire state suggests that a portrait of the entire nation would be an insurmountable task without tropes such as synecdoche. And in looking at the Michigan Avenue Bridge, Vowell found herself swept up in a "vortex," a force beyond her control.[49] Vowell's affective vortex is akin to the combination of love and hate Trilling saw as necessary for a writer to accept America. Yet Vowell seems more successful in navigating these feelings because she is able to embrace what Trilling ambivalently denied. Examining it in this way, perhaps an archive of the type I have presented is little different from Americanist criticism after all. But where criticism is often exclusively reliant on aloofness, againstness, suspicion, and superiority, perhaps these texts can encourage us to explore the wider range of affective tonalities of the imagined community of criticism.

Realizing the affects of weak nationalism expands the horizon of inquiry: the transient yet meaningful moods one feels toward the nation, the curiosity the nation evokes and the discontent it leaves us with, the hopefulness of parts fitting into a national whole, and the bind between incredulity and credulity that connects—and disconnects—us from the nation. The authors I have studied remind us through their work that "our critical task is not iconoclastic, tearing away the veil of empire to reveal the truth of its horrors; rather it is to stretch the image surface and understand our own investments in its workings."[50] At present, there are 318 million Americans. Each is an affected reader in an imagined community. Each has a theory of the nation and each feels a plentitude of affects about it. It is the miracle of the nation that every American does so. Critics have not given much thought to nationalism's weak affects, to the point that criticism hardly sees weak nationalism at all. Yet critics must become more aware of the tapestry of these attachments in the work of the nation and in their own work as well, lest we continue to miss that which is urgently in need of our interpretation.

SOURCE ACKNOWLEDGMENTS

Portions of chapter 2 first appeared as "'Macrocosm of Microcosm Me': Steinbeck's *Travels with Charley*" (*Literature Interpretation Theory* 16, no. 3 [2005] 311–32, reprinted by permission of Taylor & Francis, http://www.tandfonline.com) and as "The Discontents of Steinbeck's *America and Americans*" (*Steinbeck Review* 13, no. 1 [2016]: 36–49, reprinted by permission of the Pennsylvania State University Press).

Excerpts from Jane Smiley's "The Unteachable Ignorance of the Red States" appear by permission of *Slate*.

Excerpts from Simone de Beauvoir's *America Day by Day* (Berkeley: University of California Press, 1999) appear by permission of University of California Press.

Excerpts from the Charles Kuralt Collection, Southern Historical Collection, The Wilson Library, University of North Carolina at Chapel Hill, appear by permission of CBS News.

Excerpts from Sarah Vowell's *Lafayette in the Somewhat United States* (New York: Riverhead, 2015) and *The Wordy Shipmates* (New York: Riverhead, 2008) appear by permission of Penguin Random House.

Excerpts from Sarah Vowell's *The Partly Cloudy Patriot* (New York: Simon and Schuster, 2002) and *Take the Cannoli* (New York: Simon and Schuster, 2000) appear by permission of Simon and Schuster.

NOTES

INTRODUCTION

1. Smiley, "Unteachable Ignorance."
2. Smiley, "Unteachable Ignorance."
3. Smiley, "Unteachable Ignorance."
4. Smiley, "Unteachable Ignorance."
5. Smiley, "Unteachable Ignorance."
6. Smiley, "Unteachable Ignorance."
7. Ngai, *Ugly Feelings*, 3.
8. Obama, "Reclaiming the Promise," 625.
9. Here Smiley reminds us, as Sean McCann has noted, of a rich tradition of writers who "aspire to the task envisioned by the theorists of presidential government, but traduced by actual politicians" (*Pinnacle*, 22).
10. Geertz, *Interpretation of Cultures*, 21–22.
11. Igo, *Averaged American*, 178.
12. Doctorow, "False Documents," 216.
13. As Slavoj Žižek writes, "A nation exists only as long as its specific enjoyment continues to be materialized in a set of social practices and transmitted through national myths that structure these practices" (*Tarrying*, 202).
14. Berlant, *Queen of America*, 48.
15. Tomkins, *Affect-Imagery-Consciousness*, 2:322.
16. Tomkins, *Affect-Imagery-Consciousness*, 2:312.
17. Tomkins, *Affect-Imagery-Consciousness*, 2:324.

18. Recent interventions in affect theory have affirmed the central role of reading: consider Eugenie Brinkema's insistence that "*it is only because one must read for it that affect has any force at all*" (*Forms*, 38, italics in original). As I read the texts in this book for their synecdochical affectivity, I participate in a form of reading that, similar to Brinkema's argument, "is also an attempt to seize the passions of affect studies for textual interpretation and close reading" (*Forms*, xvi).
19. Flatley, *Affective Mapping*, 4.
20. Massumi, "Navigating Movements," 214.
21. Billig, *Banal Nationalism*, 5.
22. Spivak, *Nationalism and the Imagination*, 15.
23. Ignatieff qtd. in Billig, *Banal Nationalism*, 46.
24. For example, John Carlos Rowe writes: "To speak or write about the United States in any unified way was always already a fiction for the poststructuralists, both on the basis of the illusion of the signified operating in any representational act and in the more particular case of the fiction of national consensus. Given its explicitly multicultural and transnational composition and the rapid national legitimation demanded by its revolutionary origins, the United States calls particular, albeit not unique, attention to the fabricated, imaginary qualities of its national existence" (*New American Studies*, xix). I take no issue with the claim that narratives of national consensus frequently and unfortunately sidestep the complexities of the nation's "multicultural and transnational composition." But it is a disciplinary issue, a tendency in American literary and cultural criticism to not take narratives like the ones that are the focus of this book seriously, to dismiss texts that seek to answer the question "What is America?" as "always already a fiction." In its doing so, this example illuminates what criticism too readily dismisses, the affective power of the "fabrication" behind such narratives, as criticism presumes their "imaginary qualities" to be mere fiction. The texts in my archive should remind us that these are neither mere fictions nor demonstrations of hot nationalism exclusively.
25. Billig, *Banal Nationalism*, 93.
26. Macridis and Hulliung, *Contemporary Political Ideologies*, 192.
27. Billig, *Banal Nationalism*, 43.
28. Billig, *Banal Nationalism*, 48.
29. Billig, *Banal Nationalism*, 55.
30. Billig, *Banal Nationalism*, 56.
31. Billig, *Banal Nationalism*, 49.
32. Billig, *Banal Nationalism*, 56.
33. Fox and Miller-Idriss, "Everyday Nationhood," 549.
34. Fox and Miller-Idriss, "Everyday Nationhood," 540.

35. Sutherland, *Nationalism*, 72.
36. Anderson, *Imagined Communities*, 6.
37. Anderson, *Imagined Communities*, 6.
38. For a compendium of Tomkins's writing on this subject, see Sedgwick and Frank, *Shame and Its Sisters*, 81–105.
39. Bhabha, "DissemiNation," 297. And as Bhabha explains, such work is twofold. The nation is indeed pedagogical in how it teaches us to read its parts for wholes, turning scraps and patches into evidence of a national culture; it is indeed performative in how the resulting national narrative repeats such readings almost endlessly and across the spectrum of affects both weak and strong.
40. Clifford, "Introduction: Partial Truths," 6.
41. Hartsock, *American Literary Journalism*, 205.
42. Root, "Naming Nonfiction," 243.
43. Root, "Naming Nonfiction," 247.
44. Hartsock, *American Literary Journalism*, 187.
45. Schaub, *American Fiction in the Cold War*, 50.
46. Schaub, *American Fiction in the Cold War*, 50.
47. Lionel Trilling qtd. in Hutner, *What America Read*, 298.
48. Following a critical trajectory separate from Schaub's, Linda Wagner-Martin writes that Leslie Fielder's *Love and Death in the American Novel* similarly "solidified a movement that had been previously unacknowledged—that United States fiction was becoming the dominant genre, at the expense of poetry, drama, and non-fiction" (*History*, 5).
49. Wolfe, "New Journalism," 7.
50. Wolfe, "New Journalism," 17.
51. Wolfe, "New Journalism," 17.
52. Gornick, *The Situation and the Story*, 7.
53. di Leonardo, *Exotics at Home*, 82.
54. Donald Pease writes, "The national narrative sustains its coherence by transforming internal divisions into the symbolic demand that the subjects conscripted within its narrativity misrecognize the figures it excludes as simulacra of themselves. But when these figures surge up at these internal divides, as unintegrated externalities, they expose national identity as an artifact rather than as a tacit assumption, a purely contingent social construction rather than a meta-social universal" ("National Identities," 5). The issue is how the national narrative sustains its coherence through the tropes that allow the narrative to cohere. Coherence is the keyword: not that national narratives achieve rigorous, unified explanation—the logical sense of coherence—but that these narratives cohere by unifying, by sticking together signs—an affective coherence—through their synecdochical construction.

55. Pease, "National Identities," 5.
56. Berlant, *Queen of America*, 12.
57. Lutz, *Unnatural Emotions*, 4.
58. My use of this particular word is inspired by Moi, *Simone de Beauvoir*, 267.
59. See Tomkins, *Affect-Imagery-Consciousness*, 1:111–22 and 2:262–72.
60. Grossberg, "Affect's Future," 316. Also see Ahmed, *Politics*, 10.
61. Highmore, "Introduction: Questioning Everyday Life," 6, and Svendsen, "Moods," 422.
62. As Jonathan Flatley notes, "affects require objects, and, in the moment of attaching to an object or happening in the object, also take one's being outside of one's subjectivity" (*Affective Mapping*, 19).
63. Flatley, *Affective Mapping*, 19.
64. Seigworth and Gregg, "Inventory of Shimmers," 6. For additional context, see Flatley, *Affective Mapping*, 202, and Felski and Fraiman, "Introduction: In the Mood," vi. Theories of affect are typically separated into three broad domains: a pragmatic model that "conceives of affect as a set of embodied practices that produce visible conduct as an outer lining," a psychoanalytical model that examines affects as "primarily vehicles or manifestations of the underlying libidinal drive," and a third, naturalist model that examines affect's "capacities through interaction in a world which is constantly becoming" (Thrift, "Intensities of Feeling," 60–61).
65. Ahmed, *Politics*, 207–10.
66. Seigworth and Gregg, "Inventory of Shimmers," 1.
67. Seigworth and Gregg, "Inventory of Shimmers," 6–9.
68. Ahmed, *Politics*, 1–19.
69. Ngai, *Ugly Feelings*, 1.
70. Ngai, *Ugly Feelings*, 27.
71. Ngai, *Ugly Feelings*, 27.
72. According to Lawrence Grossberg, affects are "a-signifying (although they can produce signification), non-individualized (although they do produce individualities), non-representational (although they can produce representational forms), and non-conscious (although they produce various forms of consciousness)" (*Cultural Studies*, 193).
73. Going further, Ngai distinguishes that "affects are *less* formed and structured than emotions, but not lacking form or structure altogether; *less* 'sociolinguistically fixed,' but by no means code-free or meaningless; *less* 'organized in response to our interpretation of situations,' but by no means entirely devoid of organization or diagnostic powers" (*Ugly Feelings*, 27). What the critical reading of affects requires, then, is an awareness that affects are potentialities that may or may not happen, that they are promises without

guarantees. Such individuations and potentialities require a different variety of criticism, and a different conception of what constitutes "critical reading" to accommodate them.

74. Grossberg, *Dancing*, 128.
75. Castiglia, *Hope*, 42.
76. Anker and Felski, introduction, 4.
77. Anker and Felski, introduction, 8.
78. Anker and Felski, introduction, 15.
79. Best and Marcus, "Surface Reading," 5–6.
80. Jameson, *Postmodernism*, 15–16.
81. Jameson, *Postmodernism*, 263.
82. As Ngai has noted of the work of Ed Ruscha and John Baldessari, postmodern artists make their currency by trafficking in banality, which is not banal but an intense questioning of the legitimacy of aesthetics (see *Categories*, 147–73).
83. Felski, *Critique*, 56.
84. Rubenstein, *President*, 29.
85. See Wald, *Constituting Americans*, 1–13.
86. "The difference between metaphor and metonymy is the difference between making and seeing: making metaphors, seeing metonymies. On the one hand, a metaphor is something we make; it wasn't there before we made it; we brought it into being. On the other hand, a metonymy is something we see; we didn't make it up; it was already there" (Berger, *Figures*, 4). Synecdoche, as a subset of metonymy, is separate from metaphor because "Metaphors rhetorically challenge the similarity they grammatically claim to establish, in order to feature their departures from preexisting states of affairs. Metonymies present themselves as analogies that articulate or reaffirm preexisting states of affairs" (Berger, *Figures*, 12). To put it another way, metaphors make something up: they invent. Metonymies express the actual: they imagine. "Metonymy aspires only to emphasize or articulate the network of relations and substances of which the objects of literal reference are part" (Berger, *Figures*, 42).
87. Burke, *A Grammar of Motives*, 507.
88. Burke, *A Grammar of Motives*, 508.
89. Tell, "Burke's Encounter," 45.
90. And though as a critic he found it vulgar, Ransom employed synecdoche with effectiveness in his poetry. Randall Jarrell praised Ransom's use of the trope, writing that in his "best poems every part is subordinated to the whole, and the whole is accomplished with astonishing exactness and thoroughness" (*No Other*, 240).
91. As Michael Szalay has noted, American political parties rely on metaphor to generate "figurative registers of party identity" that generate "central

alliances" among diverse interparty factions and encourage an identification between party nominees and voters "on a visceral level" (*Hip Figures*, 16).

92. Such a tradition continues in two contemporary popular handbooks to literary terms. "To be clear," the authors of one such handbook write, "a good synecdoche ought to be based on an *important* part of the whole and, usually, the part standing for the whole ought to be directly associated with the subject under discussion" (Harman and Holman, *Handbook*, 510). Another handbook still includes terminology not used since the days of I. A. Richards. "In synecdoche, the *vehicle* (the image used to represent something else) is part of the *tenor* (the thing being represented) or vice versa. Synecdoche is distinguished from metonymy, a trope in which one thing is represented by another that is commonly and often physically associated with it" (Murfin and Ray, *Glossary*, 508, italics mine).

93. Tell, "Burke's Encounter," 58.
94. Burke, *A Grammar of Motives*, 508–9.
95. Of metaphor in general, Paul de Man wrote, "Metaphor gives itself the totality which it then claims to define, but it is in fact the tautology of its own position. The discourse of simple ideas is figural discourse or translation and, as such, creates the fallacious illusion of definition" ("Metaphor" 15). And of metonymy in particular, Gérard Genette wrote, "We see that at the limit all metonymy is convertible to synecdoche by appealing to the higher ensemble, and all synecdoche into metonymy through recourse to the relation between the constituent parts" (qtd. in Rubenstein, *President*, 30).
96. Matus, "Proxy and Proximity," 310.
97. Flatley, *Affective Mapping*, 16.
98. Ahmed, *Politics*, 10.
99. Ahmed, *Politics*, 10.
100. Ahmed, *Politics*, 194.
101. Ahmed, *Politics*, 13.
102. Ngai, *Ugly Feelings*, 3.
103. Illouz, *Cold Intimacies*, 3.
104. Lodge, *Modes*, 76.
105. Certeau, *Everyday Life*, 101.
106. Sutherland, *Nationalism*, 73.
107. After all, affects "dissolve the self-contained interiority of the individual and open it to new connections and recombinations" (Vermeulen, *Contemporary Literature*, 8).
108. Grossberg, *Cultural Studies*, 195.
109. Wald, *Constituting Americans*, 299.
110. Wall, *Inventing*, 290.

111. George Yancy and Judith Butler, "What's Wrong with All Lives Matter?," *New York Times,* January 12, 2015. https://opinionator.blogs.nytimes.com/2015/01/12/whats-wrong-with-all-lives-matter.
112. Yancy and Butler, "What's Wrong."
113. Yancy and Butler, "What's Wrong."

1. MOODINESS

1. Alice Kaplan in Cotkin, *Existential America,* 92; Cotkin, *Existential America,* 100.
2. Marks, "America Day by Day," 381.
3. Henri Peyre, "Bars, Slums, Hats and Attitudes," *New York Times,* January 3, 1954, BR5.
4. D. Trilling, "America," 210.
5. McCarthy, "Gulliver," 240.
6. Totten, "Reel to Real," 146.
7. Beauvoir, *America,* 15. As Franny Nudelman writes, McCarthy would find herself at a similar impasse in technique, especially in her reportage of the Vietnam War, wherein she abandoned "reportorial omniscience" and pursued "a painful form of self-knowledge in its stead," moving away from "detached commentary to disorienting immersion" ("Marked for Demolition," 364).
8. Beauvoir, *America,* 178.
9. Teale, "Ambiguous Satisfaction," 472.
10. Moi, *Simone de Beauvoir,* 95.
11. Moran, *Reading the Everyday,* 1.
12. Blanchot, *Infinite Conversation,* 238.
13. It joins critics like Margaret A. Simons, who has noted the role of the book, particularly Beauvoir's depiction of American race relations, in providing a theoretical model that both "support[s] the struggle against racism and construct[s] the theoretical foundations of radical feminism" (*Beauvoir,* 183). And it joins critics like Alexander Ruch, who envisions the text as a contribution toward Beauvoir's philosophical project, and Diane Rubenstein, who has reexamined the text as a contribution to both travel narrative and theory.
14. Highmore, "Introduction: Questioning Everyday Life," 1.
15. Rubenstein, "Rochester."
16. Taussig, *Nervous System,* 142. Similarly, Chiara Briganti writes, "For if the shape of the day may be a microcosm of a life, the assumption is also that in fact it isn't—a day will be followed by another day; one does not write the word 'end' at the end of the day" ("Mundane," 162).
17. Bhabha, introduction to *Nation and Narration,* 3.
18. Heidegger, *Metaphysics,* 67.
19. Heidegger, *Metaphysics,* 67–68.

20. Flatley, *Affective Mapping*, 22.
21. Felski and Fraiman, "Introduction: In the Mood" v.
22. Felski and Fraiman, "Introduction: In the Mood," vi.
23. Felski and Fraiman, "Introduction: In the Mood," vi.
24. Felski and Fraiman, "Introduction: In the Mood," vi.
25. Felski and Fraiman, "Introduction: In the Mood," vii.
26. Highmore and Taylor, "Mood Work," 6. As such, moods are individual as much as they are social; they are personal as much as they are political. This is why, as Flatley writes, "any kind of political project must have the 'making and using' of mood as part and parcel of the project. . . . Collective action is impossible if people are not, so to speak, *in the mood*" (*Affective Mapping*, 23, italics in original).
27. *Oxford English Dictionary*, 3rd ed. (2002), s.v. "mood, n.1."
28. Highmore and Taylor, "Mood Work," 9.
29. Felski and Fraiman, "Introduction: In the Mood," v.
30. Heidegger, *Being and Time*, 23.
31. Heidegger, *Being and Time*, 230.
32. Moi, *Simone de Beauvoir*, 267.
33. Heidegger, *Metaphysics*, 67.
34. Flatley, *Affective Mapping*, 21.
35. Flatley, *Affective Mapping*, 23.
36. Charles Guignon qtd. in Highmore and Taylor, "Mood Work," 9.
37. Flatley, *Affective Mapping*, 19.
38. Moi, *Simone de Beauvoir*, 267.
39. Beauvoir, *America*, xviii.
40. Beauvoir, *America*, xviii.
41. Beauvoir, *America*, xviii.
42. Beauvoir, *America*, xviii.
43. Beauvoir, *Transatlantic*, 26.
44. Certeau, *Everyday Life*, xxi.
45. Certeau, *Everyday Life*, xxi.
46. Taussig, *Nervous System*, 141.
47. Beauvoir, *America*, 5.
48. Beauvoir, *America*, 5.
49. Deutscher, *Philosophy*, 71.
50. Beauvoir, *America*, 10.
51. Beauvoir, *America*, 10.
52. Moi, *Simone de Beauvoir*, 267.
53. Svendsen, "Moods," 422.
54. Sartre in Gobeil, "Sartre Talks," in Marks, *Essays*, 17–18.

55. Moi, *Simone de Beauvoir*, 267.
56. Felski and Fraiman, "Introduction: In the Mood," vi.
57. Beauvoir, *America*, 18.
58. Beauvoir, *America*, 19.
59. Beauvoir, *America*, 19.
60. Beauvoir, *America*, 19.
61. Beauvoir, *America*, 19.
62. Beauvoir, *America*, 69.
63. Mathy, *Extrême-Occident*, 46.
64. Mathy, *Extrême-Occident*, 47.
65. Beauvoir, *America*, 24.
66. Moi, *Simone de Beauvoir*, 87.
67. Moi, *Simone de Beauvoir*, 86.
68. Moi, *Simone de Beauvoir*, 87.
69. Ngai, *Ugly Feelings*, 42.
70. Ngai, *Ugly Feelings*, 42.
71. Beauvoir, *America*, 93.
72. Beauvoir, *America*, 93.
73. Beauvoir, *America*, 67.
74. Beauvoir, *America*, 67.
75. Beauvoir, *America*, 67.
76. Certeau, *Everyday Life*, 101.
77. Highmore, "Introduction: Questioning Everyday Life," 15.
78. Teale, "Ambiguous Satisfaction," 475.
79. Beauvoir, *America*, 384.
80. Wall, *Inventing*, 120.
81. Beauvoir, *America*, 384–85.
82. Ruch, "Beauvoir-in-America," 115.
83. Beauvoir, *America*, 389.
84. Beauvoir, *America*, 389.
85. Beauvoir, *America*, 389.
86. Beauvoir, *America*, 389.
87. Much like Beauvoir found in departing New York, in trying to capture the complexities and contradictions of the North Vietnamese, McCarthy would find in *Hanoi* a "self-criticism to the point of" personal and narrative "paralysis" (Nudelman, "Marked for Demolition," 383).
88. Ruch, "Beauvoir-in-America," 123.
89. Beauvoir, *America*, 390.
90. Moi, *Simone de Beauvoir*, 208.
91. Beauvoir, *America*, 390.

92. "America with Preconceptions," 118.
93. "America with Preconceptions," 118.
94. "America with Preconceptions," 118.
95. Hutner, *What America Read*, 234.
96. D. Trilling, "America," 208–9.
97. Henri Peyre, "Bars, Slums, Hats and Attitudes," *New York Times*, January 3, 1954, BR5.
98. D. Trilling, "America," 208, 210.
99. D. Trilling, "America," 211.
100. D. Trilling, "America," 211.
101. D. Trilling, "America," 211.
102. D. Trilling, "America," 211.
103. Ngai, *Ugly Feelings*, 43.
104. Ngai, *Ugly Feelings*, 43.
105. Ngai, *Ugly Feelings*, 88.
106. See Bhabha, "DissemiNation," 297.
107. Ahmed, *Politics*, 44.
108. Ahmed, *Politics*, 43.
109. See Ngai, *Ugly Feelings*, 76–77.
110. Billig, *Banal Nationalism*, 44.
111. Moi, *Simone de Beauvoir*, 86.
112. Beauvoir, *America*, 40.
113. D. Trilling, "America," 216.
114. For the *Partisan Review* crowd of the time, one was either pro-American or pro-Soviet other, which configured the tonal veracity of their critique: William Phillips recalls Beauvoir's book as possessing "pro-Soviet and anti-American attitudes," making it clear that one implies the other without exception (*Partisan*, 124).
115. D. Trilling, "America," 216–17.
116. D. Trilling, "America," 217.
117. Dolan, *Allegories*, 61.
118. Dolan, *Allegories*, 62.
119. Beauvoir, *America*, 389.
120. See Certeau, *Everyday Life*, xxi.
121. Bhabha, "Introduction," 3.
122. Anderson, *Imagined Communities*, 7.
123. Blanchot, *Infinite Conversation*, 238.
124. Brennan, "National Longing," 51.
125. Taussig, *Nervous System*, 141.

2. CURIOSITY

1. Orville Prescott, "Books of the Times," *New York Times*, June 27, 1962, n.p.
2. *Time*, August 10, 1962, 70.
3. Cooke, "Books," 500; Scherman, "Things and People," 503.
4. Parini, introduction to *Travels*, xix.
5. Shillinglaw and Benson, "America and Americans," in *Americans*, 313.
6. Arthur Miller in Benson, *John Steinbeck*, 702.
7. Steinbeck, *Travels*, 95.
8. Steinbeck, *Americans*, 320.
9. Steinbeck, *Travels*, 151.
10. Steinbeck, *Americans*, 392.
11. Nadel, *Containment*, 20.
12. See Ngai, *Categories*, 112–13.
13. *Oxford English Dictionary*, 2nd ed. (1989), s.v. "curiosity."
14. Tomkins, *Affect-Imagery-Consciousness*, 1:337.
15. Tomkins, *Affect-Imagery-Consciousness*, 1:354.
16. Benedict, *Curiosity*, 254.
17. Benedict, *Curiosity*, 3.
18. Benedict, *Curiosity*, 246.
19. Benedict, *Curiosity*, 253.
20. Benedict, *Curiosity*, 254.
21. Manguel, *Curiosity*, 13.
22. Manguel, *Curiosity*, 13.
23. Scherman, "Things and People," 503.
24. Steinbeck, *Travels*, 5.
25. Steinbeck, *Americans*, 317.
26. Steinbeck, *Travels*, 5, 87.
27. Benedict, *Curiosity*, 245.
28. Ngai, *Categories*, 112.
29. Ngai, *Categories*, 169.
30. Sutherland, *Nationalism*, 73.
31. Steinbeck, *Travels*, 62.
32. Steinbeck, *Americans*, 331.
33. Hollinger, "Circle of 'We,'" 317.
34. Rodgers, *Age of Fracture*, 4–5.
35. Hollinger, "Circle of 'We,'" 317.
36. Tomkins, *Affect-Imagery-Consciousness*, 1:22.
37. Freud, *Leonardo*, 74.
38. Ross Posnock writes of the affect that so drove theorists of modernity like William and Henry James, "Curiosity represents the 'release' that does not

fit. . . . Its libidinal energy escapes the tyranny" of its culture's embedded "metaphysical dualisms" (*Trial*, 50).

39. Freud, *Leonardo*, 75.
40. Tomkins, *Affect-Imagery-Consciousness*, 1:354.
41. Igo, *Averaged American*, 178.
42. Igo, *Averaged American*, 143.
43. Steinbeck, *Travels*, 59–60.
44. Steinbeck, *Travels*, 5.
45. Brooks, *Body Work*, 7.
46. Brooks, *Body Work*, 96.
47. Steinbeck, *Travels*, 5.
48. Steinbeck, *Travels*, 20.
49. Roof, *Come as You Are*, xiv.
50. Roof, *Come as You Are*, 7.
51. Roof, *Come as You Are*, xv.
52. Steinbeck, *Travels*, 76.
53. Steinbeck, *Travels*, 5.
54. Steinbeck, *Travels*, 74.
55. Steinbeck, *Travels*, 78.
56. Steinbeck, *Travels*, 77.
57. Fox, "Edges," 41.
58. Steinbeck, *Travels*, 78.
59. Steinbeck, *Travels*, 196.
60. Steinbeck, *Travels*, 177.
61. Anderson, *Imagined Communities*, 6.
62. Steinbeck, *Travels*, 95.
63. Steinbeck, *Travels*, 95.
64. Steinbeck, *Travels*, 8.
65. Steinbeck, *Travels*, 10.
66. Clifford, *Predicament of Culture*, 38.
67. Roof, *Come as You Are*, 150.
68. Berlant, *Anatomy*, 4.
69. Steinbeck, *Travels*, 90.
70. Steinbeck, *Travels*, 90.
71. Steinbeck, *Travels*, 151.
72. Steinbeck, *Travels*, 90.
73. Steinbeck, *Travels*, 90.
74. Clifford, *Predicament of Culture*, 37.
75. Steinbeck, *Travels*, 90.
76. Steinbeck, *Travels*, 90.

77. Steinbeck, *Travels*, 90.
78. Steinbeck, *Travels*, 91.
79. Steinbeck, *Travels*, 91.
80. Steinbeck, *Travels*, 91.
81. Steinbeck, *Travels*, 91.
82. Steinbeck, *Travels*, 91.
83. Steinbeck, *Travels*, 91.
84. Steinbeck, *Travels*, 91–92.
85. Roof, *Come as You Are*, 12.
86. Rabinow, *Reflections*, 26.
87. Benedict, *Curiosity*, 245.
88. Anderson, *Imagined Communities*, 7.
89. Anderson, *Imagined Communities*, 6.
90. Anderson, *Imagined Communities*, 26.
91. Manguel, *Curiosity*, 37.
92. Steinbeck, *Letters*, 702–703.
93. Steinbeck, *Americans*, 392.
94. Dolan, *Allegories*, 64.
95. Nadel, *Containment*, 20.
96. Benson, *John Steinbeck*, 955.
97. Benson, *John Steinbeck*, 955.
98. Steinbeck, *Letters*, 807.
99. Steinbeck, *Americans*, 115.
100. Steinbeck, *Americans*, 317.
101. Steinbeck, *Americans*, 318.
102. Steinbeck, *Americans*, 318.
103. Patterson, *Eve*, xii.
104. Medovoi, *Rebels*, 50.
105. Igo, *Averaged American*, 287.
106. Steinbeck, *Americans*, 319.
107. Steinbeck, *Americans*, 319.
108. Steinbeck, *Americans*, 320.
109. Steinbeck, *Americans*, 320.
110. Steinbeck, *Americans*, 320.
111. Steinbeck, *Americans*, 320–21.
112. Clifford, *Predicament of Culture*, 38.
113. Roof, *Come as You Are*, xv.
114. Steinbeck, *Travels*, 186.
115. Steinbeck, *Americans*, 330–31.
116. Steinbeck, *Americans*, 331.

117. Steinbeck, *Americans*, 335.
118. Steinbeck, *Americans*, 336.
119. Nadel, *Containment*, 20.
120. Steinbeck, *Americans*, 338.
121. Steinbeck, *Americans*, 334.
122. Steinbeck, *Americans*, 337.
123. Steinbeck, *Americans*, 338.
124. Steinbeck, *Americans*, 338.
125. Benson, *John Steinbeck*, 988.
126. Steinbeck, *Letters*, 702.
127. Steinbeck, *Americans*, 353, 352.
128. Steinbeck, *Americans*, 356.
129. Steinbeck, *Americans*, 357.
130. Steinbeck, *Americans*, 356, 335.
131. Wall, *Inventing*, 11.
132. Wall, *Inventing*, 12.
133. Farber, *Great Dreams*, 64.
134. See Farber, *Great Dreams*, 57–64.
135. Steinbeck, *Americans*, 369.
136. Steinbeck, *Americans*, 374.
137. Steinbeck, *Americans*, 375.
138. Steinbeck, *Americans*, 392.
139. Steinbeck, *Americans*, 392.
140. Ngai, *Categories*, 112.
141. Steinbeck, *Americans*, 394.
142. Steinbeck, *Americans*, 397.
143. Steinbeck, *Americans*, 399.
144. Steinbeck, *Americans*, 399.
145. Eisenhower qtd. in Patterson, *Eve*, xiv.
146. Gladstein, *Americans*, 231.
147. Roof, *Come as You Are*, 7.
148. Steinbeck, *Americans*, 399–400.
149. Steinbeck, *Americans*, 400.
150. Roof, *Come as You Are*, 12.
151. Steinbeck, *Travels*, 151.
152. Steinbeck, *Americans*, 400.
153. Steinbeck, *Americans*, 400.
154. Steinbeck, *Americans*, 401.
155. Steinbeck, *Americans*, 402.
156. Steinbeck, *Americans*, 402.

157. Steinbeck, *Americans*, 404.
158. Heavilin, "Joseph Addison," 49.
159. Shillinglaw and Benson, "America and Americans," in Steinbeck, *Americans*, 313.
160. This would become most evident in his writing on the Vietnam War, in which Steinbeck's perceptions of gallantry in *Americans* may have led him to perceive gallantry where there was, in actuality, unresolvable turmoil. Steinbeck would come to see, "rather perversely" as Parini suggests, "the war in Vietnam as an opportunity for young Americans to give something back to their country, to make a sacrifice" (*Steinbeck*, 464).
161. Brinkley, "Illusion of Unity," 72.
162. Worden, "Neoliberal Style," 809.
163. Worden, "Neoliberal Style," 815–16.
164. Worden, "Neoliberal Style," 801.
165. French, *Nonfiction Revisited*, 110.
166. Bhabha, "DissemiNation," 300.
167. Steinbeck, *Americans*, 317.

3. HOPEFULNESS

1. Kuralt qtd. in V. R. Bailey, "Kuralt: Study," 101.
2. Kuralt qtd. in V. R. Bailey, "Kuralt: Study," 101.
3. Kuralt qtd. in V. R. Bailey, "Kuralt: Study," 102.
4. Kuralt qtd. in V. R. Bailey, "Kuralt: Study," 103.
5. Kuralt qtd. in V. R. Bailey, "Kuralt: Study," 104.
6. Michael Arlen qtd. in Pach, "Tet on TV," 59.
7. Tolbert, "*On the Road*: Analysis," 35.
8. Gates, *Air Time*, 177.
9. Tuchman, *Making News*, 98.
10. Gans, *Deciding What's News*, 156.
11. Epstein, *News from Nowhere*, 174. Each of the networks catered to nostalgia and its attendant affects, particularly in moments of crisis, throughout the seventies. As Natasha Zaretsky writes, competitor network NBC aired a lengthy essay on its January 10, 1974, nightly news broadcast—at the height of the oil embargo—on the Amish, who were depicted not as "a cultural anomaly" for their values that eschew contemporary technology but as having a "distinct advantage over middle-class Americans because of their commitment to moderation and restraint" (*No Direction Home*, 93–94).
12. Himmelstein, "Television News," 277.
13. Himmelstein, "Television News," 277.
14. Kuralt, *Road*, 282.
15. Ehrlich, "Myth," 334.

16. Ehrlich, "Myth," 334.
17. "Newscasting: Travels with Charley," 49.
18. Rosenberg qtd. in Ehrlich, "Myth," 327.
19. Tolbert, "*On the Road*: Analysis," 88.
20. Zaretsky, *No Direction Home*, 2.
21. Bailey and Farber, introduction to *America*, 4.
22. Bailey and Farber, introduction to *America*, 1–2.
23. Cowie, *Stayin' Alive*, 18.
24. Zaretsky, *No Direction Home*, 225.
25. Grattan, *Hope Isn't Stupid*, 1.
26. Lingis, "Murmurs of Life," 23.
27. Ahmed, *Happiness*, 181.
28. Anderson, "Becoming," 742.
29. Ahmed, *Happiness*, 272.
30. Bloch, *Principle of Hope*, 74.
31. Anderson, "Becoming," 744.
32. Eagleton, *Hope without Optimism*, 39.
33. Crapanzano, "Hope," 17.
34. Lingis, "Murmurs of Life," 23.
35. Massumi, "Navigating Movements," 211.
36. Eagleton, *Hope without Optimism*, 4.
37. Berlant, *Cruel Optimism*, 1.
38. Berlant, *Cruel Optimism*, 24.
39. *Oxford English Dictionary*, 2nd ed. (1989), s.v. "hopefulness."
40. Crapanzano, "Hope," 27. Ernesto Laclau and Chantal Mouffe also find that hope exists in the "dialectic between the universal and the particular" ("Hope," 130). Borrowing from Laclau and Mouffe's conception of hope, Castiglia has argued that the nation is a similarly "empty signifier," which enables disparate groups to converge under the umbrella of the nation (see *Hope*, 42–44).
41. Bloch, *Principle of Hope*, 3.
42. Anderson, *Imagined Communities*, 6.
43. That Kuralt was deemed "the last optimist at CBS" says much of how his "truth squad" colleagues perceived his work, as well as the discourse through which it could be seen, as mere optimism (Tolbert, "*On the Road*: Analysis," 88).
44. Taussig, "Carnival of the Senses," 45.
45. Castiglia, "Hope for Critique," 219.
46. Massumi, "Navigating Movements," 211.
47. Crapanzano, "Hope," 19.
48. Ahmed, *Politics*, 185.

49. Castiglia, "Hope for Critique," 217–18.
50. Berkowitz, *Something Happened*, 127.
51. Tolbert, "*On the Road*: Analysis," 37.
52. Nichols, *Representing Reality*, 4.
53. Fred Freed qtd. in Curtin, "Packaging Reality," 180.
54. Stam, "Television News," 29.
55. Salant in Epstein, *News from Nowhere*, ix.
56. Pach, "That's the Way It Was," 91.
57. Pach, "That's the Way It Was," 96–97.
58. Johnson, *Heartland TV*, 108.
59. Johnson, *Heartland TV*, 106.
60. Raphael, *Investigated Reporting*, 246.
61. Nichols, *Representing Reality*, 194.
62. Johnson, *Heartland TV*, 109.
63. Kuralt qtd. in Tolbert, "*On the Road*: Analysis," 20.
64. Kuralt, *Road*, 29.
65. Kuralt, *Road*, 154.
66. Berkowtiz, *Something Happened*, 177.
67. See Zaretsky, *No Direction Home*, 112.
68. Tolbert, "*On the Road*: Analysis," 101.
69. Tolbert, "*On the Road*: Analysis," 107.
70. Capozzola, "Celebrating the Bicentennial," 38.
71. Osman, "Decade of the Neighborhood," 110.
72. See Tolbert, "*On the Road*: Analysis," 73–74.
73. Tolbert, "*On the Road*: Analysis," 109.
74. Tolbert, "*On the Road*: Analysis," 90.
75. Cleary, "Early Radio Career," 230.
76. Kuralt qtd. in Cleary, "Early Radio Career," 230.
77. Kuralt, *Dateline*, 224.
78. Berkowtiz, *Something Happened*, 11.
79. Kuralt, *Dateline*, 23.
80. Kuralt, *Dateline*, 23.
81. Kuralt, *Dateline*, 23.
82. Kuralt, *Dateline*, 24.
83. Peter Carroll qtd. in Berkowitz, *Something Happened*, 6.
84. Kuralt, *Road*, 162–63.
85. Kuralt, *Road*, 162–63.
86. Kuralt, *Road*, 162–63.
87. Kuralt, *Road*, 164.
88. Kuralt, *Road*, 164.

89. Kuralt, *Road*, 164.
90. Kuralt in Tolbert, "*On the Road*: Analysis," 36.
91. Kuralt in Tolbert, "*On the Road*: Analysis," 36.
92. Kuralt in Tolbert, "*On the Road*: Analysis," 36.
93. Midgley qtd. in V. R. Bailey, "Kuralt: Study," 73.
94. Kuralt, "Roger," 1.
95. Kuralt, "Roger," 1.
96. Kuralt, "Roger," 1.
97. Kuralt, "Roger," 1.
98. Kuralt, "Roger," 1.
99. Kuralt, "Roger," 1.
100. Kuralt, "Roger," 1–2.
101. Kuralt, "Roger," 2.
102. Kuralt, "Roger," 2.
103. Kuralt, "Roger," 2.
104. Kuralt, "Roger," 2.
105. Kuralt, "Roger," 2.
106. Kuralt, "Roger," 2.
107. Kuralt, "Roger," 2.
108. Kuralt, "Roger," 2.
109. Crapanzano, "Hope," 19.
110. Isadore Bleckman qtd. in Grizzle, *Remembering*, 175.
111. Kuralt, "Roger," 2.
112. Crapanzano, "Hope," 18.
113. Kuralt, "Roger," 2.
114. Thus the segment reflects a broader cultural shift taking place in the early seventies from "disengagement rather than intervention" in the international scene (Walter Isaacson qtd. in Berkowitz, *Something Happened*, 32).
115. Capozzola, "Celebrating the Bicentennial," 38.
116. Kuralt qtd. in Ehrlich, "Myth," 333.
117. Kuralt, *Road*, 306.
118. Kuralt, *Road*, 306.
119. Kuralt, *Road*, 306.
120. Kuralt, *Road*, 306.
121. Kuralt, *Road*, 307.
122. Kuralt, *Road*, 307.
123. Kuralt, *Road*, 307.
124. Kuralt, *Road*, 307.
125. Kuralt, *Road*, 307.

126. Kuralt, *Road*, 308.
127. Kuralt, *Road*, 308.
128. Kuralt, *Road*, 308.
129. Kuralt, *Road*, 308.
130. Kuralt, *Road*, 308.
131. Kuralt, *Road*, 308–9.
132. Kuralt, *Road*, 309.
133. Kuralt, "Chandler Family," 2.
134. Ahmed, *Politics*, 184.
135. Kuralt, Chandler Family," 2–4.
136. Kuralt, *Road*, 306.
137. Kuralt, *Road*, 309.
138. Zaretsky, *No Direction Home*, 4.
139. Zaretsky, *No Direction Home*, 92.
140. Kuralt's insistence that we think of the Chandlers—an African American family—when we are told that the American family is a dying institution is an explicit refutation of neoconservative strategists' attempts throughout the seventies to link the African American family in particular to the problems of the welfare state as well as their attempts to heighten perceptions that "the family was under siege from destructive outside forces" (Zaretsky, *No Direction Home*, 231).
141. Zaretsky, *No Direction Home*, 144.
142. Zaretsky, *No Direction Home*, 163.
143. Kuralt, *Road*, 308.
144. Dawson, *Black Visions*, 91.
145. Guinn, *Road to Jonestown*, 442.
146. Ahmed, *Happiness*, 272.
147. Rodgers, *Age of Fracture*, 21.
148. Rodgers, *Age of Fracture*, 17.
149. James Reston qtd. in Farber, "Torch," 11.
150. Kuralt, *Road*, 262.
151. Kuralt, *Road*, 262.
152. Kuralt, *Road*, 262.
153. Kuralt, *Road*, 262.
154. Kuralt, *Road*, 263.
155. Kuralt, *Road*, 263.
156. Kuralt, *Road*, 263.
157. Kuralt, *Road*, 263.
158. Kuralt, *Road*, 263.

4. INCREDULITY

1. Vowell, *Patriot*, 95.
2. Vowell, *Patriot*, 96.
3. Vowell, *Patriot*, 96.
4. Vowell, *Patriot*, 96.
5. Vowell, *Cannoli*, 152.
6. Vowell, *Cannoli*, 103.
7. Vowell, *Shipmates*, 227.
8. Spitznagel, "Sarah Vowell."
9. Spitznagel, "Sarah Vowell."
10. Fisher, "Wonderful," 45.
11. Heffernan, "Mayflower Power," 11.
12. Heffernan, "Mayflower Power," 11.
13. Woloch, *Or Orwell*, ix.
14. Vowell, *Patriot*, 95.
15. Vowell, *Patriot*, 98.
16. Lyotard, *Postmodern*, xxiv.
17. Lyotard, "Narratives," 19.
18. See Tomkins, *Affect-Imagery-Consciousness*, 1:449.
19. Tomkins, *Affect-Imagery-Consciousness*, 1:450.
20. Tomkins, *Affect-Imagery-Consciousness*, 1:450.
21. Tomkins, *Affect-Imagery-Consciousness*, 1:450.
22. Lyotard, *Postmodern*, xxiv.
23. Stearns, *American Cool*, 289.
24. Stearns, *American Cool*, 296.
25. Hirschorn, "Quirked Around," 142.
26. Hirschorn, "Quirked Around," 142.
27. Ngai, *Categories*, 113. Consider by contrast, as Adam Kotsko has noticed, this decade's cultural fascination with awkwardness, especially in the broadcast-television and cable series like *The Office* and *Curb Your Enthusiasm*, in which characters try to grasp with "the often overwhelming and always unavoidable proximity of others" and their affects (*Awkwardness*, 87.)
28. Ngai, *Categories*, 169.
29. Vowell, *Assassination*, 2.
30. Vowell, *Assassination*, 139.
31. Konstantinou, *Cool Characters*, 203.
32. Sconce, "American 'Smart' Film," 350.
33. Sconce, "American 'Smart' Film," 350.
34. Sconce, "American 'Smart' Film," 352.
35. Sconce, "American 'Smart' Film," 352–53.

36. Ferguson, *Eighties People*, 133.
37. Mandel, *Disappear Here*, 23.
38. Schrecker, "Introduction," 5.
39. Woloch, *Or Orwell*, xiv.
40. Grossberg, "Reagan," 144–45.
41. Grossberg, "Reagan," 149.
42. Rodgers, *Age of Fracture*, 30.
43. Ferguson, *Eighties People*, 4.
44. Ferguson, *Eighties People*, 6.
45. Ferguson, *Eighties People*, 8.
46. Ferguson, *Eighties People*, 9.
47. Ortner, "Generation X," 423.
48. Ortner, "Generation X," 417.
49. In her ethnography of Gen Xers living in New Jersey, Ortner found that "extreme privilege . . . was also precisely the key to their anxieties. As the split opened up in the middle class, these kids felt like they were looking into the abyss, protected only by the safety net provided by their parents. On the one hand they felt very grateful. . . . On the other hand, they felt like they were in fact hanging over an abyss; hence the terror" ("Generation X," 429.)
50. Heffernan, "Mayflower Power," 11.
51. Woloch, *Or Orwell*, x.
52. Woloch, *Or Orwell*, x.
53. Woloch, *Or Orwell*, ix.
54. Tomkins, *Affect-Imagery-Consciousness*, 2:450.
55. Fox, "Edges," 35.
56. Vowell, *Cannoli*, 37.
57. Vowell, *Cannoli*, 43.
58. Vowell, *Cannoli*, 43.
59. Vowell, *Cannoli*, 44.
60. Vowell, *Cannoli*, 45.
61. Vowell, *Cannoli*, 47.
62. Vowell, *Cannoli*, 47–48.
63. Tomkins, *Affect-Imagery-Consciousness*, 2:450.
64. Berlant, *Queen*, 48.
65. Vowell, *Patriot*, 42.
66. Vowell, *Patriot*, 42.
67. Vowell, *Cannoli*, 95.
68. Vowell, *Cannoli*, 95.
69. Vowell, *Cannoli*, 95.
70. Vowell, *Cannoli*, 107.

71. Vowell, *Patriot*, 22.
72. Michael Szalay has noted that Clinton's affects were intertwined with "his neoliberal program," one that "disarticulated the twined imperatives of hip, its emphasis on individual liberty on the one hand and social justice on the other" (*Hip Figures*, 277). In doing so, Clinton valorized individual liberty as the expression of consumerism, all the while removing the teeth from the Great Society's programs committed to the welfare state.
73. Vowell, *Patriot*, 21.
74. Vowell, *Patriot*, 21.
75. Vowell, *Patriot*, 30.
76. McCann, *Pinnacle*, 18.
77. Vowell, *Patriot*, 31.
78. Vowell, *Patriot*, 123.
79. Vowell, *Patriot*, 40.
80. Vowell, *Patriot*, 80.
81. Vowell, *Patriot*, 80.
82. Vowell, *Patriot*, 82.
83. Vowell, *Patriot*, 82.
84. Ferguson, *Eighties People*, 9.
85. As Paolo Virno writes of the "sentiments of disenchantment," "it is no accident that the most brazen cynicism is accompanied by unrestrained sentimentalism. . . . Nothing is more common than the mass media technician who, after a hard day at work, goes off to the movies and cries" ("Ambivalence," 18). This is not hypocrisy as much as it is an attempt to affectively negotiate the incommensurability of a metanarrative hijacked by triumphalist affects. Vowell, much like Virno's worker, is one whose incredulity neither infringes on nor contradicts their credulity. Rather, they are dependent on one another: the representation of one leads to the other, as Vowell attempts to fashion herself out of the metanarratives she believes in and the contemporary politics she navigates. The incredulous can deploy their affective tactics for the sake of contrarianism during the day, yet at night, credulously sink into the very metanarratives they coolly disdained during the day.
86. Vowell, *Shipmates*, 63.
87. Fukuyama, "History," 18.
88. Fukuyama, "History," 18.
89. Fukuyama, "History," 18.
90. Didion, *Fixed Ideas*, 8–9.
91. Didion, *Fixed Ideas*, 8–9.
92. Rodgers, *Age of Fracture*, 258.
93. Masco, "Survival," 388.

94. Vowell, *Patriot*, 158.
95. Vowell, *Patriot*, 158.
96. Vowell, *Patriot*, 158.
97. Vowell, *Patriot*, 159.
98. Vowell, *Shipmates*, 1–2.
99. Vowell, *Shipmates*, 1–2.
100. Vowell, *Shipmates*, 52.
101. Winthrop qtd. in Vowell, *Shipmates*, 51.
102. Vowell, *Shipmates*, 52–53.
103. Vowell, *Shipmates*, 71.
104. Vowell, *Shipmates*, 72–73.
105. Prothero qtd. in Gardella, *American Civil Religion*, 59.
106. Vowell, *Lafayette*, 14.
107. Vowell, *Lafayette*, 25.
108. Vowell, *Lafayette*, 25.
109. Though there is no consensus on what constitutes American barbeque.
110. Vowell, *Lafayette*, 25.
111. Vowell, *Lafayette*, 165.
112. Vowell, *Lafayette*, 218–19.
113. Vowell, *Lafayette*, 262.
114. Vowell, *Lafayette*, 263.
115. Wainwright qtd. in Vowell, *Lafayette*, 267.
116. Wainwright qtd. in Vowell, *Lafayette*, 267.
117. Vowell, *Lafayette*, 266.
118. Spitznagel, "Sarah Vowell."
119. Vowell, "Bringing Pell Grants to My Eyes," *New York Times*, August 30, 2008, WK12.
120. Vowell, "Pell," WK12.
121. Vowell, "Hillary Clinton Made Me Cry," *New York Times*, August 1, 2016, A17.
122. Vowell, "Clinton," A17.
123. Vowell, "Join the Army, Love the Constitution, and Pray to Whomever You Like," *New York Times*, August 12, 2016, SR4.
124. Vowell, "Don't Judge Montana for a Single Body Slam," *New York Times*, May 28, 2017, SR9.
125. Vowell, "Judge," SR9.
126. Vowell, "Judge," SR9.
127. Burke, *A Grammar of Motives*, 508.
128. Vowell, "Judge," SR9.
129. Vowell, "Judge," SR9.
130. Vowell, "Judge," SR9.

131. Vowell, "Judge," SR9.
132. Bramen, *American Niceness*, 266.
133. See Bramen, *American Niceness*, 60.
134. Bramen, *American Niceness*, 10, 132.
135. See Bramen, *American Niceness*, 244.
136. Konstantinou, *Cool Characters*, 288.

CONCLUSION

1. Felski, *Critique*, 46.
2. Felski, *Critique*, 110.
3. Felski, *Critique*, 127.
4. Spivak, *Nationalism and the Imagination*, 15.
5. Billig, *Banal Nationalism*, 46.
6. Felski and Fraiman, "Introduction: In the Mood," vi.
7. L. Kennedy, "American Studies without Tears," 1.
8. L. Kennedy, "American Studies without Tears," 2.
9. Felski, *Critique*, 147.
10. Felski, *Critique*, 149.
11. Felski, *Critique*, 115–16.
12. Castronovo, "Politics of Critique," 243.
13. L. Trilling, "Promise of Realism," 29.
14. Felski, *Critique*, 17.
15. Krupnick, *Lionel Trilling*, 57.
16. Krupnick, *Lionel Trilling*, 57.
17. Sennett qtd. in Rodden, *Lionel Trilling*, 363.
18. Krupnick, *Lionel Trilling*, 149.
19. Seigworth and Gregg, "Inventory of Shimmers," 1.
20. In privileged literary genres, the issue of the "between" is gladly met with an insightful critical response. For example, of Robert Frost's "Mending Wall," Lawrence Raab has written:
    > [Frost's] repetition of *between* should . . . remind us of its two equally common meanings: between as separation, as in "something's come between us," and between as what might be shared and held in common, as in "a secret between two people" or "a bond between friends." The wall divides but it also connects, if you look at it that way. All the meaning is in how you look at it—how the poem encourages you to think about it ("On 'Mending Wall,'" 206).

    The "between" of Frost's poem is a rich moment of ambiguity: the word unites and separates simultaneously, and as Raab writes, encourages us to ponder the richness of human relationships and its language. So much, it seems, can come from the "between"—if it appears in a poem. But change the genre, or the subject, and the ponderous value of common words—and the critic's urge to interpret them—disappears. One wonders if our assumption that nonfiction does not encourage us to "think about it" as other genres do only perpetuates its neglect. And one wonders if critics, instead of seeing the bonds of being "between," see it only as a way to isolate themselves from other critics.

21. Torgovnick, "Politics of We," 268.
22. Torgovnick, "Politics of We," 268.
23. Felski, *Critique*, 128.
24. Felski, *Critique*, 147.
25. Jacobson, "Where We Stand," 265.
26. Jacobson, "Where We Stand," 266.
27. Jacobson, "Where We Stand," 266–67.
28. Cross, *Mirrors*, 271.
29. Cross, *Mirrors*, 271.
30. Cross, *Mirrors*, 271–72.
31. J. G. Kennedy, *Strange Nation*, 3.
32. Ahmed, *Politics*, 51.
33. Castiglia, *Hope*, 1.
34. Sedgwick, *Touching Feeling*, 146.
35. Tomkins, *Affect-Imagery-Consciousness*, 2:324.
36. Sedgwick, *Touching Feeling*, 135.
37. Fuss, "Love," 354–55.
38. See Sedgwick, *Touching Feeling*, 138–43.
39. Robert Koch qtd. in Felski, *Critique*, 122.
40. L. Trilling qtd. in Torgovnick, "Politics of We," 268–69.
41. Sedgwick, *Touching Feeling*, 124.
42. Grossberg, *Dancing*, 129.
43. Grossberg, *Dancing*, 128.
44. Hollinger, "Circle of 'We,'" 333.
45. Hegeman, *Patterns*, 69.
46. Norton, *Signs*, 9.
47. Beauvoir, *America*, 5.
48. Steinbeck, *Travels*, 20.
49. Vowell, *Cannoli*, 95.
50. L. Kennedy, "American Studies without Tears," 10.

BIBLIOGRAPHY

Ahmed, Sara. *The Cultural Politics of Emotion.* 2nd ed. New York: Routledge, 2015.
———. *The Promise of Happiness.* Durham NC: Duke University Press, 2010.
"America with Preconceptions." *Time.* December 14, 1953, 118–21.
Anderson, Ben. "Becoming and Being Hopeful: Towards a Theory of Affect." *Environment Planning D: Society and Space* 24 (2006): 733–52.
Anderson, Benedict. *Imagined Communities: Reflections on the Origin and Spread of Nationalism.* New York: Verso, 1991.
Anker, Elizabeth S., and Rita Felski, eds. *Critique and Postcritique.* Durham NC: Duke University Press, 2017.
———. Introduction to Anker and Felski, *Critique and Postcritique,* 1–30.
Bailey, Beth, and David Farber, eds. *America in the Seventies.* Lawrence: University Press of Kansas, 2004.
———. Introduction to Bailey and Farber, *America in the Seventies,* 1–8.
Bailey, Virginia Ruth. "Charles Kuralt, on the Road: A Study of the CBS Television News Feature." Master's thesis, University of Oklahoma, 1982.
Beauvoir, Simone de. *America Day by Day.* Translated by Carol Cosman. Berkeley: University of California Press, 1999.
———. *A Transatlantic Love Affair: Letters to Nelson Algren.* Compiled by Sylvie Le Bon de Beauvoir. New York: New Press, 1998.
Benedict, Barbara. *Curiosity: A Cultural History of Early Modern Inquiry.* Chicago: University of Chicago Press, 2001.
Benson, Jackson J. *John Steinbeck, Writer: A Biography.* New York: Penguin, 1984.

Berger, Harry, Jr. *Figures of a Changing World: Metaphor and the Emergence of Modern Culture.* Bronx NY: Fordham University Press, 2015.

Berkowitz, Edward D. *Something Happened: A Political and Cultural Overview of the Seventies.* New York: Columbia University Press, 2006.

Berlant, Lauren. *The Anatomy of National Fantasy: Hawthorne, Utopia, and Everyday Life.* Chicago: University of Chicago Press, 1991.

———. *Cruel Optimism.* Durham NC: Duke University Press, 2011.

———. *The Queen of America Goes to Washington City: Essays on Sex and Citizenship.* Durham NC: Duke University Press, 1997.

Best, Stephen, and Sharon Marcus. "Surface Reading: An Introduction." *Representations* 108, no. 1 (2009): 1–21.

Bhabha, Homi K. "DissemiNation: Time, Narrative and the Margins of the Modern Nation." In Bhabha, *Nation and Narration,* 291–322.

———. Introduction to Bhabha, *Nation and Narration,* 1–8.

———, ed. *Nation and Narration.* New York: Routledge, 1990.

Billig, Michael. *Banal Nationalism.* Thousand Oaks CA: Sage Publications, 1995.

Blanchot, Maurice. *The Infinite Conversation.* Translated by Susan Hanson. Minneapolis: University of Minnesota Press, 1992.

Bloch, Ernst. *The Principle of Hope.* Vol. 1. Translated by Neville Plaice, Stephen Plaice, and Paul Knight. Cambridge MA: MIT Press, 1986.

Bramen, Carrie Tirado. *American Niceness: A Cultural History.* Cambridge MA: Harvard University Press, 2017.

Brennan, Timothy. "The National Longing for Form." In Bhabha, *Nation and Narration,* 44–70.

Briganti, Chiara. "Giving the Mundane Its Due: One (Fine) Day in the Life of the Everyday." *ESC* 39, no. 2–3 (2013): 161–80.

Brinkley, Alan. "The Illusion of Unity in Cold War Culture." In *Rethinking Cold War Culture,* edited by Peter J. Kuznick and James Gilbert, 61–74. Washington DC: Smithsonian Institution Press, 2001.

Brinkema, Eugenie. *The Forms of the Affects.* Durham NC: Duke University Press, 2014.

Brooks, Peter. *Body Work: Objects of Desire in Modern Narrative.* Cambridge MA: Harvard University Press, 1993.

Burke, Kenneth. *A Grammar of Motives.* 1945. Berkeley: University of California Press, 1969.

Capozzola, Christopher. "'It Makes You Want to Believe in the Country': Celebrating the Bicentennial in an Age of Limits." In Bailey and Farber, *America in the Seventies,* 29–49.

Castiglia, Christopher. "Hope for Critique?" In Anker and Felski, *Critique and Postcritique,* 211–29.

———. *The Practices of Hope: Literary Criticism in Disenchanted Times.* New York: New York University Press, 2017.

Castronovo, Russ. "What Are the Politics of Critique? The Function of Criticism at a Different Time." In Anker and Felski, *Critique and Postcritique*, 230–51.

Certeau, Michel de. *The Practice of Everyday Life.* Translated by Steven Rendall. Berkeley: University of California Press, 1984.

Cleary, Johanna. "Creating 'America's Storyteller': The Early Radio Career of Charles Kuralt." *Journal of Radio Studies* 11, no. 2 (2004): 226–38.

Clifford, James. "Introduction: Partial Truths." In *Writing Culture: The Poetics and Politics of Ethnography*, edited by James Clifford and George E. Marcus, 1–26. Berkeley: University of California Press, 1986.

———. *The Predicament of Culture: Twentieth Century Ethnography, Literature, and Art.* Cambridge MA: Harvard University Press, 1988.

Cooke, Robert J. "Books." In McElrath, Crisler, and Shillinglaw, *John Steinbeck: The Contemporary Reviews*, 500.

Cotkin, George. *Existential America.* Baltimore: Johns Hopkins University Press, 2003.

Cowie, Jefferson. *Stayin' Alive: The 1970s and the Last Days of the Working Class.* New York: New Press, 2012.

Crapanzano, Vincent. "Reflections on Hope as a Category of Social and Psychological Analysis." *Cultural Anthropology* 18, no. 1 (2003): 3–32.

Cross, Charles R. *Room Full of Mirrors: A Biography of Jimi Hendrix.* New York: Hyperion, 2005.

Curtin, Michael. "Packaging Reality: The Influence of Fictional Forms on the Early Development of Television Documentary." *Journalism Monographs* 137 (July 1992): 168–214.

Dawson, Michael C. *Black Visions: The Roots of Contemporary African-American Political Ideologies.* Chicago: University of Chicago Press, 2001.

de Man, Paul. "The Epistemology of Metaphor." In *On Metaphor*, edited by Sheldon Sacks, 11–28. Chicago: University of Chicago Press, 1979.

Deutscher, Penelope. *The Philosophy of Simone de Beauvoir: Ambiguity, Conversion, Resistance.* New York: Cambridge University Press, 2008.

Didion, Joan. *Fixed Ideas: America since 9/11.* New York: New York Review Books, 2003.

di Leonardo, Micaela. *Exotics at Home: Anthropologies, Others, and American Modernity.* Chicago: University of Chicago Press, 1998.

Doctorow, E. L. "False Documents." *American Review* 26 (November 1977): 215–32.

Dolan, Frederick M. *Allegories of America: Narratives, Metaphysics, Politics.* Ithaca NY: Cornell University Press, 1994.

Dunphy, Mark. "Beat by Beat: Simone de Beauvoir's *America Day by Day* as Beat Memoir." *Simone de Beauvoir Studies* 19 (2002–3): 72–78.

Eagleton, Terry. *Hope without Optimism*. Charlottesville: University of Virginia Press, 2015.

Ehrlich, Matthew C. "Myth in Charles Kuralt's *On the Road*." *Journalism and Mass Communication Quarterly* 79, no. 2 (Summer 2002): 327–38.

Epstein, Edward Jay. *News from Nowhere: Television and the News*. New York: Random House, 1973.

Farber, David. *The Age of Great Dreams: America in the 1960s*. New York: Hill and Wang, 1994.

———. "The Torch Had Fallen." In Bailey and Farber, 9–28.

Felski, Rita. *The Limits of Critique*. Chicago: University of Chicago Press, 2015.

Felski, Rita, and Susan Fraiman. "Introduction: In the Mood." *New Literary History* 43, no. 3 (Summer 2012): v–xii.

Ferguson, Kevin L. *Eighties People: New Lives in the American Imagination*. New York: Palgrave Macmillan, 2016.

Fisher, Marc. "It's a Wonderful Life." *American Journalism Review*, July-August 1999, 40–45.

Flatley, Jonathan. *Affective Mapping: Melancholia and the Politics of Modernism*. Cambridge MA: Harvard University Press, 2008.

Fox, Jon. "The Edges of the Nation: A Research Agenda for Uncovering the Taken-for-Granted Foundations of Everyday Nationhood." *Nations and Nationalism* 23, no. 1 (2017): 26–47.

Fox, Jon, and Cynthia Miller-Idriss. "Everyday Nationhood." *Ethnicities* 8, no. 4 (2008): 536–76.

French, Warren. *John Steinbeck's Nonfiction Revisited*. New York: Twayne Publishers, 1996.

Freud, Sigmund. "Leonardo da Vinci and a Memory of His Childhood." In *The Standard Edition of the Complete Psychological Works of Sigmund Freud*, translated and edited by James Strachey, 63–139. Vol. 10. London: Hogarth, 1957.

Fukuyama, Francis. "The End of History?" *National Interest*, Summer 1989, 3–19.

Fuss, Diana. "But What about Love?" *PMLA* 132, no. 2 (2017): 352–55.

Gans, Herbert. *Deciding What's News*. New York: Pantheon Books, 1979.

Gardella, Peter. *American Civil Religion: What Americans Hold Sacred*. New York: Oxford University Press, 2014.

Gates, Gary Paul. *Air Time: The Inside Story of CBS News*. New York: Harper and Row, 1978.

Geertz, Clifford. *The Interpretation of Cultures*. New York: Basic Books, 1973.

Gladstein, Mimi Reisel. "*America and Americans*: The Arthurian Consummation." In *After "The Grapes of Wrath": Essays on John Steinbeck*, edited by Donald V. Coers, Paul D. Ruffin, and Robert J. DeMott, 228–37. Athens: Ohio University Press, 1995.

Gobeil, Madeleine. "Sartre Talks of Beauvoir." In *Critical Essays on Simone de Beauvoir*, edited by Elaine Marks, 15–18. Boston: G. K. Hall, 1987.

Gornick, Vivian. *The Situation and the Story: The Art of Personal Narrative*. New York: Farrar, Straus and Giroux, 2001.

Grattan, Sean Austin. *Hope Isn't Stupid: Utopian Affects in Contemporary American Literature*. Iowa City: University of Iowa Press, 2017.

Grizzle, Ralph. *Remembering Charles Kuralt*. Guilford CT: Globe Pequot Press, 2001.

Grossberg, Lawrence. "Affect's Future: Rediscovering the Virtual in the Actual." In *The Affect Theory Reader*, edited by Gregory J. Seigworth and Melissa Gregg, 309–38. Durham NC: Duke University Press, 2010.

———. *Cultural Studies in the Future Sense*. Durham NC: Duke University Press, 2010.

———. *Dancing in Spite of Myself: Essays on Popular Culture*. Durham NC: Duke University Press, 1997.

———. "Rockin' with Reagan, or the Mainstreaming of Postmodernity." *Cultural Critique* 10 (Autumn 1988): 123–49.

Guinn, Jeff. *The Road to Jonestown: Jim Jones and the Peoples Temple*. New York: Simon and Schuster, 2017.

Harmon, William, and C. Hugh Holman. *A Handbook to Literature*. Upper Saddle River NJ: Prentice Hall, 1996.

Hartsock, John C. *A History of American Literary Journalism: The Emergence of a Modern Narrative Form*. Amherst: University of Massachusetts Press, 2001.

Heavilin, Barbara A. "'A Love for Joseph Addison': Wit, Style and Truth in Steinbeck's *America and Americans*." *Steinbeck Review* 6, no. 2 (2009): 39–54.

Hegeman, Susan. *Patterns for America: Modernism and the Concept of Culture*. Princeton NJ: Princeton University Press, 1999.

Heffernan, Virginia. "Mayflower Power." *New York Times Book Review*, November 30, 2008, 11.

Heidegger, Martin. *Being and Time*. Translated by John Macquarrie and Edward Robinson. New York: Harper and Row, 1962.

———. *The Fundamental Concepts of Metaphysics: World, Finitude, Solitude*. Translated by William McNeill and Nicholas Walker. Bloomington: Indiana University Press, 1995.

Highmore, Ben. "Introduction: Questioning Everyday Life." In *The Everyday Life Reader*, edited by Ben Highmore, 1–34. New York: Routledge, 2002.

Highmore, Ben, and Jenny Bourne Taylor. "Introducing Mood Work." *New Formations* 82 (2014): 5–12.

Himmelstein, Hal. "Television News and the Television Documentary." In *Television: The Critical View*, edited by Horace Newcomb, 255–91. New York: Oxford University Press, 1987.

Hirschorn, Matthew. "Quirked Around." *Atlantic*, September 2007, 142–44, 147.

Hollinger, David A. "How Wide the Circle of 'We'? American Intellectuals and the Problem of Ethnos since World War II." *American Historical Review* 98, no. 2 (1993): 317–37.

Hutner, Gordon. *What America Read: Taste, Class, and the Novel, 1920–1960.* Chapel Hill: University of North Carolina Press, 2009.

Igo, Sarah E. *The Averaged American: Surveys, Citizens, and the Making of a Mass Public.* Cambridge MA: Harvard University Press, 2007.

Illouz, Eva. *Cold Intimacies: The Making of Emotional Capitalism.* Malden MA: Polity Press, 2007.

Jacobson, Matthew Frye. "Where We Stand: US Empire at Street Level and in the Archive." *American Quarterly* 65, no. 2 (June 2013): 265–90.

Jameson, Frederic. *Postmodernism, or The Cultural Logic of Late Capitalism.* Durham NC: Duke University Press, 1991.

Jarrell, Randall. *No Other Book: Selected Essays.* Edited by Brad Leithauser. New York: HarperCollins, 1999.

Johnson, Victoria E. *Heartland TV: Prime Time Television and the Struggle for U.S. Identity.* New York: New York University Press, 2008.

Kennedy, J. Gerald. *Strange Nation: Literary Nationalism and Cultural Conflict in the Age of Poe.* New York: Oxford University Press, 2016.

Kennedy, Liam. "American Studies without Tears, or What Does America Want?" *Journal of Transnational American Studies* 1, no. 1 (2009): 1–13.

Konstantinou, Lee. *Cool Characters: Irony and American Fiction.* Cambridge MA: Harvard University Press, 2016.

Kotsko, Adam. *Awkwardness: An Essay.* Winchester UK: Zero Books, 2010.

Krupnick, Mark. *Lionel Trilling and the Fate of Cultural Criticism.* Evanston IL: Northwestern University Press, 1986.

Kuralt, Charles. "Chandler Family." Charles Kuralt Collection, Wilson Library, University of North Carolina at Chapel Hill, folder 364.

———. *Dateline America.* New York: Harcourt Brace Jovanovich, 1979.

———. *On the Road with Charles Kuralt.* New York: G. P. Putnam's Sons, 1985.

———. "Waiting for Roger." Charles Kuralt Collection, Wilson Library, University of North Carolina at Chapel Hill, folder 383.

Laclau, Ernesto, and Chantal Mouffe. "Hope, Passion, Politics." In Zournazi, *Hope*, 122–49.

Lingis, Alphonso. "Murmurs of Life." In Zournazi, *Hope*, 22–41.

Lodge, David. *Modes of Modern Writing.* Ithaca NY: Cornell University Press, 1977.

Lutz, Catherine. *Unnatural Emotions: Everyday Sentiments on a Micronesian Atoll and Their Challenge to Western Theory.* Chicago: University of Chicago Press, 1988.

Lyotard, Jean-François. "Apostil on Narratives." In *The Postmodern Explained: Correspondence 1982–1985*, translated by Julian Pefanis and Morgan Thomas, 17–23. Minneapolis: University of Minnesota Press, 1993.

———. *The Postmodern Condition: A Report on Knowledge*. Translated by Geoff Bennington and Brian Massumi. Minneapolis: University of Minnesota Press, 1984.

Macridis, Roy C., and Mark L. Hulliung. *Contemporary Political Ideologies: Movements and Regimes*. 6th ed. New York: HarperCollins, 1996.

Mandel, Naomi. *Disappear Here: Violence after Generation X*. Columbus: Ohio State University Press, 2015.

Manguel, Alberto. *Curiosity*. New Haven CT: Yale University Press, 2015.

Marks, Elaine. *Critical Essays on Simone de Beauvoir*. Boston: G. K. Hall, 1987.

———. Review of *America Day by Day*, by Simone de Beauvoir. *French Review* 27, no. 5 (1954): 381–82.

Masco, Joseph. "'Survival Is Your Business': Engineering Ruins and Affect in Nuclear America." *Cultural Anthropology* 23, no. 2 (2008): 361–98.

Massumi, Brian. "Navigating Movements." In Zournazi, *Hope*, 210–43.

Mathy, Jean-Philippe. *Extrême-Occident: French Intellectuals in America*. Chicago: University of Chicago Press, 1993.

Matus, Jill. "Proxy and Proximity: Metonymic Signing." *University of Toronto Quarterly* 58, no. 2 (Winter 1988–89): 305–26.

McCann, Sean. *A Pinnacle of Feeling: American Literature and Presidential Government*. Princeton NJ: Princeton University Press, 2008.

McCarthy, Mary. "Mmle. Gulliver en Amérique." In *"A Bolt from the Blue" and Other Essays*, edited by A. O. Scott, 239–45. 1953. New York: New York Review Books, 2002.

McElrath, Joseph R., Jr., Jesse S. Crisler, and Susan Shillinglaw, eds. *John Steinbeck: The Contemporary Reviews*. New York: Cambridge University Press, 1996.

Medovoi, Leerom. *Rebels: Youth and the Cold War Origins of Identity*. Durham NC: Duke University Press, 2005.

Moi, Toril. *Simone de Beauvoir: The Making of an Intellectual Woman*. 2nd ed. New York: Oxford University Press, 2008.

Moran, Joe. *Reading the Everyday*. New York: Routledge, 1995.

Murfin, Ross, and Supryia M. Ray. *The Bedford Glossary of Critical and Literary Terms*. Boston: Bedford/St. Martin's, 2009.

Nadel, Alan. *Containment Culture: American Narratives, Postmodernism, and the Atomic Age*. Durham NC: Duke University Press, 1995.

"Newscasting: Travels with Charley." *Time*, January 19, 1968, 48–49.

Ngai, Sianne. *Our Aesthetic Categories: Zany, Cute, Interesting*. Cambridge MA: Harvard University Press, 2015.

———. *Ugly Feelings*. Cambridge MA: Harvard University Press, 2007.
Nichols, Bill. *Representing Reality: Issues and Concepts in Documentary*. Bloomington: Indiana University Press, 1991.
Norton, Anne. *The Republic of Signs: Liberal Theory and American Popular Culture*. Chicago: University of Chicago Press, 1993.
Nudelman, Franny. "'Marked for Demolition': Mary McCarthy's Vietnam Journalism." *American Literature* 85, no. 2 (2013): 363–87.
Obama, Barack. "Reclaiming the Promise to the People: A Brighter Day." *Vital Speeches of the Day* 70, no. 20 (August 2004): 625.
Ortner, Sherry B. "Generation X: Anthropology in a Media-Saturated World." *Cultural Anthropology* 13, no. 3 (1998): 414–40.
Osman, Suleiman. "The Decade of the Neighborhood." In *Rightward Bound: Making America Conservative in the 1970s*, edited by Bruce J. Schulman and Julian E. Zelizer, 106–27. Cambridge MA: Harvard University Press, 2008.
Pach, Chester, Jr. "And That's the Way It Was: The Vietnam War on the Network Nightly News." In *The Sixties: From Memory to History*, edited by David Farber, 90–118. Chapel Hill: University of North Carolina Press, 1994.
———. "Tet on TV: US Nightly News Reporting and Presidential Policy Making." In *1968: The World Transformed*, edited by Carole Fink, Philipp Gassert, and Detlef Junker, 55–82. New York: Cambridge University Press, 1998.
Parini, Jay. Introduction to Steinbeck, *Travels with Charley: In Search of America*, vii–xxii.
———. *John Steinbeck: A Biography*. New York: Henry Holt and Company, 1995.
Patterson, James T. *The Eve of Destruction: How 1965 Transformed America*. New York: Basic Books, 2012.
Pease, Donald E. "National Identities, Postmodern Artifacts, and Postnational Narratives." In *National Identities and Post-Americanist Narratives*, edited by Donald E. Pease, 1–13. Durham NC: Duke University Press, 1993.
Phillips, William. *A Partisan View: Five Decades of the Literary Life*. New York: Stein and Day, 1983.
Posnock, Ross. *The Trial of Curiosity: Henry James, William James, and the Challenge to Modernity*. New York: Oxford University Press, 1991.
Raab, Lawrence. "On 'Mending Wall' by Robert Frost." In *Touchstones: American Poets on a Favorite Poem*, edited by Robert Pack and Jay Parini, 203–8. Lebanon NH: University of New England Press, 1996.
Rabinow, Paul. *Reflections on Fieldwork in Morocco*. Berkeley: University of California Press, 1977.
Raphael, Chad. *Investigated Reporting: Muckrakers, Regulators, and the Struggle over Television Documentary*. Champaign: University of Illinois Press, 2005.

Rodden, John. *Lionel Trilling and the Critics: Opposing Selves.* Lincoln: University of Nebraska Press, 1999.

Rodgers, Daniel T. *Age of Fracture.* Cambridge MA: Harvard University Press, 2011.

Roof, Judith. *Come as You Are: Sexuality and Narrative.* New York: Columbia University Press, 1996.

Root, Robert, Jr. "Naming Nonfiction (a Polyptych)." *College English* 65, no. 3 (2003): 242–56.

Rowe, John Carlos. *The New American Studies.* Minneapolis: University of Minnesota Press, 2002.

Rubenstein, Diane. "'I Hope I Am Not Fated to Live in Rochester': America in the Work of Beauvoir." *Theory & Event* 15, no. 2 (2012). https://muse.jhu.edu/article/478361.

———. *This Is Not a President: Sense, Nonsense, and the American Political Imaginary.* New York: New York University Press, 2008.

Ruch, Alexander. "Beauvoir-in-America: Understanding, Concrete Experience, and Beauvoir's Appropriation of Heidegger in *America Day by Day.*" *Hypatia* 24, no. 4 (2009): 104–29.

Schaub, Thomas Hill. *American Fiction in the Cold War.* Madison: University of Wisconsin Press, 1991.

Scherman, David E. "Things and People." In McElrath, Crisler, and Shillinglaw, *John Steinbeck: The Contemporary Reviews,* 503.

Schrecker, Ellen. "Introduction: Cold War Triumphalism and the Real Cold War." In *Cold War Triumphalism: The Misuse of History after the Fall of Communism,* edited by Ellen Schrecker, 1–26. New York: New Press, 2006.

Sconce, Jeffrey. "Irony, Nihilism, and the New American 'Smart' Film." *Screen* 43, no. 4 (Winter 2002): 349–69.

Sedgwick, Eve Kosofsky. *Touching Feeling: Affect, Pedagogy, Performativity.* Durham NC: Duke University Press, 2003.

Sedgwick, Eve Kosofsky, and Adam Frank. *Shame and Its Sisters: A Silvan Tomkins Reader.* Durham NC: Duke University Press, 1995.

Seigworth, Gregory J., and Melissa Gregg. "An Inventory of Shimmers." In *The Affect Theory Reader,* edited by Gregory J. Seigworth and Melissa Gregg, 1–25. Durham NC: Duke University Press, 2010.

Shillinglaw, Susan, and Jackson J. Benson. Introduction to *America and Americans: Selected Nonfiction,* edited by Susan Shillinglaw and Jackson J. Benson, ix–xviii. New York: Penguin, 2002.

Simons, Margaret A. *Beauvoir and "The Second Sex": Feminism, Race, and the Origins of Existentialism.* Lanham MD: Rowman and Littlefield, 1999.

Smiley, Jane. "The Unteachable Ignorance of the Red States." *Slate*, November 4, 2004. http://www.slate.com/articles/news_and_politics/politics/2004/11/why_americans_hate_democratsa_dialogue_8.html.

Spitznagel, Eric. "Sarah Vowell, Queen of the Literary Hipster Nerds, Explains Her Begrudging Respect for the Monarchy." *Vanityfair.com*, March 17, 2011. https://www.vanityfair.com/hollywood/2011/03/sarah-vowell-question-time.

Spivak, Gayatri. *Nationalism and the Imagination*. New York: Seagull Books, 2010.

Stam, Robert. "Television News and Its Spectator." In *Regarding Television*, edited by E. Ann Kaplan, 23–43. Lanham MD: University Publications of America, 1983.

Stearns, Peter N. *American Cool: Constructing a Twentieth-Century Emotional Style*. New York: New York University Press, 1994.

Steinbeck, John. *"America and Americans" and Selected Nonfiction*. Edited by Susan Shillinglaw and Jackson J. Benson. New York: Penguin, 2002.

———. *Steinbeck: A Life in Letters*. Edited by Elaine A. Steinbeck and Robert Wallstein. New York: Viking Press, 1975.

———. *Travels with Charley: In Search of America*. 1962. New York: Penguin, 1997.

Sutherland, Claire. *Nationalism in the Twenty-First Century: Challenges and Responses*. New York: Palgrave, 2012.

Svendsen, Lars. "Moods and the Meaning of Philosophy." *New Literary History* 43, no. 3 (2012): 419–31.

Szalay, Michael. *Hip Figures: A Literary History of the Democratic Party*. Stanford CA: Stanford University Press, 2012.

Taussig, Michael. "Carnival of the Senses." In Zournazi, *Hope*, 42–63.

———. *The Nervous System*. New York: Routledge, 1992.

Teale, Tamara. "Her 'Ambiguous Satisfaction': Simone de Beauvoir in the Southwest." *Journal of the Southwest* 41, no. 4 (1999): 461–76.

Tell, David. "Burke's Encounter with Ransom: Rhetoric and Epistemology in 'Four Master Tropes.'" *Rhetoric Society Quarterly* 34, no. 4 (Autumn 2004): 33–54.

Thrift, Nigel. "Intensities of Feeling: Towards a Spatial Politics of Affect." *Geografiska Annaler* 86B, no. 1 (2004): 57–78.

Tolbert, Jane Thornton. "The Charles Kuralt *On the Road* Series: A Structural and Production Analysis. Master's thesis, University of Florida, 1975.

Tomkins, Silvan. *Affect-Imagery-Consciousness*. Vol. 1, *The Positive Affects*. New York: Springer, 1962.

———. *Affect-Imagery-Consciousness*. Vol. 2, *The Negative Affects*. New York: Springer, 1963.

Torgovnick, Marianne. "The Politics of We." In *Eloquent Obsessions: Writing Cultural Criticism*, edited by Marianne Torgovnick, 260–78. Durham NC: Duke University Press, 1994.

Totten, Gary. "Simone de Beauvoir's *America Day by Day*: Reel to Real." In *Issues in Travel Writing: Empire, Spectacle, and Displacement*, edited by Kristi Siegel, 135–49. New York: Peter Lang, 2002.
Trilling, Diana. "Simone de Beauvoir's America." In *The Avon Book of Modern Writing*, edited by William Phillips and Philip Rahv, 208–17. New York: Avon Publications, 1953.
Trilling, Lionel. "The Promise of Realism." In *Speaking of Literature and Society*, edited by Diana Trilling, 27–33. New York: Harcourt, 1980.
Tuchman, Gaye. *Making News: A Study in the Construction of Reality*. New York: Free Press, 1978.
Vermeulen, Pieter. *Contemporary Literature and the End of the Novel: Creature, Affect, Form*. New York: Palgrave Macmillan, 2015.
Virno, Paolo. "The Ambivalence of Disenchantment." In *Radical Thought in Italy: A Potential Politics*, edited by Paolo Virno and Michael Hardt, 13–36. Minneapolis: University of Minnesota Press, 1996.
Vowell, Sarah. *Assassination Vacation*. New York: Simon and Schuster, 2005.
———. *Lafayette in the Somewhat United States*. New York: Riverhead, 2015.
———. *The Partly Cloudy Patriot*. New York: Simon and Schuster, 2002.
———. *Take the Cannoli: Stories from the New World*. New York: Simon and Schuster, 2000.
———. *The Wordy Shipmates*. New York: Riverhead, 2008.
Wagner-Martin, Linda. *A History of American Literature: 1950 to the Present*. New York: Wiley-Blackwell, 2013.
Wald, Priscilla. *Constituting Americans: Cultural Anxiety and Narrative Form*. Durham NC: Duke University Press, 1994.
Wall, Wendy L. *Inventing the "American Way": The Politics of Consensus from the New Deal to the Civil Rights Movement*. New York: Oxford University Press, 2008.
Wolfe, Tom. "The New Journalism." In *The New Journalism*, edited by Tom Wolfe and E. W. Johnson, 3–54. New York: Harper and Row, 1973.
Woloch, Alex. *Or Orwell*. Cambridge MA: Harvard University Press, 2016.
Worden, Daniel. "Neoliberal Style: Alex Haley, Hunter S. Thompson, and Countercultures." *American Literature* 87, no. 4 (2015): 799–823.
Zaretsky, Natasha. *No Direction Home: The American Family and the Fear of National Decline, 1968–1980*. Chapel Hill: University of North Carolina Press, 2007.
Žižek, Slavoj. *Tarrying with the Negative: Kant, Hegel, and the Critique of Ideology*. Durham NC: Duke University Press, 1993.
Zournazi, Mary, ed. *Hope: New Philosophies for Change*. New York: Routledge, 2003.
———. Introduction to Zournazi, *Hope*, 14–20.

INDEX

Abu Ghraib, 195
affect: in *America Day by Day*, 40; avoidance of, 130–33, 175, 176; complexity of American, 111, 222; of criticism, 22, 211–14, 219–23; of curious writers, 76, 79; defining nation by, 1, 5–7; of hopefulness, 34–35, 124–28, 133, 157, 159, 161, 162, 223; in Jane Smiley's essay, 3–4; of John Steinbeck, 72–74, 82, 116; and moodiness, 44, 46, 51, 52; in nationalist rhetoric, 7, 11–12, 17–19, 36; obscuring of, 24–25, 197, 206; of *On the Road* segments, 119–24, 143, 148, 157, 158, 161; reading of, 8–9, 14–15, 20–26, 209–12; of Reagan era, 176–78; of Sarah Vowell, 166–70, 179, 182–89, 192–95, 201, 248n85; source of, 42; strength of, 64, 75, 124, 126, 159, 169, 173, 190–91, 205, 206, 219; and synecdoche, 26–27, 29–32, 137, 216–17, 232n107; theories of, 2–3, 6, 8, 19–22, 39, 171–72, 221, 228n18, 230n62, 230n64, 230n72; waning of, 24, 25, 190; weakness of, 7–8, 13–14, 75, 128–29, 176, 189, 205–7. *See also* emotion
Affect-Imagery-Consciousness (Tomkins), 8, 21
affective disobedience, 124, 125, 157
Affect Theory Reader (Seigworth and Gregg), 21
Affordable Health Care Act, 202
African Americans: and "All Lives Matter" movement, 32; equality of, 108, 109, 156, 158; families of, 156, 245n140; nationalism of, 157; news coverage of, 136, 151; as priests, 120. *See also* race and racism
againstness, 212–15, 223. *See also* hate; love/hate relationship
Ahmed, Sara, 21, 29, 124
Alaska, 193

Algren, Nelson, 48
All Lives Matter movement, 32
America: in 1930s, 98, 108; in 1940s, 16, 61; in 1950s and '60s, 79–80, 82, 98, 100, 102–3, 105, 115, 122; in 1960s and '70s, 117–19, 122, 123, 130, 132, 134–35, 138, 147, 155, 156, 158–59, 177, 178, 205, 241n11, 244n114, 245n140; in 1980s, 10, 34, 159, 168, 173, 175–79, 188, 197, 198, 201; in 1990s, 175, 178; as body, 98–99, 101, 102, 105, 106, 110–11; complexity of, 56–59, 79–80, 82, 83, 85–86, 101, 116, 123, 133, 191, 221–23, 235n87; French view of, 39, 53–54, 56, 59–61; history of, 174, 183–84, 186–88, 191, 193–94, 196–200; identity of, 82–83, 102–3, 106, 122, 124, 129–30, 132, 133, 139, 155, 159, 168, 178, 179, 193–95, 206, 228n24; imperialism of, 215–16; John Steinbeck's construction of, 74–76, 88–93, 95–98, 101, 105–9, 111–16; John Steinbeck's curiosity about, 72, 78, 81, 84; literary canon of, 182, 183; local and national in, 121–23, 133–41, 162; problems in, 109–14, 121–24, 129, 130, 136–38, 146–48; representation in *On the Road*, 120–21, 147–48, 152–53, 155–57, 241n11; representation in presidential libraries, 186; "right" and "wrong" impressions of, 38, 47–48; Sarah Vowell's assessment of, 189, 197; Simone de Beauvoir's hostility toward, 61–63, 66; values of, 152–53, 156, 158, 162, 177; as watch, 101, 102. *See also* nation
"America" (Ginsberg), 181

America and Americans (Steinbeck): analysis of, 34; criticism of, 71–72, 78, 116; curiosity and discontent in, 75, 76, 78, 82, 99, 102, 109, 112–15, 241n160; difficulty writing, 90; on genetic tape of nation, 106, 107, 196; genre of, 100–101, 103; nationalism associated with, 10, 100; nation imagined in, 73–75; paradox in, 105–7, 110; redemption in, 113–14; tone of, 112
America Day by Day (Beauvoir): analysis of, 33–34; on complexity of America, 59, 68, 222; everyday life in, 39–40; nationalism associated with, 10; responses to, 37–39, 61–69, 71–72, 233n13, 236n114; tone of, 63; typographical errors in, 62–66
American Dilemma (Myrdal), 80
American dream, 17, 106, 107
American exceptionalism. *See* America: identity of
American flag, 192
American Revolution Bicentennial, 120, 135, 156, 192
Americans, 101, 192–93, 205. *See also* America: identity of
"Americans and the Future" (Steinbeck), 110
Amish, 241n11
Anderson, Benedict, 14, 39, 68, 124
anti-intensity emotionology, 173, 179, 191. *See also* emotion
Arcola IL, 137–40
Arrol's Drug Store, 138–40
The Autobiography of Malcolm X, 115
Avon Book of Modern Writing, 62

Bach, Richard, 177
Baez, Joan, 216

Bailey, Virginia, 135, 141, 142
Baldessari, John, 231n82
banality: in *America Day by Day*, 37–38; of John Steinbeck's nationalism, 75, 108; of nationalist affects, 12, 19, 211; of national narratives, 121; of "nice," 205; of nonfiction, 15, 17; in postmodern art, 231n82; of *On the Road* segments, 128, 162; Sarah Vowell's response to, 187; strength of, 14
barbecue, 196, 197
Bastille Day, 53
Baudrillard, Jean, 39
Beat poets, 38. *See also* poetry
Beauvoir, Simone de: on complexity of America, 56–59, 222, 235n87; criticism of, 61–67, 71–72, 105; impressions of America, 38–41, 47–55, 60, 233n13; moodiness of, 8–10, 33–34, 41–42, 46–47, 61; writing style of, 41, 45, 47, 50, 54–55, 57, 63
Benedict, Barbara, 76, 79
Benson, Jackson J., 72, 101, 108, 114
Berkowitz, Edward, 122
Berger, Harry, Jr., 231n86
Berlant, Lauren, 7, 19, 89, 126, 183
Best, Stephen, 24
betrayal, 64, 220
between-ness, 21–23, 40–41, 44–46, 213, 214, 221, 250n20
Bhabha, Homi K., 40, 63–64, 229n39
Bible, 144, 146, 181–82, 195. *See also* faith
Billig, Michael, 11–13
binary thinking, 53–54, 68
"Blackie" (television segment), 160–63
Black Lives Matter movement, 32–33
Black Nationalism, 157
Blanchot, Maurice, 39
Bloch, Ernst, 125, 141, 145

blue states, 2, 3, 4, 203. *See also* Democrats
Bosler WY, 134
Bovary, Emma, 187
Bowery, 50–51. *See also* New York City
Bramen, Carrie Tirado, 205
The Breakfast Club, 188
Brennan, Timothy, 69
Briganti, Chiara, 233n16
Brinkema, Eugenie, 228n18
Brinkley, Alan, 115
Broderick, Matthew, 198, 199
Brooks, Peter, 84–85
Buffalo SC, 133
Burke, Kenneth, 27–29, 31, 141, 204
Bush, George H. W., 178–79
Bush, George W.: effect on national metanarrative, 192, 193, 195; inauguration of, 165, 169, 173, 191, 202; invasion of Iraq, 189; nationalism associated with, 10, 168; Sarah Vowell's opposition to, 165–67, 170, 173, 191, 200; votes for, 1. *See also* presidencies
Butler, Judith, 32

Cambodia, 142, 147
Camp David Accords, 160
capitalism: in 1960s America, 108–9, 115, 119; affects of, 25; as American trait, 156; nationalism associated with, 10; and New England foliage, 118; news coverage of, 137, 138; in Reagan era, 176. *See also* economy; poverty
Capozzola, Christopher, 134–35, 147
Carrothers OH, 142, 145
Castiglia, Christopher, 129, 130, 242n40
Castronovo, Russ, 211

CBS Evening News with Walter Cronkite, 34, 117, 119, 141–42. *See also* reporting
CBS Reports, 132
CBS television, 136–37, 242n43
Certeau, Michel de, 31, 49, 57, 68, 108, 127
Chandler, Alex, 149–57, 245n40
Chandler, Cleveland, 150
Chandler, Fortson, 154
"Chandler Reunion" (television segment), 148–57
Chicago, 88–97, 101, 113, 184–85, 197–98
Chicago Tribune, 166–67
children, 110, 112, 118, 119, 154, 156
Civil Rights movement, 10
Cleary, Johanna, 136
Cleveland OH, 142, 146
Clifford, James, 15, 89, 104
Clinton, Bill, 129, 165, 168, 185, 201, 248n72. *See also* presidencies
"Coffee Cups" (television segment), 138–41, 149
Cold War: end of, 180; national attitude during, 98, 109; nationalism associated with, 10, 35, 42, 66, 168, 176; and synecdoche, 32, 72, 100, 191, 192; triumphalism of, 178–91
college football, 103–5
colonialism, 167, 171
Columbia University, 214
"Coming Home" (television segment). *See* "Chandler Reunion" (television segment)
community: and affect, 14–15, 216–17, 222, 223; in America, 58, 80, 134, 135; and Cold War triumphalism, 190; effect of hopefulness on, 127, 128, 132–33, 145, 162; individuality within, 188–89; and irony, 175; John Steinbeck's search for, 72–74, 88, 97–98, 111, 113; metanarratives of, 196–97; of mobile home owners, 87; and national opinion polls, 82–83; and nonfiction texts, 18, 68; through opposition, 166, 168–69, 172, 178, 182; representation of, 28, 79, 201–2; synecdoches of, 139–40, 169, 177, 192, 194, 197. *See also* families; people; self
Connecticut, 136
contrarianism. *See* incredulity
"cool," 173
corn, 137, 138
Cosman, Carol, 38
Cotkin, George, 37
Cotton, John, 193
counterculture, 115, 134, 206. *See also* culture
Covarrubias, 77, 78
Covici, Pascal, 98, 101–2, 106, 108, 110
Crapanzano, Vincent, 125, 146
criticism: and affect theory, 22, 211–20, 230n73; of American writers, 71; of G. W. Bush, 165–66; of John Steinbeck, 71–72, 78, 116; limits of, 218–21; of nation, 182, 183; of nonfiction, 15–17; of *On the Road* segments, 119–21, 128, 132, 161, 162; of politics of others, 169; of Sarah Vowell, 167; of Simone de Beauvoir, 38–42, 61–69; suspicion associated with, 11–12, 22–26, 28, 31, 35–36, 128, 130, 162, 182, 209–12, 214–15, 218–23; and synecdoche, 27, 28; tone of, 54, 62–64, 67; of weak nationalist texts, 9, 11, 223. *See also* New Criticism
Cronkite, Walter, 117, 118, 119, 145
Cross, Charles R., 217
Cuba, 193, 194

The Cultural Politics of Emotion (Ahmed), 21
culture: in 1950s and '60s, 79–80, 82, 109; in 1980s, 175–78; of awkwardness, 246n27; blind spots in, 217, 218; components of national, 14, 229n39; and curiosity, 77; of Generation X, 179; John Steinbeck's analysis of, 91, 94–95; Lionel Trilling's attitude toward liberal, 213; Lionel Trilling's definition of, 220, 222; of mobile home owners, 86–87; in *On the Road* segments, 134–35, 157; and Simone de Beauvoir's impressions of America, 52–53; synecdoches of, 89, 92, 104. *See also* counterculture; popular culture
curiosity: criticism's effect on, 210; definition of, 75; effects of, 77–78; of John Steinbeck, 34, 72, 79, 80, 83, 85, 87–90, 94–98, 101, 109, 114; nationalism associated with, 79, 218, 223; relationship to discontent, 75–76, 78, 79, 81–82, 86, 89, 95, 99; theories about, 81, 237n38; in *Travels with Charley*, 73–74
Custer, George Armstrong, 193

Dateline America (Kuralt), 137–38, 140–41
"Dear Dead Congressman" (Vowell), 187, 188
de Man, Paul, 232n95
Democrats, 3, 4, 170, 200, 201, 204. *See also* blue states
Deutscher, Penelope, 49
Didion, Joan, 191
discontent: in *America and Americans*, 75, 99, 102, 104–5, 109, 111–15, 241n160; with American government and corporate leaders, 138, 148, 159, 169, 171, 177–81, 185, 189, 192–96, 198, 200; with community image, 172; in *Dateline America*, 138; relationship to curiosity, 75–76, 78, 79, 81–82, 86, 89, 95, 99; tone of John Steinbeck's, 72, 73, 87–88, 90, 97–100, 102, 104–5, 108–15; in *Travels with Charley*, 83–84, 102, 113; in *Wordy Shipmates*, 194
distrust, 129, 182
The Dixie Chicks, 216
Doctorow, E. L., 7
Dolan, Frederick M., 66
"Don't Judge Montana for a Single Body Slam" (Vowell), 203–4
Duluth MN, 134
Dunphy, Mark, 38

Eagleton, Terry, 125, 126
East of Eden (Steinbeck), 72
École Normale Supérieure (ENS), 46, 54, 55
economy, 177–79. *See also* capitalism; Generation X
Ehrlich, Matthew, 121
Eisenhower, Dwight, 112. *See also* presidencies
elections, 1–2, 5, 188, 200–204. *See also* presidencies; voting
emotion: and affect theory, 21, 22; betrayal as, 220; and concept of nation, 6, 7, 13, 20; cultural expressions of, 25; in Jane Smiley, 3–4; maturity of, 173; reading of, 8; and reason, 9, 28, 43, 46, 68; of Sarah Vowell, 174; sociality of, 29–30; source of, 42. *See also* affect; anti-intensity emotionology; feelings; mood; moodiness

"The End is Near, Nearer, Nearest" (Vowell), 180
"The End of History" (Fukuyama), 190
Episcopal Church, 120
epistemophilia: in Cold War era writing, 100; description of, 81–82; and knowledge of nation, 84–85, 90, 97; in *Travels with Charley*, 88–91, 93, 95, 96, 101, 112, 114. *See also* feelings
E Pluribus Unum, 103–5, 112
Epstein, Edward Jay, 120
Esalen Institute, 177
ethnicity, 104–5, 156. *See also* race and racism
"Eve of Destruction" (McGuire), 102, 110
everyday life: in *America Day by Day*, 39–41, 52–53, 67; contrasts in, 60–61; incredulous nationalists' view of, 183, 187; and moodiness, 44–46, 50, 68; nature of, 40, 233n16; in *On the Road* segments, 140; reading of, 49–50, 57–58, 67–69; in Reagan era, 178
Existential America (Cotkin), 37
existentialism, 37–38, 45, 52

faith, 144, 146, 151–53, 156–58, 162, 180–82, 189, 194–95. *See also* Bible
families, 143–44, 147, 149, 150, 152–58, 245n140. *See also* community; people
Farber, David, 109
Fargo ND, 134
fear, 1–2, 7, 247n49
feelings, 21, 118. *See also* emotion; epistemophilia; sensations
Felski, Rita, 43, 44, 51, 210, 211, 212
Ferguson, Kevin L., 175, 178, 188, 198
Ferraro, Geraldine, 201
Ferris Bueller's Day Off, 197–98

fiction. *See* novels
Fielder, Leslie, 229n48
Fisher, Marc, 167
Fitzgerald, F. Scott, 182
Flatley, Jonathan, 230n62, 234n26
Flaubert, Gustave, 187
Fort Motte SC, 134
Fox, Jon, 13–14, 180
Fraiman, Susan, 43, 44, 51, 210
France, 39, 40, 52–54, 56, 59–62, 142
freedom, 157, 159, 177
French, Warren, 116
French Review, 37
Freud, Sigmund, 80, 81, 82
Frost, Robert, 250n20
Fukuyama, Francis, 190, 191
Fuss, Diana, 219

gangs, 107–8
Gans, Herbert, 120
Gaulle, Charles de, 142
Geertz, Clifford, 6, 7
General Motors, 142
Generation X: affect of, 25, 168, 173, 175–76, 191; coping strategies of, 187, 201; economy of, 177–79; effect of Reagan era politics on, 179–80, 189, 191, 206; fears of, 247n49; synecdoches of, 35
Genette, Gérard, 232n95
Gettysburg Address, 174
Gianforte, Greg, 202–5
Ginsberg, Allen, 181, 183, 189
Gladstein, Mimi, 112
Gobeil, Madeline, 50
"God Will Give You Blood to Drink in a Souvenir Shot Glass" (Vowell), 186
Gore, Al, 165, 195
Gornick, Vivian, 18
Grammar of Motives (Burke), 27

Grand Canyon, 38
Grant, Ulysses S., 186
Grattan, Sean Austin, 123
Great Depression, 98, 154. *See also* poverty
The Great Gatsby (Fitzgerald), 182
Greenspan, Alan, 185
Gregg, Melissa, 21, 214
Grossberg, Lawrence, 177, 221, 230n72
Guantanamo Bay, 193, 194
Guardian, 202
Guinzburg, Thomas H., 100
Guyana. *See* Jonestown, Guyana

Hall, Anthony Michael, 188
Hannibal MO, 134
Harlem, 136. *See also* New York City
Hartsock, John C., 16
hate, 110, 112. *See also* againstness; love/hate relationship
Hawaii, 171, 196
Heavilin, Barbara A., 114
Heffernan, Virginia, 167, 179
Hegel, Georg Wilhelm Friedrich, 58–59, 68
Hegeman, Susan, 221–22
Heidegger, Martin, 42–44
Hendrix, Jimi, 216–17
Highmore, Ben, 40, 43
Hill, Gladys, 101, 102
Himmelstein, Hal, 120
Hirschorn, Michael, 173–74
history, 174, 183–84, 186–88, 190
Hollinger, David A., 80
hope: America as "last best," 193, 195; characteristics of, 124–26, 242n40; difference from hopefulness, 123, 127–28, 146–48, 159, 162; difference from optimism, 124; in *On the Road* segments, 151, 154, 155, 157–58, 161; in Reagan era, 176–77

hopefulness: affect of, 34–35, 122, 159, 162, 223; about America, 113–14, 151, 153, 157–59; characteristics of, 124, 126–29; in *On the Road* segments, 118–23, 135–37, 139–51, 153–58. *See also* optimism; promise
hopelessness, 125, 133
Howard University, 150
Hughes, John, 197–98
Huston, John, 101, 102
Hutchinson, Anne, 167
Hutner, Gordon, 61
hyperbole, 166, 167, 170, 200

Ignatieff, Michael, 11, 28, 210, 211
Igo, Sarah E., 82–83, 102–3
"Ike Was a Handsome Man" (Vowell), 185
Illinois, 160–63
Illouz, Eva, 30
Imagined Communities (Anderson), 39
imperialism, 183, 215–17
incredulity: effects of, 184, 204; legitimacy of, 174; meaning of, 171–72; nationalism associated with, 168–69, 182–83, 186, 218, 223; post 9/11, 191, 192; as reaction to Reagan era, 176, 179; of Sarah Vowell, 35, 167–68, 171, 173, 182, 185, 189, 191, 192, 195–97, 199–200, 248n85; and slackening, 175–76
Individualism Reconsidered (Riesman), 16
in media res. See between-ness
Invalides, 60. *See also* Paris
Iran, 160
Iran-Contra, 204
Iraq, 189
irony, 175, 176, 179, 185, 189, 196–97, 206

Jackson, Jesse, 204
Jacobson, Matthew Frye, 215–17

James, Henry, 237n38
James, William, 237n38
Jameson, Frederic, 24, 25, 190
Jarrell, Randall, 231n90
John Birch Society, 10
Johnson, Lyndon B., 186
Johnson, Victoria E., 132
Jonathan Livingston Seagull (Bach), 177
Jonestown, Guyana, 148, 157

Kennedy, J. Gerald, 217
Kennedy, John F., 187
Kennedy, Liam, 210–11
Kerouac, Jack, 182, 183, 189
Kinsey reports, 80
knowledge, 80–82, 84–85, 90, 93, 97
Konstantinou, Lee, 174
Korean War, 139
Kotsko, Adam, 246n27
Krupnick, Mark, 213
Kuralt, Charles: affect toward country, 9, 34–35, 222; criticism of, 119–20, 128, 242n43; fall foliage segment by, 117–19; nationalism associated with, 10; radio reporting by, 136–37; technique of, 141, 142, 145–59, 161, 245n140; on tone of *Road* stories, 133. See also *On the Road with Charles Kuralt*

Laclau, Ernesto, 242n40
Lafayette, Marquis de, 193, 196–200
Lafayette in the Somewhat United States (Vowell), 196, 198
Lafayette Square, 199
LaGuardia Airport, 49
Lambert, Harold Lee, 143
Lambert, Jane, 143
Lambert, Roger, 143–46
Lambert, Sam, 142

Lawrence KS, 3
"Leaves" (television segment), 117–19, 133
"L'Envoi" (Steinbeck), 101
Leonardo da Vinci, 81
Lincoln, Abraham, 167, 193
Lindbergh, Charles, 139
Lingis, Alphonso, 123
Little Big Horn, 120
Lodge, David, 30
The Lonely Crowd (Riesman), 80
Lonesome Harry (Steinbeck character), 90–96, 101
Long Island NY, 78, 84. See also New York City
Los Angeles Times, 121
losers, 176, 177, 179
love, 110, 219, 220. See also love/hate relationship
Love and Death in the American Novel (Fielder), 229n48
love/hate relationship, 64, 81, 222. See also againstness; hate; love
Lutz, Catherine, 19
Lyotard, Jean-François, 35, 171, 173

Manguel, Alberto, 77, 79
Marcus, Sharon, 24
Marilyn (Warhol), 25
Marks, Elaine, 37–38
Massumi, Brian, 126, 129
McCann, Sean, 227n9
McCarthy, Mary, 38, 39, 52, 66, 233n7, 235n87
McCarthyism, 10
McGuire, Barry, 102
media. See reporting
Medovoi, Leerom, 102
"Mending Wall" (Frost), 250n20
metaphor, 231n86, 231n91, 232n95
metonymy, 231n86, 232n92, 232n95

Mexico, 193
"Michigan and Wacker" (Vowell), 184–85
Michigan Avenue Bridge, 184–86, 203, 222
Midgley, Leslie, 141–42
Milk, Harvey, 148
Miller, Arthur, 72
Miller-Idriss, Cynthia, 13–14
Minneapolis MN, 135
Mississippi, 149–51, 156
Missouri, 1, 2
mobile home owners, 86–87, 107
"Modell of Christian Charity" (Winthrop), 194
Moi, Toril, 39, 45, 50, 54, 65
Montana, 180, 202–5
mood: and affect theory, 20–22; connotation of, 54–55; definition of, 43; of everyday life, 41, 67; function of, 42–45, 50–51, 234n26; nationalism associated with, 223; of Paris, 60; polls showing national, 82–83. *See also* emotion
moodiness: connotation of, 44; nationalism associated with, 10, 218; reading of, 44–45, 61–62, 69; as response to everyday life, 34, 45–46, 50, 52, 54, 57; of Sarah Vowell, 167; of Simone de Beauvoir, 8–9, 39, 40, 46–48, 50–51, 66–68. *See also* emotion
moral judgment, 172, 175, 176, 177, 179, 191
Moran, Joe, 39
Moscone, George, 148
Mouffe, Chantal, 242n40
Munch, Edvard, 25
Murray, Pauli, 120
Myrdal, Gunnar, 80

Nadel, Alan, 75, 100
nation: American writer's view of, 84–85; constructed image of, 73, 75, 77, 79, 83, 88–92, 94–98, 200, 206; definition of, 1, 4, 20, 105, 131, 165, 169–70; identity of, 18, 180–81, 229n54; intensity of attachment to, 181–83, 187–88, 206, 212, 217–18; moods of, 82–83; narratives of, 11, 14, 18, 121–23, 129–33, 136, 141, 142, 148, 154–58, 168–74, 179, 181–87, 189–98, 200, 201, 205–6, 228n24, 229n39, 229n54, 248n85; nonfictions of, 15, 17–18, 69; outsiders' view of, 41, 45–48, 54–55, 61, 63, 66–67, 182, 189; promise of, 124, 126, 127, 129, 130, 135, 158–61, 242n40; relationship of parts to whole in, 14, 80–83, 86, 89, 91, 93, 97, 99–110, 112–16, 121, 129, 132, 136, 140–41, 145, 148, 150, 162, 166, 178, 193, 196, 197, 199, 201, 203–4, 229n39; "right" and "wrong" impressions of, 64–69; synecdoches of, 27–28, 73, 92, 94–99, 102, 167–68, 177, 181, 189–90, 215–16; writers' affect toward, 8–9, 17–18, 22–23, 27, 222. *See also* America
nationalism: conflicting feelings of, 87, 157, 182–83, 206; critics' attitudes toward, 42, 210–12, 218, 221–22; effect of hopefulness on, 129–30; incredulous, 35, 168, 170, 173, 185, 186, 189, 192, 201, 202, 206; reading about, 24, 221; us/them mentality of, 1–2, 13, 191
nationalism, hot: affects of, 11, 12, 126; causes and characteristics of, 64–65, 159; of Diana Trilling, 42, 62, 63, 66–67; of Donald Trump, 201, 202, 205; of John Steinbeck, 104–5, 111; and presidencies, 170; and synecdoche, 26, 36; tone of, 52, 62–65, 68

nationalism, weak: complexity of, 7, 19, 33, 36, 162, 216–17, 222–23; critiques of, 9–12, 26, 75, 218, 222–23; curiosity's effect on, 78, 79; effect of hopefulness on, 127, 159–60; language of, 12–15; of *On the Road* segments, 124, 156, 157; in Reagan era, 176; representation through, 203–4; strength of, 13–14, 31, 129; vs. strong, 5, 8, 11, 12, 64, 168–70, 179–80, 202; unity through, 32, 156
Native Americans, 203
nature, 133
NBC television, 241n11. *See also* reporting
neoconservatives, 35, 177, 178, 189–90, 201, 205–6
New Criticism, 16, 28. *See also* criticism
New England, 117–18
New Hampshire, 117–18
New Jersey, 247n49
New Journalism, 17. *See also* reporting
news. See *CBS Evening News with Walter Cronkite*; reporting
Newton, Wayne, 199
New York City, 50, 55, 62, 67, 199. *See also* Bowery; Harlem; Long Island NY
New York Intellectuals, 16
New York Times, 37, 71, 102, 136, 200
New York Times Book Review, 71
New York Times Sunday Review, 203
Ngai, Sianne, 21–22, 30, 63, 64, 75, 79, 230n73, 231n82
"nice," 204–5
Nichols, Bill, 132–33
9/11, 10, 35, 168, 191–94, 200, 206
Nixon, Richard, 186, 195
nonfiction: affects of, 24, 26, 28, 82, 206; as genre, 15–16, 17, 250n20; by John Steinbeck, 72, 92; nationalist texts as, 18, 19, 36, 115–16; of Sarah Vowell, 170; search for community through, 73, 80. *See also* travel writing
Norman, Princess Chandler, 150–51, 153–54
Norton, Anne, 222
novels, 15–16, 69, 73, 85–86, 92, 98, 229n48
novelty, 75–78, 81–82, 87
Nudelman, Franny, 233n7

Obama, Barack, 4, 10, 129, 170, 200
Oberlin College, 55–56
Ochs, Phil, 216
Oklahoma, 180
On the Road (Kerouac), 182
On the Road with Charles Kuralt: affect of, 119, 121; analysis of, 34; contrast with traditional news, 138; criticism of, 119–21, 128, 132, 161, 162; first segment of, 117; local and national coverage by, 135; nationalism associated with, 10; national narrative of, 129–30, 133, 158; popularity of, 119, 133, 141–42, 145, 148; subjects and format of, 118, 123, 129, 130, 133–37, 140, 148, 160; synecdoche in, 139–40, 158. *See also* Kuralt, Charles; stories
optimism, 123, 124, 126, 128, 155, 158, 159, 178, 242n43. *See also* hopefulness
The Organization Man (Whyte), 80
Orly, 60. *See also* Paris
Ortner, Sherry B., 178, 247n49
Osman, Suleiman, 135

Pach, Chester, Jr., 131
Paine, Thomas, 186

"Paradox and Dream" (Steinbeck), 105–7
Parini, Jay, 72, 241n160
Paris, 60, 67
Parks, Rosa, 187
Partisan Review, 62, 65, 236n114
The Partly Cloudy Patriot (Vowell), 180, 185, 187, 196
"The Partly Cloudy Patriot" (Vowell), 192
patriotism, 98, 112, 132, 146–48, 181, 192–93, 197, 206
Patterson, James, 102
Pease, Donald, 18, 229n54
people: and Blackie, 160–61; effect of hope on, 124–25, 127; news about, 132, 133, 139; as parts of America, 110–16, 129, 140; quirkiness of, 174; as representatives of nation, 91–94, 107–8, 159, 166, 167, 181, 182, 189–90, 199, 203–4; "smart," 174–75, 179. *See also* community; families; self
Peyre, Henri, 37, 62
Phillips, William, 62, 236n114
"Place of Sorrows" (television segment), 120
poetry, 181, 229n48, 231n90, 250n20. *See also* Beat poets
politics: in America, 55, 134, 205; of conformity and unity, 58, 102–3; and diversity in Montana, 203–5; of hopefulness, 123–26, 128–30, 158–59; and incredulity, 169, 171, 179; Lionel Trilling's attitude toward, 213–14; metaphor in, 231n91; nationalism associated with, 10, 11, 35, 170–71; news coverage of, 132, 134, 137, 138; in nonfiction texts, 115; in *On the Road* segments, 146, 158; post 9/11, 193, 194, 200, 202; of Reagan era, 176, 177, 181, 206;

Sarah Vowell's attitude toward, 165, 168, 199–201; of Simone de Beauvoir's impressions, 52–53, 65–66; and synecdoche, 1–4, 27–28, 32, 68, 199, 203–4, 215–16; in *Travels with Charley*, 86. *See also* presidencies
Pop Art, 25
popular culture, 197, 198. *See also* culture
Posnock, Ross, 237n38
poverty, 149–52, 154–56. *See also* capitalism; Great Depression
Prairie MS, 149
Prescott, Orville, 71
presidencies, 167, 168, 170–71, 185–86. *See also* elections; politics; Reagan era; *and specific presidents*
promise, 124, 126–30, 135, 136, 141, 159–61, 200, 230n73. *See also* hopefulness
Prothero, Stephen, 195
Puritans, 167, 171, 193, 194, 195
"The Pursuit of Happiness" (Steinbeck), 110

"Quantrill's Raid," 3
Queens NY, 53. *See also* New York City
quirkiness, 170, 173–76, 182, 183, 186, 189, 198, 206, 246n27

Raab, Lawrence, 250n20
race and racism, 117, 136, 151, 154–57, 233n13. *See also* African Americans; ethnicity; white supremacy
Rahv, Philip, 62
Rainbow, Paul, 96
Rankin, Jeannette, 201, 204
Ransom, John Crowe, 28, 219, 231n90

reading: of affect, 8–9, 14–15, 20–26, 82, 219, 221; from critical perspective, 35–36, 69, 209; for curiosity, 78; in everyday life, 33–34, 46–49, 57–58, 67–69; of moodiness, 44–46, 61–62; of national descriptions, 6, 64, 80–81; of synecdoche, 28–29, 33

Reagan, Ronald, 177, 178, 180, 189, 200. *See also* presidencies

Reagan era: affects of, 175, 176, 192, 206; economic policies of, 178–79; nationalism associated with, 9, 10, 35, 168, 170, 173; rhetoric of, 129, 159, 181, 195–98; tropes of, 168, 177, 178, 191, 193, 195. *See also* presidencies

reason, 9, 28, 43, 46, 68

red states, 1–4, 203. *See also* Republicans

reporting: about nation, 82–83, 86–87, 122, 142; John Steinbeck's dissatisfaction with, 87–88; of Montana election, 202–3; in Reagan era, 177; synecdoches in, 137–38; tone and subjects of, 120–21, 130–32, 135, 136, 144–45, 148, 158, 160, 162, 233n7, 241n11; in *Travels with Charley*, 91, 93, 95. *See also* CBS *Evening News with Walter Cronkite*; New Journalism

Republicans, 3, 4, 185, 202, 203. *See also* red states

Richards, I. A., 232n92

Riesman, David, 16, 80

Rodgers, Daniel T., 158–59, 177, 192

Roof, Judith, 85, 89, 95, 112

Root, Robert, Jr., 16

"Rosa Parks, *C'est Moi*" (Vowell), 187

Rosenberg, Howard, 121

Rowe, John Carlos, 228n24

Rubenstein, Diane, 26, 40, 233n13

Ruch, Alexander, 233n13

Ruscha, Ed, 231n82

Russia, 193. *See also* Soviet Union

Ryan, Paul, 203

Salant, Richard, 131

San Francisco, 148

Sartre, Jean-Paul, 50

Schaub, Thomas Hill, 16

Schrecker, Ellen, 176

Sconce, Jeffrey, 175

The Scream (Munch), 25

Sedgwick, Eve Kosofsky, 219, 220

Seeger, Pete, 216

Seigworth, Gregory J., 21, 214

self: Americans' focus on, 79–80; curiosity's effect on, 77, 86; definition through quirkiness, "smartness," and use of irony, 176, 182–83, 186, 206; legitimacy of, 174; perception in news coverage, 132, 134; in Reagan era, 177–78; relationship to nation, 74, 91, 92, 97, 109–10, 113, 114, 116, 122, 157, 165–66, 168, 172, 180–81, 187–89, 201–2; as representative of society, 204. *See also* community; people; Vowell, Sarah: self-definition of

Sennett, Richard, 213

sensations, 49, 51, 52, 58–59, 67, 81, 84–85. *See also* feelings

Shillinglaw, Susan, 72, 114

sight, 85, 116. *See also* epistemophilia; sensations

Simons, Margaret A., 233n13

Sixteen in Webster Groves, 132

60 Minutes, 119

slackening, 175–76, 185, 204, 205

Slate, 1–3

"smartness," 182, 186, 189, 192, 206
Smiley, Jane, 1–5, 9, 13, 17, 203, 211, 227n9
Smith, Henry Nash, 80
sobriety, rhetoric of, 121, 130–33, 135, 136, 158, 162
Something Happened (Berkowitz), 122
Soviet Union, 10, 66, 181, 236n114. *See also* Russia
Spivak, Gayatri, 11, 28, 210, 211
"The Star-Spangled Banner," 216
Stearns, Peter, 173
Steinbeck, John: affect toward country, 9, 82, 116, 222; career of, 72; construction of national identity, 90, 95–96, 102–3; correspondence of, 98; criticism of, 71–72, 78, 116; curiosity of, 34, 72, 79, 80, 83, 85, 87–90, 94–98, 101, 109, 114; on genetic tape of nation, 106, 107, 196; knowledge of America, 84–85; nationalism of, 10, 99, 100, 104–6, 111; use of "more," 90; use of "thing," 90, 105; on Vietnam War, 241n160; writing style of, 72, 85–87, 89, 99–103
Steuben, Friedrich Wilhelm von, 197–99
Stiff, Bill, 160–61
stories, 183–84, 186, 206–7. *See also* nation: narratives of; *On the Road with Charles Kuralt*
Streep, Meryl, 196, 197
Sutherland, Claire, 14, 31
Svendsen, Lars, 50
Synar, Michael, 187, 188
synecdoche: affective power of, 30–31, 75, 76, 82, 123, 162, 169, 192, 217; in *America Day by Day*, 48, 57, 68; defining nation by, 1, 5–7, 27–28, 36, 72–74, 80, 83, 99, 122, 222;

function of, 27–29, 57, 100, 103, 108, 113, 127, 141, 145, 203–4, 231n86, 232n92, 232n95; of Generation X, 34–35; of G. W. Bush, 167, 191; of hopefulness, 35, 123, 124, 127–30; for imperialism, 215–16; incitement to read through, 20–21, 28–30, 218; of intellectuals, 65–66; interpretations of, 41; John Steinbeck's use of, 79, 85, 86, 89, 91, 92, 94, 96, 97, 99, 101–4, 106, 107, 111, 114–16; moods as, 43; in nationalist texts, 9, 14–15, 19, 26–27, 33, 116, 229n54; New Criticism's hostility toward, 28; in news reporting, 136–38; in *On the Road* segments, 118, 122, 135–41, 146, 148, 149, 150, 152–58, 161–62; in poetry, 231n90; political use of, 2, 32, 68, 159, 202, 215–16; and Reagan era, 177, 178, 181, 189–91, 195; Sarah Vowell's use of, 167–70, 182–87, 189–95, 197, 199, 200, 206; and strength of theory, 5, 8. *See also* trope
Szalay, Michael, 231n91, 248n72

Take the Cannoli (Vowell), 11, 180, 189, 203
Taussig, Michael, 40, 128
Taylor, Jenny Bourne, 43
Teale, Tamara, 38, 58
Tet Offensive, 131, 147
Texas, 193
Thanksgiving, 148, 149, 151–53
thick description, 6
This American Life, 35, 167, 180
Time, 61, 71
Time-Life World War II series, 186
Tocqueville, Alexis de, 39
Tolbert, Jane, 130, 135, 136, 141, 150
Tomkins, Silvan, 4, 7, 8, 14, 31, 75, 81, 172, 219

INDEX 277

tone: of criticism, 52, 62–65, 68; effect of, 57; of John Steinbeck, 72, 73, 76; of *Partisan Review*, 236n114; of Sarah Vowell, 166–68, 170, 176, 185–86, 197, 203, 206; of Simone de Beauvoir, 46, 54–55
Torgovnick, Marianna, 214, 220
Totten, Gary, 39
Travels with Charley (Steinbeck): affect toward America in, 73, 75, 76, 82, 116, 222; analysis of, 34; comparison to *America and Americans*, 101, 102, 106, 112, 113, 115; creation of national identity in, 89; criticism of, 71–72; difficulty writing, 73, 90, 95–96; John Steinbeck's curiosity in, 77, 78, 83–84, 88, 99, 114; nationalism associated with, 10; paradox in, 105; setting of, 79–80, 82, 86, 97, 98
travel writing: content and tone of, 47, 53, 54, 60, 85, 89, 98–99; critical responses to, 40, 69; as everyday reading, 33–34. *See also* nonfiction
Trilling, Diana, 38, 42, 62–66, 105
Trilling, Lionel, 16, 35–36, 212–15, 217, 218, 220–22
triumphalism: absence of, 185; criticism of, 177; of G. W. Bush administration, 191, 192; of Reagan era, 175, 176, 178, 179, 189–91, 195, 198, 206; Sarah Vowell on, 9, 35; strong affects of, 205
trope: affects generated by, 8; for America, 98–99, 106, 110; in Cold War era writing, 72; for hope, 125; for knowledge of nation, 84–85; in national narratives, 18; in poetry, 231n90; of Reagan era, 168, 177, 178, 191, 193, 195; and synecdoche,

28–31, 104, 159, 218, 232n92; theory of, 28. *See also* metaphor; metonymy; synecdoche
Trump, Donald, 12, 170–71, 201–2, 205
Tuchman, Gaye, 120

Ugly Feelings (Ngai), 21–22
Unfamiliar Fishes (Vowell), 171, 196
United Auto Workers, 142
United Kingdom, 62
United States. *See* America
unity. *See* community
University of Notre Dame, 104
"The Unteachable Ignorance of the Red States" (Smiley), 1–5, 9, 13, 17, 203, 211
U.S. Congress, 203, 204
U.S. Constitution, 199
USS *Abraham Lincoln*, 191
utopia, 7, 183, 189

Vanity Fair, 167, 200
Veterans Day, 142, 143
Vietnam War: effect on nation, 118–19, 147–48, 155; John Steinbeck on, 241n160; library display on, 186; Lionel Trilling's attitude toward, 213; nationalism associated with, 10; news coverage of, 117, 121, 131, 233n7, 235n87; in *On the Road* segments, 141–43, 146–47; Sarah Vowell's reference to, 193, 194
Virgin Land (Smith), 80
Virno, Paolo, 248n85
voting, 188, 199. *See also* elections
Voting Rights Act (1965), 186
Vowell, Sarah: affect toward country, 9, 166–69, 172–73, 180, 183, 194–95, 222–23; favorite book of, 182; on General Lafayette, 198–99;

incredulity of, 35, 167–68, 171, 173, 182, 185, 189, 191, 192, 195–97, 199–200, 248n85; nationalism associated with, 10–11; obscuring of affect, 25, 197, 206; on representation of Montana, 203–5; self-definition of, 165–69, 174, 180–82, 186, 188, 189, 190, 197, 198, 200, 201; stories of, 183–84, 194; tone of, 166–68, 170, 176, 185–86, 197, 203, 206

Wagner-Martin, Linda, 229n48
Wainwright, Evelyn Wotherspoon, 199
"Waiting for Roger" (television segment), 141–49, 155, 160, 244n114
Wald, Priscilla, 31
Wall, Wendy L., 32, 58, 109
War Advertising Council, 58
WarGames, 197, 198
Warhol, Andy, 25
War on Terror, 168, 189, 192
Washington DC, 36, 199
Watergate, 147
Webster Groves MO, 132
White House, 36, 199
white supremacy, 10. *See also* race and racism
Whitmore, Jenny, 161
Whyte, William H., 80
Williamsburg VA, 198
Winthrop, John, 194
Wolfe, Tom, 17
Woloch, Alex, 168, 176–77, 179, 180
Worden, Daniel, 115
The Wordy Shipmates (Vowell), 10–11, 167, 171, 193, 194
work ethic, 150–51, 153, 157, 158
World War II, 10, 16, 52, 56, 58, 98, 197
Wounded Knee, 193

Zaretsky, Natasha, 122, 241n11
Žižek, Slavoj, 227n13

CPSIA information can be obtained
at www.ICGtesting.com
Printed in the USA
BVHW031514100619
550610BV00001B/145/P

9 781496 215482